THE BRIGHTEST DAY

THE BRIGHTEST DAY

Alan Savage

This first world edition published in Great Britain 2005 by
SEVERN HOUSE PUBLISHERS LTD of
9–15 High Street, Sutton, Surrey SM1 1DF.
This first world edition published in the USA 2005 by
SEVERN HOUSE PUBLISHERS INC of
595 Madison Avenue, New York, N.Y. 10022.

British Library Cataloguing in Publication Data

Savage, Alan, 1930-
    The brightest day. - (The French Resistance series ; v. 4)
    1. Gruchy, Liane de (Fictitious character) - Fiction
    2. World War, 1939-1945 - Underground movements - France - Fiction
    3. War stories
    I. Title
    823.9'14 [F]

    ISBN 0-7278-6246-4

Typeset by Palimpsest Book Production Ltd.,
Polmont, Stirlingshire, Scotland.
Printed and bound in Great Britain by
MPG Books Ltd., Bodmin, Cornwall.

And not by eastern windows only,
When daylight comes, comes in the light,
In front the sun climbs slow, how slowly,
But westward, look, the land is bright.

Arthur Hugh Clough

PART ONE

Sisters

And lovelier things have mercy shown
To every failing but their own,
And every woe a tear can claim
Except an erring sister's shame.
George Gordon, Lord Byron

One

Cherchez La Femme

'I have Pound Seventeen,' Sergeant Rachel Cartwright said. 'At last! I'll speak.' Major James Barron leapt up from his desk and strode across the small office to the radio. A big man, with heavy shoulders and rugged features, he moved with the natural grace of the athlete he had been before the War. As required by his position, he wore civilian clothes, although on this chilly spring day in 1943 he had added a jumper beneath his jacket, and his fair hair, even when cut short, was as always untidy.

'Pound Two,' he snapped into the microphone, speaking French. 'Where the devil have you been?'

'It has been terrible, monsieur, terrible,' said the voice on the receiver. 'The Boche have been everywhere. I have not dared use the set. Even now, I am taking a terrible risk.'

'Where are Pound Eleven and Pound Twelve? It has been five months.'

'When the Germans came in, before Christmas, they had to leave. They are too well known to be hidden here.'

'Where have they gone?'

'I do not know exactly, monsieur. They went south.'

'And you have heard nothing?'

'Nothing, monsieur. Now I must go. There is someone coming. Pound Seventeen out.'

James stared at the set in frustration, and Rachel stood against him and put her arms round his waist.

'If Liane had been taken, the Germans would have shouted it from the rooftops.' A tall, slender young woman, black hair carefully confined in a bun, her pertly pretty features enhanced by the horn-rimmed spectacles, she had struck up an intimate

3

relationship with her boss during the three years they had worked and virtually lived together in this tiny office, trying to control their group of French Resistance fighters on behalf of the Special Operations Executive of the Secret Intelligence Service. The nature of their work precluded any close friendships outside of the office; their relative social standing had bridged the gap between enlisted 'man' and officer. James was the son of a schoolmaster, Rachel the daughter of a general and, while James was a professional soldier who had wound up in Special Operations Executive after Dunkirk, mainly because of his knowledge of and connections in France, Rachel had joined up because her family had expected her to do so, as they had expected her to volunteer for any unusual or especially taxing job that was offered. She had thought it a bit of a jolly in the beginning, but that had been before she had met James.

But however genuinely fond she was of him and, she believed, he was of her, and however sexually intimate they might be, she knew that he was actually in love with Liane de Gruchy, the beautiful French aristocrat who had become a leader of the Resistance and the most wanted woman in France; and who had disappeared since the Germans had over-run Vichy after the Allied invasions of North Africa.

'She could still be dead,' James muttered. 'Unknown to anyone.'

'Liane is indestructible,' Rachel said loyally. In fact, for all their rivalry, she had met and admired the famous Frenchwoman, who could so easily have fled France for the security of England; she had an English mother and had been educated in England. But she had chosen to stay, and fight, and risk her life almost daily. Obviously her luck had to run out eventually, but until they *knew* . . .

'Listen,' she said. 'The Germans have taken over all of Vichy, right? So there is no longer any safe haven in any town or village. So where would Liane go? Surely to where her group originated, back in 1940.'

James turned, slowly. 'The Massif Central?'

'Doesn't it make sense? She must know those hills like the back of her hand. And they are her people down there.'

'It's also where she and her group were all but wiped out, two years ago.'

4

'I don't believe that would have put her off going back. And I'll bet Moulin is with her.' Jean Moulin, prefect of Chartres before the War, had been arrested and savagely tortured by the Gestapo, but had escaped and made his way into the then-safe haven of Vichy. Now he was General de Gaulle's personal representative amongst all of the various Resistance groups in France, but he was an old friend of the de Gruchy family, and as he was known to be with Liane when the German occupation of Vichy had commenced, it seemed a natural conclusion that they were still together.

James snapped his fingers. 'I'm going to see the brigadier. We'll send someone in to find them.'

'Permission to volunteer, *sir*.'

James kissed her. 'You must be stark, raving mad.'

'I've been before, sir.'

'And got taken by the Gestapo. Do you want to repeat that experience?'

Involuntarily, Rachel touched the bodice of her dress. 'I still have nightmares. But I was betrayed. Monterre is dead.'

'Do you suppose he was, or is, the only traitor in the Resistance? You'll mind the shop. That's an order.'

Rachel watched the door close and lit a cigarette. She was not an habitual smoker – James did not like it; she had indulged occasionally back in 1939, when she had been a bright young thing on the London social scene, at least a hundred light years past – but found the occasional cigarette good for the nerves. She loved France. She had holidayed there regularly before the War, and indeed spoke the language better than James, who still used the schoolboy variety. She had thoroughly enjoyed her two previous missions to the Resistance, the excitement and the camaraderie, the feeling that one was *doing*, rather than sitting behind a desk ordering others to do, up to the moment she had been arrested by the Gestapo.

That had been the most terrible moment of her life, but the succeeding moments had been more terrible yet. She could still see Johann Roess' smiling face in front of her as he had ordered her to be stripped naked before beginning to torment her, as she could still hear Joanna Jonsson's calm voice commanding her release. Oh, Joanna! The Swedish-American double agent had to be the most heroic woman she had ever known, as well as the most enigmatic. Rachel knew that their superiors had never actually trusted her, even after she had risked her position with the Germans, not to mention her life, to rescue *her,* Rachel. And now Joanna had vanished back into Germany, regarded as a traitor by her own people, but very probably dead or in a concentration camp.

Rachel sighed and began work on the pile of transcripts of recent German news items that had just arrived, dividing them into two piles; those, the larger pile, items that could not possibly interest the Pound Section, and those that just might. She was actually looking for some mention of Joanna's name, some indication that she might have survived – Joanna had always been a great survivor – and then found herself frowning as she blinked at the sheet of paper. Carefully she placed it on James' desk, and the telephone rang. She picked up the receiver.

'Pound.'

'Oh, sergeant, I'm sorry to bother you.'

Rachel gave another sigh. Their landlady, while absolutely reliable, had never been able to get together with the concept of code usage. 'Yes, Mrs Hotchkin. Is something the matter?'

'Well, there's this person here, says she's to see the major.'

'What?' Their office, tucked away in a shabby building in the depths of London's East End, was top secret. 'Did you say *she*?'

'She's a French lady. Says you would know her as de Gruchy.'

'Jesus! Is she very good-looking? Does she have blonde hair?'

'Well, as to looks, I wouldn't care to say. But her hair is brown.'

'And she calls herself de Gruchy?' The situation had to be dealt with, and in James' absence it had to be her responsibility. 'You'd better send her up.'

'Would you like me to come up with her?' Mrs Hotchkin was a large, powerful woman. But if this stranger was an enemy agent who had somehow learnt of the section and where to find it, she would probably be armed.

'No, no, Mrs Hotchkin, I can manage,' she said. Rachel

6

discovered that her heart was beating quite powerfully. She went to her desk, opened the drawer and took out the Browning automatic pistol that lay there. She checked that it was loaded. She had only fired it on the range, and her only experience of being under fire herself had been in that frantic battle in the cave eighteen months before, when she had had James on one side of her and Liane on the other. She reminded herself that this woman could still be Liane, somehow escaped to England, with dyed hair; but not even Mrs Hotchkin could have second thoughts as to Liane's beauty.

There was a tap on the door. Rachel stood against the wall beside it, the pistol held in both hands.

'It's open.' The door swung in, the woman stepped through and Rachel kicked it shut, at the same time presenting the pistol to the back of the intruder's head. 'Raise your hands.'

'Rachel?' The young woman ignored the command and turned to face her.

'Oh, my God!' Rachel lowered the pistol. 'Amalie Burstein?'

Amalie de Gruchy was Liane's youngest sister. She was indeed attractive rather than pretty and had curling dark brown hair escaping from a cloche. Her coat and dress were expensive, as befitted a de Gruchy.

'I thought that dragon downstairs was going to eat me.' She spoke English with no trace of accent. 'Is James here?'

'If you mean Pound One, you should say so. He's not here at the moment.' She laid down the pistol, took Amalie's coat and hung it on the hook behind the door. 'But what are you doing here? *How* are you here?' Amalie had been plucked from France the previous year, as much wanted by the Germans for killing one of their senior officers as was her sister. But once Amalie was safely in England, to live with her also exiled parents, Rachel had assumed her to be permanently retired.

Amalie was pouting at her rebuff. 'I was sent here. May I sit down?'

Rachel gestured to the spare chair. 'Sent here by whom?'

Amalie sat down. 'Some old geyser. A brigadier general.'

'The brigadier sent you here? You know him?'

'I don't. Well, I didn't until he came to Ashley Hall.'

Rachel all but scratched her head. 'I am in a total fog. You have been at Ashley Hall?' This was the main training establishment for would-be female agents. Rachel had trained there herself, as had Joanna Jonsson.

'Terrible place. Do you know it? But of course you do. Mummy knows the commandant. And I was so bored, sitting down there in the country, and so worried about Liane . . . How is she?'

'When I find out, I'll let you know. So, you have been trained as an agent. Rather like ferrying coals to Newcastle, wasn't it?'

'Oh, no. I knew nothing about spying and codes and unarmed combat and that sort of thing. Or explosives.'

'But I'll bet you were the only one in your class who had actually ever killed a man. Did you say explosives?'

Amalie giggled. 'I was the youngest, too.'

Rachel recalled that this girl was only twenty-two and had already seen her home destroyed and her family scattered, her husband of only a few months hanged, had herself been imprisoned briefly by the Gestapo, attempted suicide, committed murder . . . and yet appeared perfectly normal. Because she was Liane's sister?

'I am now an explosives expert,' Amalie claimed proudly. 'Show me what you want blown up, and I'll do it for you.'

'And so the brigadier found you . . . ?'

'No, no. I found him. Well, Mummy did.'

Rachel made a mental note that one day she had to meet Madame de Gruchy. James, who *had* met her, had told her that her maiden name had been Howard, with a distant connection to *the* Howards, and that there could be no doubt where her daughters got their looks from. 'And then I told him I wanted to go back to France. I want to be back with Liane.'

'Your mother goes along with this?'

'Mummy knows I want to work in the Secret Service. She doesn't know I'm going back to France.'

'You'll have to talk to James about that. Would you like a cup of tea?'

'I seem to have lived off tea for the past four months. You wouldn't have any Gruchy?'

'At a hundred pounds a bottle? I'll make some tea.' She

went into the little flat that adjoined the office and poured some water. 'Do you ever hear anything of Madeleine?' she asked over her shoulder.

Amalie followed her into the kitchenette. 'That's not very likely, is it?'

'She's your sister.'

'Who married a German, remember?'

'She helped your mother and father, and you, escape from France.'

'So blood is thicker than water. Her husband's people killed my husband. She's a Nazi. Do we have to talk about her?'

'I just thought you might be interested in a news item we received this morning.' Rachel put down her cup, led the way back into the office and picked up the transcript she had placed on James' desk.

'Aren't those things top secret?' Amalie asked, following her.

'Not all of them. I thought this might interest James.' Amalie took the sheet of paper; it had been translated into English. She read it aloud.

'Nazi war hero Colonel Frederick von Helsingen invalided home from Russia, seriously wounded. Frederick von Helsingen is the only son of millionaire businessman Johann von Helsingen, one of the Fuehrer's closest associates, and is married to French wine heiress Madeleine de Gruchy.' She snorted. 'Heiress? Even if there is anything left to inherit after the War, she is not going to see any of it. She should be locked up for the rest of her life.'

'Is that all you can say? Didn't Helsingen pull rank to get you out of a Gestapo cell?'

'He did that to impress Madeleine. I hope he's shot all to pieces.'

'Here's James,' Rachel said with some relief.

'James!' Amalie cried, throwing herself into his arms.

He kissed her. 'You're looking great.'

'You mean you're not surprised to see her?' Rachel asked.

'The brigadier told me she had volunteered.' He looked down at Amalie, who was still in his arms. As Liane's sister, she was one of his favourite people. 'Do you seriously want to go back?'

9

'She wants to be with Liane,' Rachel said acidly.

'Is there something wrong with that?' Amalie demanded.

'Of course not,' James said. 'But you do realize that you are still under sentence of death?'

'So is Liane. And Pierre is already dead. What have I got to live for that is so special? Except for Liane.'

James hugged her again. Save for Liane herself, he had been the last to see Pierre de Gruchy, their only brother, alive, before he had been cut down by German bullets during the disastrous attack on Dieppe the previous summer.

'You'll see Liane again,' he promised. 'Now go home and keep you mouth shut, and I'll contact you in a couple of days.'

'You're not just pushing me aside. I *am* going back?'

'Unless the brigadier changes his mind.'

She kissed him again and glanced at Rachel, who was holding her coat. 'Two days,' she said and left the office.

James closed the door. 'She's a ball of fire.'

'You're not seriously sending her back to France?'

'Pound's idea. He thinks she may stir things up.'

'Stir things up?' Rachel cried. 'She's a menace. The moment she lays eyes on a German, she's liable to shoot him. You're sending her to her death, James, and God knows how many other people she'll take with her. Including Liane.'

'I'm not *sending* her anywhere,' James said mildly, sitting at his desk. 'I'm taking her with me when I go.'

'You're doing *what*?' Rachel also sat down, but involuntarily.

'De Gaulle is very upset at losing contact with Moulin, and the brass agree with us that he is probably with Liane and that they are probably in the Massif. They want me to find them, and the boss thinks that Amalie may be very helpful; she knows that area almost as well as Liane. Besides, they have a job for us to do, and Amalie is important for that. She's qualified as an explosives expert.'

'So she told me. What is she going to blow up, apart from herself?'

'Wolfram.'

'Say again?'

'Don't you know what wolfram is?'

'Never heard of it.'

10

'It's the basic element from which tungsten is made. Don't tell me you've never heard of tungsten?'

'I think I have. But don't ask me what it's for.'

'Tungsten, my dearest girl, is a basic component of armour plate, or armour-piercing ammunition. No modern army can fight without armour, and no armour can be made without tungsten. Now, Germany does not have any natural wolfram. They used to get their supplies from Portugal, but that source is drying up, thanks to our diplomatic efforts. So they have had to look elsewhere, and it so happens that there are quite a few small wolfram mines in France, including a relatively big one quite close to the Massif. My orders are to locate Liane, activate her people and have them destroy that mine.'

'Shit! Then that's the end of you. Oh, James . . . you'll be betrayed.'

'Now, who is going to do that? As you mentioned this morning, Monterre is dead. And no one is going to lure me across the border.' He grinned. 'Simply because there is no border any more. What's this?' He picked up the sheet of paper.

'A news transcript I thought might interest you.'

He scanned it. 'Poor old Madeleine.'

'You had something going for her once, didn't you?'

'Once. Before I met Liane. I really never thought of her as a widow.'

'Helsingen isn't dead.'

'From this report,' James said, 'he could as well be.'

As the train pulled into the station, the band struck up the national anthem, and at the same moment Adolf Hitler marched on to the platform, preceded by his black-uniformed guards and followed by his entourage of generals and party officials. The Fuehrer went straight up to a group of women that was already waiting, but he had a greeting for only one.

'Frau von Helsingen,' he said. 'Madeleine.'

He stretched out his hands and Madeleine de Gruchy took them, giving a little bob of a curtsey. The tallest of the sisters, at twenty-seven six years younger than Liane and five older than Amalie, she was handsome rather than beautiful, but her full figure, her splendid long, wavy brown hair, her expensive clothes, and the air of chic she exuded combined to make her

11

a striking woman. Hitler's lips brushed her gloved knuckles. 'I am told the injuries are not life-threatening.'

'I do not believe so, my Fuehrer.' Madeleine's voice was low.

'And they were suffered defending the Reich, eh?' He stared into her eyes as he spoke; even he, with his capacity for self-deception, could understand that it was difficult to claim a man was defending the Fatherland when he was several hundred miles away in a foreign country.

But Madeleine merely said, 'Yes, my Fuehrer.'

The train was stopping and doors were opening. The conductors, having been forewarned, hastily stopped anyone leaving the train until their most important passenger had been disembarked. Now four medical orderlies lifted the stretcher from its compartment, followed immediately by two doctors. A trolley had been wheeled forward and the stretcher was placed on this. Frederick von Helsingen was all but invisible, his head wreathed in bandages, his body lost beneath the blankets, but his eyes were open and only slightly drowsy. He could recognize the face leaning over him.

'My Fuehrer,' he muttered and tried to move his arm. 'Heil Hitler!'

'Do not exert yourself, my dear Frederick,' Hitler said. 'I congratulate you. You are in good hands now. I will see you when you are well.'

He stepped back. Madeleine made to go forward but was brushed aside as Herr von Helsingen stepped in front of her. She waited while her husband spoke with his father, then it was her turn.

'Oh, my darling,' he said. 'I am so sorry.'

'Just to have you home is a treat.' She looked above him at the doctor.

'He must go to the hospital first,' the doctor said.

'But he will be coming home?'

'Of course.'

Madeleine made to squeeze Frederick's hand but could not find it. 'I will see you soon,' he said.

The trolley was wheeled away. Madeleine looked left and right at the people milling about, at the other wounded soldiers being greeted by their loved ones . . . and had her arm grasped by those powerful fingers she knew so well.

'I think I had better see you home,' Joanna Jonsson said.

'There was no hand,' Madeleine whispered. 'My God, there was no hand!'

'You just couldn't find it,' Joanna suggested.

Madeleine glanced at her. While she, personally, had never liked the Swedish-American woman, she knew that Joanna was Liane's oldest and dearest friend and was prepared to accept that they had been lovers at finishing school in Switzerland, from which they had both been expelled when discovered in bed together. But they also shared a terrifying secret. Of everyone in Germany, only she knew that Joanna was a double agent. Her problem was that she did not know which side Joanna rated higher. But as Joanna knew all of Madeleine's secrets, including the fact that she had more than once aided her sisters, who were the two most wanted female terrorists – in German eyes – in France, there was nothing she could do save accept Joanna as she came. Besides, she was such an overwhelming personality. Quite apart from being the daughter of an American millionairess and a Swedish diplomat, she was nearly six feet of flowing blonde sexuality, her yellow hair cascading as always past her shoulders. If her features were perhaps a shade too bold for beauty, her body might have been sculpted by some Norse god, which clearly made her the more compelling to those with the Nazi Aryan ideology at heart. In the course of her tortuous activities, Joanna had worked her way through those, until arriving at very nearly the top.

'I didn't see Heinrich at the station,' Madeleine remarked as they drove back to her apartment in Joanna's car. They sat in the back and there was a glass partition shutting off the chauffeur's ears.

'He is a very busy man.'

'Busier than the Fuehrer?'

'As a matter of fact, yes.'

'Do you sleep with him?'

'When he requires it.'

'He is such a slimy character. I don't see how you can.'

13

'You need to remember that Heinrich controls the entire police force, secret and public.'

'And you enjoy prostituting yourself? Are you still going to marry Franz Hoeppner?'

'Whenever he next has leave, yes.'

'You had better hope that he doesn't come home like Freddie. Or in a wooden box. Does he know about Himmler?'

'He knows that I work for Heinrich, as I once worked for Oskar Weber. He understands what that involves.'

'And he accepts it?'

'He is a realist, and he loves me.' The car stopped outside the Helsingens' apartment block. 'Would you like me to come up?'

'Thank you, no. I'm quite all right.'

'Then listen. Freddie is coming home?'

'Of course he is. As soon as he has been checked out.'

'Well, when he does come home, I want you to ask him what conditions are really like in Russia.'

'You are up to your old tricks. Doesn't Himmler tell you what's going on?'

'He tells me the same as Goebbels tells everybody else: that Stalingrad was just a clever plan to lure all the Soviet forces away from Moscow and bleed them white; that this coming summer the Reich will launch the greatest armoured assault in history, which will smash Stalin for ever. I want to know what the soldier on the ground feels about it.'

'And you want me to ask my husband to betray his country?'

'I am asking you to get you husband to tell you the truth. The truth can never be a betrayal. I'll be in touch.'

The door closed. Joanna tapped on the glass panel, which promptly opened. 'The Albert.'

'Herr Himmler left instructions that when you were finished at the station you were to be taken to his office, Fräulein.'

'Oh? Well, in that case, take me to Gestapo Headquarters.'

She leant back on the cushions, feeling pleasantly anticipatory. Hers had been an exciting but often pleasant war, if one overlooked the first few traumatic days of the German invasion of France when, no doubt relying too heavily on her

American neutrality, she had drifted into the immediate war zone and watched her much loved half-brother cut to pieces by the bullets of a strafing Messerschmitt, and with her friend Liane de Gruchy had had to submit to gang rape by a party of German deserters. Both women had been shattered by the experience but, while Liane had instantly determined on revenge, she had only wanted to get away from it all, back to the safety of the States.

It had been while she had been waiting in London for the ship that would hopefully carry her across the Atlantic that had come that chance meeting with James Barron, a man she had only previously met at Amalie's wedding to Henri Burstein, and whom she had not really liked, because he had so obviously had something going for Liane ... and Liane was equally obviously responding. But she had known he was in Military Intelligence, without quite knowing what, and she had suddenly wanted to pour out her heart to him. James had immediately recognized her potential, possessing both an American and a Swedish passport, well known in the social whirl of Europe, and especially that of Berlin, where she had worked as a gossip columnist for an American newspaper. And she was a willing subject, aware that she was going back to nothing in the States, and suddenly realizing that she could fight beside Liane, even if at a distance.

Thus had begun that frenetic but beguiling life, living in Berlin but travelling to England, via Sweden, as and when she chose, with whatever information she had been able to glean. It should have ended with the entry of America into the war, now nearly eighteen months ago. James had wanted to pull her out immediately, but she had preferred to continue with her mission, and the only way she could do that was to allow herself to be 'turned' by Oskar Weber, the German spymaster. That had launched her on another dizzy merry-go-round; to the world – and particularly the American world – a despicable traitor; to the Gestapo an invaluable courier who, using her Swedish passport, could enter and leave England at will; and to James Barron, despite the doubts of his superiors, an even more destructive mechanism in the very heart of the German secret service.

Where would it end? She had come close to catastrophe

more than once before, not least when rescuing James' side-kick Rachel Cartwright from the Gestapo. But she had survived, by both her looks and her femininity. She had even survived Weber's fall from power, as his master, Heinrich Himmler, had appropriated her for his own 'secretary'. And she was engaged to be married to one of the nicest men she had ever met; the fact that Franz Hoeppner wore the uniform of a German officer did not mean that he was a Nazi, but the fact that he was a career soldier who put duty above every-thing, and was now serving in Russia, meant that she had no idea when, or if ever, she would see him again. She had just seen what could happen, in the shattered body of his best friend, Frederick von Helsingen.

The car stopped in the so familiar courtyard. Sentries clicked to attention as Joanna strode past them; they all knew who she was.

'The Reichsfuehrer said you were to go straight up, Fräulein,' said an adjutant.

Joanna nodded and went up the stairs. A secretary opened the double doors for her, and she stepped into the large, beau-tifully furnished office she knew so well, pausing to throw her right arm out in front of herself. 'Heil Hitler!'

'Joanna!' Himmler beamed at her as he greeted her as if he had not seen her for at least a week instead of the previous night. He was, as always, flawlessly dressed in a black uniform with death's head shoulder badges, waist and cross belts highly polished, as were his boots, with his somewhat bland features rendered positively gentle by the rimless glasses he wore. The odd thing about him was that Joanna knew he genuinely believed he had a gentle nature; that on the occasion he had personally witnessed the execution of several hundred Jewish men and women in Russia he had been physically sick; but that he had signed an order for the next batch of executions without a moment's hesitation, steeling himself for what he considered to be his duty. She supposed any criminal psychiatrist would find him a fascinating study; the catastrophe lay in the fact that a man who definitely needed psychiatric help controlled the lives, and deaths, of millions of human beings. And as she had confessed to Madeleine, she slept with him whenever he summoned her to his bed. 'You'll never guess who has come to visit.'

16

His voice was as mild as his appearance, but Joanna turned her head sharply to look at the other man in the room, standing to one side. He also wore a black uniform and was a small man with lank dark hair and a toothbrush moustache, obviously worn in imitation of his fuehrer.

'Fräulein! I trust you are well?'

His eyes gleamed at her. Joanna was aware that there were a great many people in Germany, at least in the corridors of power, who disliked and distrusted her, either because they disliked traitors as a matter of principle, or they disliked her flamboyant looks that seemed able to bewitch so many men who should have known better. But as far as she knew, Johann Roess was the only one who actively hated her. They had clashed often in the past, and she knew that Roess – who had succeeded Oskar Weber as commandant of the SD, the Sicherheitsdienst, the secret department within the Gestapo that wielded absolute power subject only to Himmler's overrule – dreamt of her eventually being delivered into his hands. He had achieved his goal last autumn, when she had seemed to share in his predecessor's disgrace, had actually had her in his cells awaiting the torture he called interrogation, and had been interrupted by Himmler himself. She had not laid eyes on him since that never-to-be-forgotten day. Now she forced a smile but, even forced, Joanna Jonsson's smile suggested a world of untold pleasure.

'I am very well, Colonel Roess. And yourself?'

'I am as well as can be expected, Fräulein.'

'Of course you had that bump on the head, given you by . . .' She paused, staring at him, her mouth open, as if she had forgotten.

'Given me by that bitch Liane de Gruchy,' Roess almost snarled.

'Colonel, please,' Himmler said. 'There is a lady present.' It was Roess' turn to stare with his mouth open, and his surprise was genuine. But he was not going to question his boss's opinion. 'Why don't you both sit down?' Himmler said. 'This meeting is about this female.' Himmler opened the file on his desk. Joanna sank into the chair in front of his desk, hoping that the sudden colour she could feel in her cheeks was not giving her away.

'This woman has been a thorn in the side of the Reich since

17

July 1940, when she murdered a German officer. I understand you knew her then, Joanna.'

'I was friends with her before the War, Herr Reichsfuehrer. You know that.'

'You were her lover,' Roess snapped. Himmler raised his eyebrows.

'We were . . . friends, at school,' Joanna said.

'And you were with her in the first days of the invasion, when you *claim* to have been assaulted by German soldiers.'

'I was in France to attend the wedding of Mademoiselle de Gruchy's sister and—'

'You mean Frau von Helsingen?' Himmler interrupted.

'No, sir. This was her other sister.'

'Who is also guilty of murdering a German officer,' Roess interjected.

'What a family,' Himmler commented. 'But you say you and this woman were assaulted by German soldiers?'

'We were raped, Herr General. Repeatedly.'

'My word. How did this happen?'

'We had taken shelter in a deserted house and were found there by these men. I understand they were deserters.'

'Were these people ever caught?'

'Oh, yes, sir.'

'And what happened to them?'

'They were hanged, sir. By order of General Rommel, who was commanding that district at the time.'

'Oh, Rommel. Poor fellow.'

'Sir?' Joanna had only met the general on that one occasion, but she had liked him.

'Well, he is being pushed from pillar to post in North Africa. His great days are behind him.'

'Ahem,' Roess said. 'Fräulein Jonsson has not explained what she was doing in the company of Fräulein de Gruchy, north of Paris, if they were no longer close friends.'

'As I have said, sir, I was attending the wedding of Amalie de Gruchy when the invasion took place. There were several officers at the ceremony, and they all had to rejoin their regiments as rapidly as possible. The transport situation was very bad, and so Liane offered to drive them up to the Belgian border. I accompanied her.'

'Why? These men were going to fight against the Reich.'

'I knew that, and I also knew they would be beaten. But as you may remember, sir, at that time I was working as a journalist, and I thought there might be a story in it.'

'Of course. There you are, Roess. We have drifted away from the point, which is that this woman has eluded capture for three years, while committing God alone knows how many crimes against the Reich. I really had supposed that once we took over Vichy she would fall into our hands. We knew she was using there as a base. But this has not happened.'

'Until now, sir,' Roess said.

Joanna's head jerked. 'You have captured her?'

'Not yet. But we know where she is to be found.' Joanna waited, scarce able to breathe. Roess smiled. 'We have information that she has returned to her original haunt, the Massif Central. You know the Massif well, do you not, Fräulein?'

'Explain,' Himmler said.

'Fräulein Jonsson was a member of the task force we sent into Vichy in the autumn of 1941, to destroy the de Gruchy gang. It was reportedly a success. The gang was wiped out, so it was claimed. Liane de Gruchy was killed. So it was claimed. These claims were made by Fräulein Jonsson.'

Himmler again looked at Joanna. But she had got her nerves back under control. 'The assault was commanded by Colonel Weber. The guerillas were hiding in a cave. We penetrated the cave, and there was a violent battle. It was dark and very difficult to tell friend from foe. But Liane de Gruchy was there. I saw her and I shot her, seconds after she had shot Colonel Weber. I knew she went down. But I was concerned about the colonel, who was very badly hurt. Also, we had used up most of the time we had been allowed before our planes would have to take off again; General Heydrich, who had devised the operation, was most insistent that we should not delay long enough to become engaged with any Vichy police who might approach the scene. At that time, as you may recall, Herr Reichsfuehrer, the Fuehrer was most anxious to preserve good relations with Vichy. So Captain Karlovy and I determined to abort and get out, with Colonel Weber. I was certain Liane de Gruchy was dead. I was apparently mistaken. I am sorry.'

Roess snorted. Himmler turned to him. 'You do not believe this? You are accusing Fräulein Jonnson of lying?'

'I deal in facts, Herr Reichsfuehrer. And the fact is that Liane de Gruchy did not die in that battle. How she survived I do not know, but it is also a fact that since then she has continued her reign of terror throughout France.'

'Including laying you out on the one occasion you got too close to her,' Joanna reminded him.

Roess glared at her. 'Including giving the British detailed information on the defences of Dieppe, which enabled them to carry out their raid last year. I saw her there.'

'But like Fräulein Jonsson,' Himmler pointed out, 'you were unable to kill or capture her. The woman seems to have more lives than a cat. And that raid was not successful, was it? However, I regard it as essential, if you and Fräulein Jonsson are going to work together, that there is absolute trust between you. As for what happened in the cave and afterwards, I wish to see General Heydrich's precise instructions.'

'There are no written instructions, sir,' Roess said. 'General Heydrich apparently gave Colonel Weber only verbal orders.'

'Because what he was doing was illegal. And he is now dead. Well, get hold of this fellow Karlovy and have him corroborate the Fräulein's story.'

'Captain Karlovy is also dead, sir. He was killed in Russia a few month ago.'

'And Weber is now in Russia himself. But as he was unconscious when all this was going on, he can hardly tell us much about it. I'm afraid you and the Fräulein will just have to kiss and make up, Roess. I am speaking figuratively.'

Joanna was just getting her breath back. 'Would you repeat that, Herr Reichsfuehrer? I am to work with Colonel Roess?'

'On this assignment, yes. As the colonel has pointed out, you know the area. You also know Fräulein de Gruchy. I am informed that one of the reasons she has evaded captured for so long is that she is a mistress of disguise. I am sure that she will not be able to fool you. I am making the elimination of this woman top priority. The news from Russia has not been good this winter. That, combined with the Allies' success in North Africa, means that the people of the various occupied countries under our control are becoming restless, assuming that we may soon be forced to make peace.'

'Did not Roosevelt and Churchill declare that they would only accept unconditional surrender?' Joanna ventured.

'That is pure rhetoric. They would be happy to make peace, if we offered it. This war is bleeding them white. So Russia is holding out longer than we had expected, and it looks as if we may lose North Africa. Those are peripherals. The Allies have no means of getting at us in Fortress Europe, except by bombing, and that is not going to get them anywhere. We hear all this aimless chatter about the Second Front. Propaganda. If we couldn't find a way to invade Great Britain in 1940, when we were strong and they were weak, how are they going to find a way to invade Europe when our armed forces are still the strongest in the world?'

Neither Roess nor Joanna, who both had access to the Top Secret reports and directives that emanated from OKW, the military headquarters, dared suggest that their employer might be drawing a somewhat rosy picture. 'No, no,' Himmler went on. 'The only course left to the Allies is to stir up the people of the occupied territories. We know they are encouraging every aspect of resistance, with this futile V for victory code. But we must not underestimate these people.

'The key to the problem is leadership. Without leadership these bandits are just bandits. We must concentrate on removing the leaders. We are devoting a great deal of time and resources to destroying this fellow Tito in Yugoslavia. Now in France there is this fellow Moulin. He must be caught and executed, as publicly as possible. The same goes for his sidekick, de Gruchy. Our information suggests that they are working together, and therefore are together, at least some of the time. Go and find them. It would be preferable to take them alive but, if necessary, take them dead. And there must be no more mistakes. If I cannot see Liane de Gruchy standing in front of this desk, in chains, I wish to see a photograph of her body, unmistakably dead, on this desk. Now go and do your duty.' He smiled at them. 'I have every confidence in your success.'

Two

Wolfram

'Well,' Roess said, as they went down the stairs, 'we have been given a challenge but, as the Reichsfuehrer said, I am sure we will succeed. However, I think we should lay our plans very carefully, do you not agree, Fräulein?'

'I suppose we should,' Joanna said.

'Well, then, as this is highly confidential, I think we should discuss it in private, should we not? We shall go to my apartment.'

'Sadly, I have things to do.'

'Suppose I made my request into an order?'

They had reached the open air, where their two cars waited. 'In that case,' Joanna said, 'I would have to report to Reichsfuehrer Himmler that, having failed on so many occasions to insert one of your electrodes between my legs, you now wish to replace them with your prick.'

He stared at her with his mouth open, taken aback by her deliberate vulgarity. 'I am sure he would be amused,' Joanna said. 'But then again, perhaps not.'

Roess recovered, although his cheeks were crimson, as he glanced at the expressionless sentries, uncertain if they had overheard. 'We are to work together.'

'So it seems. But not to sleep together. I would like you to remember that, Colonel Roess. When do we leave?'

'Tomorrow morning, early.'

'Then I shall report to your office, tomorrow morning. Early.'

In the security of her suite at the Albert Hotel, Joanna discovered that she was wringing wet with sweat. She ran a bath and sank into the bubbles. Her brain was spinning. The previous year Weber had sent her to assist Roess in finding Amalie de Gruchy, who had disappeared following her shooting of the German Colonel Kessler. She had found Amalie, because Madeleine had told her of the secret childhood hideaway shared by the sisters. Thanks to that knowledge, she had been able to get the girl out of the country without Roess suspecting it, but that had been by using the haven of Vichy. That haven no longer existed and, in any event, a year ago she had had an independent role, as it were; this time she was required to operate as Roess' second-in-command. And Himmler was a totally different personality to Weber. Oskar had been so much in love with her he would support her in anything she did or wished. Heinrich was too cold a fish to be in love with anyone save himself. He enjoyed going to bed with someone so well endowed and so utterly compliant as she always was when in his company. But if he ever felt she were letting him down . . .

Over the winter she had actually given some thought to getting out while she could. When, last year, MI5 had felt it necessary to arrest the German agent with whom she had been dealing for the previous two years, James had considered that her position was compromised. He had offered to provide her with documentation to show the State Department that she was actually a British agent and not a traitor. She had opted to return to Germany. Why? As she was no longer employed as a courier she could convey no more information to the Pound Unit.

Was she really in love with Franz Hoeppner? If she were going to love any man, she supposed it would be him. He was an utter gentleman, an idealist – that he believed in Hitler was an error of judgement, not a crime, because he certainly did not support all of Hitler's decisions – and he loved her. But as she now knew, despite Himmler's bombast, that Nazi Germany was bound to be defeated, what sort of life did the future hold for a man like Hoeppner? And thus, his wife? Did that make her a moral coward? Or was it just that she was hooked on the glamour, and the danger, of being at the centre of events? That like an addicted gambler she dreamed of pulling off one more big coup, such as her discovery of the

German plans for the invasion of Russia, which had first made her reputation within the ranks of the SIS? She wanted to be a heroine. In real terms, she *was* a heroine. But only a handful of people knew that. She wanted to be able to scream it from the rooftops when the War was over. But first there was the business of surviving until then, and making sure that Liane did too.

'What exactly do you have on de Gruchy and Moulin?' Joanna asked as she sat opposite Roess in the train.

'People answering their description have been seen around the village of Aumont. A man who walks with a limp and who speaks in a peculiarly hoarse voice. You know, of course, that Moulin once cut his own throat?'

'To end torture by the Gestapo.'

'And that fool Kluck actually had him nursed back to life and then let him escape.'

'Kluck was your predecessor as commandant of the Paris Gestapo, was he not?' Joanna inquired in her most dulcet tones. 'I met him once, in 1940. He tried to talk me out of making a fuss about being raped.'

'And he did not succeed.'

'Have I ever made a fuss? I just wondered where he was now?'

'Sitting behind a desk in Warsaw, dealing with Poles.'

'I am sure he will be good at that. Do you realize that there must be several thousand people in France who have a hoarse voice and walk with a limp?'

'But only one of them is likely to be accompanied by Liane de Gruchy.'

'Who gave you this information?'

'Do you remember the name Monterre? A fellow who used to belong to the de Gruchy gang but abandoned them and betrayed them to that idiot Hoeppner, who was then commanding the Bordeaux garrison.'

Joanna did not know if Roess was aware of her engagement and was thus deliberately being rude, but she decided against taking offence at this moment; there were more important matters. 'I remember Monterre very well,' she said. 'A nasty piece of work. But I understood he committed suicide.'

'That was the official verdict. It seemed superficially logical. He was found seated in his van with the top of his head blown off. His own pistol was in his hand, and forensic evidence indicated that this pistol had been placed in his mouth and the trigger squeezed. The gendarmerie had no doubt that it was suicide. But Monterre had a sister, a married woman named Juliette Dugard. She claims never to have been a member of any Resistance group, but she did know of her brother's activities. They saw each other quite regularly, and he told her that he was mortally afraid that he would be found out and executed by his erstwhile associates. In particular, he was terrified that Liane de Gruchy would return to Limoges and deal with him.'

'Limoges! Isn't that where you had your unfortunate meeting with Liane?'

'Yes,' Roess snapped. 'I did not know who she was. I thought she was a most attractive woman who had, well, fallen for me.'

'There's no accounting for the ability to self-deceive.' Roess glared at her but she merely smiled. 'But she was actually using your lust for her to get herself out of Paris and back to her own people. When she discovered that you intended to leave the train at Limoges and stay with her for a while, she realized that she was bound to be identified. So she decided to get out while she could.'

Roess was frowning. 'How do you know all this?'

Joanna continued to smile. 'Colonel Hoeppner made a full report.'

'That woman is a devil incarnate, a bitch for the darkest pit of hell.'

'A place I am sure you know well. But what has she to do with Monterre's death? Simply because he was afraid of her?'

'Simply because Monterre's sister is certain that she saw her, in Oradour, a little town a few kilometres north of Limoges, a couple of days after her brother's death. She is quite well known in those parts.'

'And that is evidence that she killed Monterre? How circumstantial can you get? Anyway, why didn't this woman report her suspicion to the gendarmerie?'

'She did, and they told her to forget about it. They are all terrorists at heart.'

25

'So, are you saying that Liane is back in Limoges? I can't believe that. And didn't Reichsfuehrer Himmler say she was in the south?'

'She is in the south. Not long after her brother's death, Juliette Dugard split with her husband and returned to her original home in Aumont. She is working there now, in a bar-restaurant, and it was there she saw Moulin and de Gruchy. They came to the village several times, buying supplies. They moved quite openly. That whole area is riddled with terrorists. Once again Dugard reported her suspicions and, needless to say, the local police did not follow it up, but they did make a routine report to the nearest Gestapo office, who reported it to Berlin.'

'But they did nothing about it themselves?'

'They visited Aumont but nothing came of it. You know how those fools operate. Anyone of any sense can spot a Gestapo agent a mile away, and they just clam right up.'

'Aren't they going to identify us right away?'

'Of course. But we are not going in undercover. I have been given the use of a Milice Français battalion stationed in Lyons, and I have also been given permission to call in the local gendarmerie, who are now under our control. Once we have interviewed this woman and made sure that what she says is true, we are going to take that whole area apart. And this time, Fräulein, there are going to be none of the problems you seem to have had with Weber's mission. If we have to fight these people in darkness, then, when we have won, we will wait for daylight to identify the dead and photograph them.'

Joanna stared out of the window. Oh Liane! Of course she would believe that she was safe in a place like Aumont, where everyone was on her side. Everyone save one. If only she had some way of getting in touch with James, because it seemed that the only hope of getting Liane out of this mess would be an airlift.

'We're just about there, major,' said Flight Lieutenant Brune. A short, somewhat chubby young man, he had made these flights several times before, more than once with James as a passenger, and handled the Lysander as he might a fast car on an empty road, so that even the hedge-hopping tactics he

26

necessarily employed when flying over France never appeared frightening. Now he added, 'So I'm going up.'

As no one was expecting them, it had to be a parachute drop. He gunned the engine and the little machine soared upwards. James squeezed Amalie's hand. 'OK?'

'Oh, yes,' she said. Like him, she wore a black boiler suit, an all-in-one jacket and trousers fastened by a zip up the front, which fitted over the dress she wore as a French peasant woman (James also wore rough civilian clothes) and, also like him, she had flown with Brune before, when escaping from France. Now she was obviously on a high at the prospect of going back, going home. James remembered Rachel's warning; Amalie was clearly going to need a tight rein. But once she was reunited with Liane, the one person in the world she truly worshipped, she should settle down.

There was a little ping and a red light glowed. The despatcher got out of his seat behind them and opened the door. There was no wind but the night air whistled by and the cabin chilled. James and the despatcher dragged the first of the large lozenge-shaped containers to the door, nodded to each other and pushed it out. 'Going round,' Brune said. The two men grasped grab rails as the Lysander banked and looked down at the billowing white as the parachute opened. 'Next,' Brune said.

The second container went out, and the plane circled again.

'Remember,' James said, 'the first thing we do is find each other.' He moved into the doorway, received another nod from the despatcher and stepped out. As always his stomach seemed to rise up into his throat, but it went down again as soon as the parachute opened. He could see nothing above the canopy, but assumed that Amalie had also jumped, as the noise of the aircraft, distant from the moment he had left it, now faded altogether. Without a wind the night was still. He looked down into blackness; there was no moon. They had jumped on an old map reference, and he had no certainty as to what was beneath him. It should be the lightly wooded slopes of a hill, but it could now also be occupied by a German unit. On the other hand, surely they would be showing lights. He stared down and at last made out trees, and peaks to either side. Brune had done his job with his usual exactitude and dropped

27

them into the required valley. Now he could see the crumpled white of one of the earlier parachutes, and it became a matter of avoiding the trees by pulling the cords to and fro in an attempt to guide the last few feet of the descent.

A moment later he was on the ground, stumbling behind his parachute as he gathered it in, not a difficult job on an airless night. In a few moments he had it under control and had freed the straps. Then he could look around him. Close at hand were both the containers and . . . 'Hey,' Amalie called.

She was caught up in a tree, only about fifty feet away from him, and about twelve feet from the ground. He stood beneath her. 'Well, come on down.'

'How do I do that?'

'Use your knife to cut yourself free, and drop.'

'Twelve feet? I'll break something.'

'My dear girl, you have just dropped a thousand feet.'

'And I think I have already broken something.'

'Cut yourself free. I'll catch you.'

'Oh. Right.' A moment later she was plummeting downwards. He caught her easily enough but staggered to and fro for some moments before he could set her on the ground. 'Oof!' she commented. 'What about my parachute?'

He considered the tree. In the darkness handholds were difficult to discern. And if he were to fall and hurt himself, or even twist an ankle, their mission would be finished before it had properly begun. 'Shine you torch.'

Amalie fumbled in her haversack, produced her torch and played it on the tree. James took off his own haversack, grasped a branch and swung himself up.

'Do be careful,' she said. He got to within reach of the silk and sawed at it with his knife. Slowly it came free, until he could grasp it and tug. Then it began to rip and a moment later he did nearly fall.

'Look out!' Amalie cried.

'Sssh! On a still night sound will travel for ever.' A few more tugs, and the last of the material clouded down. 'Bundle that up, and mine.' He climbed down, went to the first container and cut away the 'chute. Amalie followed more slowly, and he peered at her through the gloom.

'Is something the matter?'

28

'I am in pain.'

'Damnation. Where?'

'My legs were apart when I landed on that branch. I think I have hurt myself.'

'It will be just a bruise. It'll wear off.'

'Suppose I have broken something? Will you look at it?'

'Amalie, we are not here to play games. If you are in real pain, sit down over there while I unload the containers.'

She pouted, sat down, and grunted, then lay down, rolling on to her stomach. So perhaps she had really hurt herself. If she had done something like breaking her pelvis he would have some serious decisions to make. But for the time being he could concentrate on the containers. Such important items as the sticks of gelignite, the strings of hand grenades, the tommy-guns and ammunition and rations, not to mention their sleeping bags, were stacked to one side. But the radio was the most vital. It had been cocooned in several layers of cloth and rubber and, as far as he could ascertain in the darkness, was in working order. He placed the box of batteries beside it and returned to Amalie. 'Can you move?' She pushed herself up to her knees. 'Good girl. We have to shift this equipment from these open slopes to the shelter of that little wood.'

Amalie held his hand to get to her feet. 'You don't believe I am hurt, do you?'

'Help me get this gear to those trees, and I'll look at you.'

'Would you? I'd like that.'

He reflected that while Rachel had sensed that this girl could be dangerous in her inability to restrain her anxiety to get at the Germans, she had not considered the possibility that she might prove a problem in other ways as well. Or had she?

It took them over an hour to transfer all the gear to the trees, and then the containers and the parachutes, then they drank a thermos of coffee. 'What happens now?' Amalie asked.

'The idea was that we go into Aumont together and make a few discreet enquiries. I need you along because my French is clearly foreign. But if you are incapable of moving . . .'

'I can move. How far distant is it?'

'Several miles.'

'I will manage it. Will you look at me?'

He sighed but there was nothing for it. She released her zip and slipped the suit down. 'You will have to take it right off,' he said, 'if the bruise is between your legs.'

'What about my knickers?'

'I think you can keep them on for the time being.'

'Oh.' She sounded disappointed, but she discarded the suit and hitched her skirt up to her waist.

James switched on his torch and shone it on the pale flesh, moving up to the silk covering her groin. She had certainly hurt herself, but the damage was on the inside of her thighs, where the flesh was broken and there was some blood. 'You'll live,' he said. 'In fact, you'll be as right as rain in a couple of days. I'll just put something on these cuts.' He opened the First Aid box, found the analgesic ointment and coated the bruises.

It was Amalie's turn to sigh. 'Do you know that it is eighteen months since a man has touched me there?'

'Well, I wouldn't rush it. You're going to be sore for a few days. There we go. Now, try to get some rest. We'll make a move at first light.'

He took off his own suit, unfolded their sleeping bags, and she inserted herself with sighs and grunts.

'I do not think you like me,' she remarked as she settled.

'Don't be ridiculous. You're one of my favourite people. When you're behaving yourself.'

'But you will not have sex with me. You do not find me attractive. Do you know that apart from those brutes of the Gestapo, only you and Henri have ever touched me there? If Liane were here, you would have sex with *her*.'

'That's another point. I've never been big on incest. Now for God's sake, go to sleep.'

Philipe Chartrin asked, 'Did you hear the plane?' He was a tall young man, but thin, with hatchet features. He stood in the doorway of the small underground bedroom, twisting his hands together, as he always did when in the presence of the woman he worshipped.

Liane de Gruchy was seated on a stool in front of the mirror that hung above the small dressing-table, brushing her hair; no matter what her circumstances, she believed in always looking her best (unless she intended to look her worst, which she could do very efficiently). She wore only the shirt in which she had slept, and that was simply because the cellar was chill. To be in her presence when she was in such deshabille had Philipe's heart pounding. Twenty-three years old, he knew she was ten years his senior, but how he dreamt of sharing her bed, without the shirt! In the four months she had been sheltering beneath his father's farm, he had done no more than touch her hand.

She turned to face him, still sitting, the shirt riding up sufficiently to allow a glimpse of the pale vee at her groin before settling again. That she treated him, as she treated all men, as if he were a brother, was no comfort. He knew her reputation; that when she chose to exert herself, sexually, there was no woman in the world could match her. She was only a few inches over five feet tall, and her body was slender; if her breasts appeared larger than they were, it was because everything about her was so perfectly proportioned. Her hair was a pale blonde, absolutely straight, drifting past her shoulders. But all of her beauty was subsumed by her face, for the flawlessly chiselled features were overlaid with a sheen of soft kindliness that made a man, in addition to wanting to make love with her, even more anxious to hold her and guard her against the world. The knowledge that controlling so much sheer delight was an ice-cold brain that had killed, time and again, that those perfectly shaped hands had more than once been stained with blood, could drive a man mad. And none of it mattered, beside her voice, the purest liquid velvet.

'I hear nothing down here,' she said. 'What time was this plane?'

'Just after midnight. Close and low. It circled twice and then left.'

'How many engines?'

'I think only one.'

'Thank God!' Liane said. 'We are not forgotten. If it circled, there was a drop. Does Monsieur Moulin know?'

'I wished to tell you first.'

'You are a good boy. Now go and wake Monsieur Moulin and tell him what you have told me. Hurry, now.'

Philipe hesitated, cast a last longing look at her legs and

31

left the room. Liane got up and closed the door, then dressed in shirt and trousers and canvas boots. She added her beret, placed her Luger automatic pistol in her knapsack, slung the sack and her tommy-gun from her shoulder, then went into the central cellar where the wine barrels and the cured meat were stored. She encountered Jean Moulin emerging from the other concealed bedroom. 'Do you believe it?' he asked, his voice a thin croak that went with his emaciated frame and trembling hands; if no one could ever doubt his courage, the evidence of what he had suffered was plain to see.

'I intend to find out,' Liane said.

'After so long . . .'

'The important thing is that they are still looking, and now they have found us.' She led the way up the stairs into the farmhouse kitchen. 'Odile.'

Madame Chartrin was laying the table for breakfast. 'You know of the plane?'

'Philipe told me. Now we must find what it dropped. Philipe?'

'I am here, mademoiselle. I am ready.' He held up his shotgun.

'I will come too,' Gabrielle announced The girl was seventeen, six years younger than her brother, but already nearly matching his height. On her the sharp Chartrin features were softened in an attractive delicacy and, if she would never be beautiful, with her abundance of curling dark hair and her full figure she was worth a second glance from any man.

Odile embraced her. 'Be careful.' She would say no more than that; she knew that all of their lives hung by a shoestring.

Charles Chartrin, a heavier edition of his son, was just returning to the house from milking the cows. At his heels the Pyrenean Mountain dog, Rufus, panted. 'You think it could be from London?'

'Single engined, it must be the Lysander. Flying low and circling, it must be a drop. Where, do you reckon?'

'Two, maybe three, valleys away.'

Liane nodded and turned back to Moulin, who stood in the doorway, his face sombre. He wished to accompany her, but he knew that his half-crippled body would only slow her up. She blew him a kiss. 'Back for lunch.'

Philipe snapped his fingers for Rufus to follow them, and he and Gabrielle hurried behind Liane, out of the walled enclosure, to set out across the pasture, which here undulated gently upwards towards the low hillside that masked the next valley, until the cow pasture was behind them. He carried a haversack with some bottles of water and stayed just behind her, content both to let her lead and to watch her steady, tireless movements. Rufus roamed in front of them while Gabrielle came last, her long hair fluttering in the morning breeze, as did the skirt of her dress.

Liane was exhilarated. Escaping the Limoges area last year had been traumatic, especially with Jean needing regular rest and unsteady on his feet. They had been taken entirely by surprise when the Germans had suddenly crossed the border in such strength; at that time no one in Vichy had heard more than a rumour of the Torch landings and, if Petain's government had been thrown into confusion, equally no one had expected the Germans to react so swiftly and so violently. For the previous several months Moulin had worked secretly and successfully, travelling about the country, seeing various Resistance leaders and instilling in them some idea of homogeneity. They could never be considered an underground army; even had they possessed sufficient weaponry to mount any kind of rising, the different commanders all had different ideologies and thus different agendas. But he had been able to persuade most of them to accept the concept of General de Gaulle as leader of the Free French, as he liked to call his movement, and Jean had reckoned he had some ten thousand men and women prepared to rise up whenever the Allies launched their long-promised invasion, and in the meanwhile who were willing to carry out a systematic disruption of German installations and infrastructure. If blowing up trains and bridges was very dangerous and not always successful, other measures such as pouring sand into engine oil or 'misinterpreting' orders so that the wrong train was misdirected to the wrong place were simple and nearly impossible for the enemy to pin down.

Now the various groups were entirely splintered. No one knew what was happening to anyone else. Liane had known immediately that she and Jean had to leave Limoges; nor did she dare tell Anatole, the baker, Pound Seventeen, anything more of their intentions than that they were going south. She did not entirely trust Anatole, and she certainly did not trust his ability to withstand Gestapo questioning. But she had told him to convey that information to Pound One, James Barron, as soon as possible. James would surely recognize that she was heading back to the Massif.

But had he? Or had something happened to Anatole? Or had he simply betrayed them? The problems were that they had had to abandon radio contact, as there was no way they could carry the cumbersome transmitter with them, and it had taken them two months to get down here. She had at least been sure of a welcome, and especially from the Chartrins, who she had known back in 1940 before her group had been forced to move north after Weber's raid. Charles Chartrin and his son had fitted out two of the cellar rooms for them to live in, and although the gendarmerie had come to the farm, quite recently – part of a routine search, they had explained – they had clearly neither expected nor wanted to find anything.

In the meantime they had resumed recruiting, slowly and carefully, never letting on who they actually were but claiming to represent a central controlling force that would one day call the people of the Massif into action. That had been interesting and useful work, and hopefully would be rewarding, but without support from London it had also been pointlessly frustrating. But now . . . She topped the rise, only slightly out of breath, and waited for Philipe and Gabrielle to catch her up. From her knapsack she took her binoculars and swept the valley below. The sun was steadily rising behind her, but much of the valley remained in gloom.

'Must be the next one over,' she decided.

'I saw something move.' Philipe did not have binoculars, but he had countryman's eyes. 'In those trees.'

'I see it too,' Gabrielle said.

Liane levelled the glasses again and kept them focused for several seconds. 'Yes,' she said at last. 'In those trees.'

'They could be Germans.'

'Germans would not be hiding in a wood. Let's get down there.' She started down the slope and, after a moment's hesitation, the Chartrins followed. Rufus caught the spirit and charged ahead. They moved towards the wood at a steady pace, but Liane unslung her tommy-gun, just in case. The people in the wood remained concealed until they were within a hundred yards, then a man stepped from the trees. Liane halted, peering at the shabby clothes, the countryman's beret. Then she shouted, 'James!' and ran forward, Rufus beside her, now barking excitedly.

James ran too, checking as the dog charged him.

'Down, Rufus!' Liane commanded, and the large beast halted a few feet short of its target, panting. Liane went past him, and she and James threw their arms round each other. 'Oh, James,' she said. 'It's been so long. There were times I thought you had abandoned us.'

He kissed her mouth. 'Abandoned you? It took us this long to get hold of Anatole.'

She pulled her head back. 'Something has happened?'

'You were never too happy about him, as I remember. But come . . .' He held her hand and led her towards the trees.

Liane stared at her sister, just stepping from shelter. 'Amalie? Amalie!' She released James to embrace the younger woman. 'But what are you doing here?'

'I have come back to be with you. To fight the Boches.'

Liane looked at James. 'She's got clearance,' he said.

'And I thought you would be safe until the War ends,' Liane grumbled. 'But it is good to see you.' She hugged her again, and then indicated the two young people, who were slowly approaching. 'This is Philipe Chartrin and Gabrielle. You remember the Chartrins, Amalie?'

'I remember them very well. As I remember you, Philipe. But Gabrielle, how you have grown.'

Gabrielle simpered. 'She is a woman now,' Philipe said proudly. 'But Madame Burstein, we were so sorry to learn about your husband.'

'He was avenged,' Amalie said. 'And will be again.'

'We must get back to the farm,' Liane said. 'We are here because Philipe heard the Lysander. Others may have heard it too.'

'We cannot hurry,' James said. 'Amalie hurt herself landing.'

'Is it bad?'

35

'It is awkward,' Amalie said. 'It makes walking difficult.'

'Then Philipe will carry you.'

'There is also some gear,' James said. 'In the next valley. Where we landed.'

Liane's eyes gleamed. 'Guns? Ammunition?'

'A few. But more importantly, a radio.'

'Thank God for that. We have felt so cut off. Is this *matériel* hidden?'

'From anything but a serious search by someone who knows there is something to find.'

'I think we should look at it, and make sure of the radio, at least. Philipe, Gabrielle, take Madame Burstein to the farm. We will be back later.'

'You do not wish me to stay with you, mademoiselle?'

'I have told you what I wish you to do. And take Rufus with you. ' She kissed Amalie. 'We will have a long talk, this afternoon. Show me where you have hidden this gear, James.'

The pair of them set off, and Amalie looked at Philipe. 'You do not have to carry me, if you are prepared to walk slowly and rest from time to time.'

'It would be a pleasure to carry you, madame, at least from time to time.'

'Well, when I get tired. Which way is it?'

'Over here. You are happy for the mademoiselle to go off with that Englishman?'

'They are old friends.'

'They are lovers.'

'You are an observant boy. Yes, they are lovers. They have been lovers for years, whenever they have been able to get together, which hasn't been very often.'

'She gives her body to him,' Philipe said, half to himself. 'But he will not marry her. He is a swine.'

'Of course he is not a swine,' Amalie snapped. 'He would marry her, if he could. But he is an army officer and she will not leave France while we are fighting the Boche.'

'You say he is an army officer? Then what is he doing here?'

'He is our boss. He has come to tell us what to do next.'

'Mademoiselle Liane has a boss: Monsieur Moulin.'

'This man is Monsieur Moulin's boss as well.'

'I think Mr Barron looks very nice,' Gabrielle ventured.

Philipe hunched his shoulders.

Liane and James climbed the hill and went down into the next valley. 'Is she really hurt?' Liane asked.

'Just bruised between her thighs. She landed in a tree.'

'But why is she here at all? After all the trouble Joanna took, the risk she ran . . .'

'To tell you the truth, Li, after not hearing from you for so long, the brigadier began to feel that you were out of action, and so—'

'He sent Amalie to replace me? One day I must meet this brigadier of yours and teach him the facts of life. How is Joanna?'

'I have no idea.'

Liane stopped walking. 'What's happened to her?'

'Again, I don't know that anything has happened to her. We offered her an out last summer, but she evaded our surveillance and returned to Germany. Since then nothing.'

Liane resumed walking. 'Why did she return to Germany if you were no longer employing her?'

'Again, I have no idea. There was some talk that she had a German boyfriend . . .'

Liane smiled. 'You think that will upset me? Do I not also have a boyfriend?'

'Yours is on the same side as yourself.'

'So, do you now consider her an enemy?'

'I personally do not know what to consider her. But there are lots of people who do.'

They reached the top of the hill and looked down into the next valley. 'It will have to be sorted out when the War is over; Joanna, Madeleine . . .' She sighed. 'Will the War ever be over, James?'

He put his arm round her shoulder to hug her. 'It's coming closer every day. You know about Stalingrad?'

'There is a rumour that the Germans were defeated.'

'Defeated? An entire army, over a million men, was wiped out.'

She looked up at him. 'Does it mean anything for us?'

'It means that Hitler is being squeezed everywhere. He's

37

hanging on to North Africa by his bootstraps, he's being bombed day and night, and now he's come a real cropper in Russia . . . Oh, did you know that Helsingen has been invalided home from the Russian front, badly injured?'

'I did not know that. Oh, poor Madeleine.'

'Did you ever know Helsingen?'

'No. He came on the scene after I was already an outlaw. But I know he helped Amalie, or got his friend Hoeppner to do so. Is he going to die?'

'We have only the report that he was wounded.'

'Then perhaps he will survive. Where are your goods?'

'In that wood.'

'Well, at least they are not visible from the air.' She went down the slope, her hair fluttering behind her.

He kept at her shoulder. 'What is the situation here?'

'Quiet. There is a German presence and they, or the gendarmerie, make searches every so often, but not very purposefully. That is because no one knows I am here, or Jean, and because we have been carrying out no operations.' She glanced at him. 'I assume that is now about to end?'

'Would that bother you?'

'I would welcome it. I have been feeling very guilty, sitting here and doing nothing for all this time. But just to be back in touch with you makes it all worth while.'

'Liane . . .' He caught her arm, and she turned against him. Her kiss was hungry, but when his hands slipped down to her buttocks she shook her head.

'Let's go into the trees. Out here is too exposed.'

They hurried and found the containers where he had left them, half buried beneath their leaves and branches. She opened the first one. 'It is a start. But there will never be enough.' Again she turned into his arms. 'Love me, James. Oh, love me.' Although the sun was now high, the day remained chilly, but as he and Amalie had intended to return to the wood had their reconnoitre not been successful, their sleeping bags remained where they had left them. Liane stripped with the simple grace that depicted all of her actions and slipped into the quilted warmth. James joined her a few seconds later, and their bodies nestled against each other.

'Did you sleep with Amalie?' she asked.

38

'Would you be jealous if I had?'

She smiled as she kissed him. 'I am in no position to be jealous of you, James.'

'Well, I didn't.'

'Didn't she want to?'

'Yes, she did. But I knew I was coming to see you.'

She kissed him again. 'It would have done her good.'

'Maybe. But at the time she wouldn't have enjoyed having me between her legs.' His hands slipped between Liane's legs. Although they had had so few shared moments since 1940, they both knew what the other wanted.

She sighed, put her hands down to hold him and feel him swell. 'What am I to do with her, James?'

'She wants to fight. To kill Germans. And she'll be useful to you; she's an explosives expert.'

'Amalie?'

'She's been to school.'

'I sometimes think all she wants to do is die. Oh, James ... James ...'

To have an orgasm with Liane de Gruchy had to be to open the gates of paradise. She gave herself without the least hesitation in any direction, and if from time to time he could not stop himself from wondering if she had behaved like that with all the men she had seduced – even that rat Johann Roess on a memorable occasion – or indeed the women, he knew that was the secret of her success. For had not an even more famous Liane, the immortal courtesan de Pougy, written that the only way to make a man believe that you love him while having sex with him, is to love him while having sex with him.

As there was, and never had been, any reason for her to *pretend* to love him, other than his obvious adoration of her, he refused to believe that such an observation applied to him. But he also knew that she could be the most single-minded woman he had ever encountered, and *her* only reason for living was to see France finally liberated; although, perhaps unlike her sister, she had every intention of staying alive until that happened. So it was no surprise when, after lying quiescent in his arms for a few moments, she asked, 'So tell me what you wish me to do?'

But then, if there were a more single-minded man in the world than anyone *she* had ever known, it was himself. 'I have come to tell you about wolfram,' he said.

'James!' Jean Moulin embraced him. 'It is good to see you. After so long . . .'

'I have a letter for you, from General de Gaulle.' James gave him the envelope then sat silently with Liane and Amalie while he read the message.

'Promises, promises,' Moulin said. 'And the usual bombast. But that is the nature of the beast. He certainly seems very confident. He talks of great things about to happen.' He raised his head. 'Would that be this year?'

'Everyone is talking about this year,' Amalie said.

'No one is supposed to be talking about it at all,' James said. 'And certainly not someone in General de Gaulle's position.'

'He says,' Moulin went on, 'that when it happens, I must be ready to put fifty thousand Frenchmen into the field.'

'And women,' Liane reminded him.

'He does not mention women at all. Fifty thousand! He is starting to believe his own propaganda. Even if I could raise fifty thousand men, how am I to arm them? Will your government provide arms and ammunition for such a number, James?'

'We haven't got it spare. With respect, Jean, I think we should leave the big things to the big boys and get on with the task in hand. Do you know where this wolfram mine is situated?'

'Yes.' The map was spread on the kitchen table, and Moulin indicated the area. 'Can it not be bombed?'

'Not if we intend to destroy the mine itself.' James laid several photographs beside the map. 'These were taken by the RAF. You'll see there are barracks here, and here. One of them is for the labour force. Then there is the office, and quarters for the management staff.'

'And two watch towers,' Liane commented.

'Is that a problem?'

'I shouldn't think so.' She indicated the dark areas fringing the photos. 'Are these woods?'

40

'Yes.'

'Then there will be no problem. And the nearest town is . . . ?'

'Ten miles away. But there will be telephone communication. How long would it take you and your people to get there?'

She checked the scale and peered at the map again, studying the terrain. 'A week. With twenty men.'

'And two women,' Amalie said.

'Have you that number?'

She nodded. 'I can raise that number.'

'And arms?'

'Thanks to what you brought we have six tommy-guns and eight pistols. My people are all farmers, so they will have shotguns.'

'You also have the two dozen grenades.'

She nodded again. 'They will be vital.'

James turned to Moulin. 'Any idea how well the mine will be guarded?'

'In such a remote area, I would say not more than twenty men.'

'One for one,' Amalie declared.

'Every one armed with an automatic weapon.'

'Can you do it?' James asked Liane.

'Yes.'

'You understand, I would come with you, if I could. But I have been expressly ordered to make contact and return to London. As soon as we can set up some landing lights I must call Brune for a pick-up.'

'Of course I understand, my darling.' Liane squeezed his hand. 'But when you get home, send us some more weapons, please.'

'When will you be ready to move?'

'As soon as we can contact all our people.' She looked at Moulin.

He nodded. 'I will start tomorrow.'

'Well, then . . .' She stood up, still holding James' hand. 'We are for bed.'

Captain Kaufman scrambled to his feet, hastily buttoning his tunic. If he had never seen Colonel Roess before, he had heard

41

the name. Now he goggled at the little man, who was today wearing his black uniform, and at the tall blonde woman beside him. Beauty and the beast, he thought; he was a classicist.

'Herr Colonel! Heil Hitler! Will you not sit down? And the Fräulein. If I had known you were coming . . .'

'So would everyone else.' Roess sat before the desk. Joanna fetched the other chair in the room to sit beside him.

'Oh, no, Herr Colonel. But . . .' He looked at Joanna and then back at Roess. 'Is there a problem? Here? In Lyons?'

'You would not say so? Now you will tell me that you do not know the name Juliette Dugard?'

'Juliette Dugard. Oh, yes, I know of Juliette Dugard. A madwoman.'

'What makes you say that?'

'Well, her brother committed suicide, you know.'

'Our information is that he was murdered.'

'That is what she says. She claims he was murdered by the Resistance. By the famous Liane de Gruchy. But there is no proof. Now she claims to have seen this de Gruchy quite close to here, in the village of Aumont. Well, Herr Colonel, I ask you . . . and again there is no proof.'

'I am not interested in proof, captain. I am interested in Liane de Gruchy. What steps have you taken to follow this matter up? Have you carried out searches?'

'Searches, Herr Colonel? This is a huge area, and I have only a few men—'

'You have the use of the Milice Français and the gendarmerie.'

'I do not trust them. Certainly the Milice Français. All Frenchmen hate us at heart; they only join outfits like the Milice to avoid the labour battalions. I did request the gendarmerie to make enquiries, but they turned nothing up.'

'But you trust *them*. Very good, Captain Kaufman. I wish Madame Dugard brought in for questioning. Do it discreetly, we do not want to alarm the neighbourhood. And when you have done that, you may pack your bags.'

'Sir?'

'It is my opinion that you are not temperamentally suited for this assignment. You may do better in Russia.'

*　　*　　*

42

Joanna stood at the window of her hotel room and looked out at the rolling hills. Liane was out there. Did she know what was happening in here? Had she any inkling of the net that was closing around her? And there was nothing *she* could do about it, with Roess always at her side, save . . .

She heard him now, tapping on her door. 'Are you awake, Fräulein?'

'Yes.'

'Well, dress yourself and come down. They brought in Madame Dugard last night.'

'I'll be down in a minute.' She put on her clothes, picked up her shoulder-bag and checked that her Luger pistol was loaded. Beside it there lay a knife with a six-inch blade. The moment of decision. She hated using knives. And she actually hated killing people. She was about to take a terrible risk. But if Liane's life was at stake . . . She picked up the pistol again, extracted the magazine and removed the first two bullets. Then she removed the bullet from the chamber. The bullets she placed in her shoulder-bag. Then she slapped the magazine back into the gun butt and went to the door. God save Liane, she thought. But she would rather do it herself.

Three

Catastrophe

'Do you really trust this woman?' Joanna asked, as she got into the car beside Roess.

'As a woman? Good God, no. She is French.'

'But you are prepared to trust her information.'

'She is a woman whose brother was murdered. I am prepared to trust her desire for vengeance.'

'But you have only her opinion that he *was* murdered. The gendarmerie in Limoges do not think so. So this woman claims to have seen Liane in Oradour not long after her brother's death. Has this sighting been confirmed by anyone else? And if it were, why should she not be in Oradour? It is only a few kilometres north of Limoges. The mere fact that she was there does not mean she had anything to do with Monterre's death.'

'Jut what are you trying to say, Fräulein?'

'The first is that we may be engaging on a wild goose chase at the behest of an hysterical woman determined to avenge her brother, dreaming up sightings of de Gruchy in every corner.'

'You did not suggest this to Reichsfuehrer Himmler.'

'I had not had the time to think about it.'

'Well, as we are here, we must follow it up.' The car had arrived at Gestapo Headquarters.

'But there is another aspect of the situation that concerns me,' Joanna said, as the door was opened.

Roess, about to step out, checked himself. 'What is that?'

'Do you not find the whole thing too pat? This woman claims to have seen Liane de Gruchy in Oradour. No one else seems to have done so. Now she claims to have seen her here

44

in the south. No one else has. Is it not possible that it is all a subterfuge, that she is actually working *with* Liane? After all, we have only her say so that she is not a member of the Resistance.'

'What would be the purpose of this subterfuge?'

'Well, she claims to have seen Liane in the Limoges area, when it seems doubtful that she was there. Now she claims to have seen her down here. So we, predictably, come rushing down here to find her, when it is extremely possible that she is somewhere else, far away, about to blow up something or murder someone.'

Roess got out of the car. 'If I thought that, I would take this woman apart, inch by inch.'

Joanna joined him. 'It would be simpler to find out the truth.'

Roess acknowledged the salutes of the sentries as he strode into the building. 'Oh, I intend to do that.'

Joanna walked at his shoulder. 'With your whips and your electrodes. I could do it for you much more quickly and effectively.' He turned to face her. 'I can do it without destroying her, and in a tenth of the time,' Joanna said. 'You need to remember that I was trained by Oskar Weber.'

He considered for a moment, then said, 'Very well. It should be amusing to watch.'

'I work alone.'

'Why?'

'A woman needs to have her secrets. It will only take me half an hour.'

Another brief consideration, then he nodded. 'Very well. You may have half an hour, then I will take over.'

Kaufman was waiting for them, sweating. 'Good morning, Herr Colonel. Fräulein. Heil Hitler!'

'Where is the prisoner?' Roess demanded.

'In my office.'

'Your office? Why is this?'

'Well, Herr Colonel, she is not actually a prisoner. She has come here to supply us with information. As soon as we told her what we wanted, she came of her own free will.'

Roess looked at Joanna, who shrugged. 'The office will do very well.' In fact, she thought, it will be ideal.

45

'Very well. Proceed. You have half an hour. Show the Fräulein to your office, Kaufman, and I will have coffee.'

'Of course, Herr Colonel.' Kaufman signalled an orderly and then escorted Joanna up the stairs to his office and opened the door. 'My people are close, if you need assistance.'

'I never need assistance,' Joanna assured him and stepped inside, locking the door behind her.

The woman seated in the chair before the desk turned to look at her. Juliette Dugard was a large woman, almost as tall as Joanna herself, and equally well built. Unlike Joanna, her features were also large, and coarse, and her hair a straggly and unkempt dark brown. She wore a somewhat shapeless dress, clearly hastily put on. 'I was told the Gestapo wished to interview me,' she said.

Joanna sat behind the desk. 'I am the Gestapo. Tell me about Liane de Gruchy.'

'She is a devil. She is all sweetness and light on the outside, with her soft voice and her charming smile, but underneath she is a cold-hearted killer.'

'Of traitors and Germans, certainly.' Juliette's head jerked. 'And you claim to know her,' Joanna said. 'And to have seen her, recently.'

'Not a week ago. In Aumont, in the bar where I work.'

'Was she wearing any form of disguise?'

'Oh, well, she wears a headscarf and those sunglass things. Very chic. But there is no need for her to be disguised. Vlabon is her friend.'

'Who is Vlabon?'

'The patron. Everyone in Aumont is her friend.'

'Except you.'

Once again Juliette jerked. 'She murdered my brother.'

'So you say. Is Mademoiselle de Gruchy by herself when she comes to Aumont?'

'No, no. She is always accompanied by a man.'

'The same man?'

'No, no. Sometimes it is a young man, sometimes someone older. Sometimes there is a young girl.'

'Do you know these people?'

'No. Not the young ones. De Gruchy called the boy Philipe.'

'And the girl?'

46

'Gabrielle. I think they are brother and sister.'

'And the older one?'

'He she calls Jean. He walks with a limp and has a hoarse voice. I believe he is the man Moulin.'

'And you can identify these people? Mademoiselle de Gruchy and these two men? And the girl? Do you know their surnames?'

'No. I have tried asking Monsieur Vlabon, and he tells me to mind my own business. But if your people are in the bar when next they come in, I will point them out to you. But afterwards, you must give me protection.'

'We intend to take care of you. There is just one more question I have to ask. These people, do you know where they live, where they come from to visit Aumont?'

'I believe it is on a farm in the Massif. But I do not know, exactly.'

'I see. Now, Madame Dugard, I have to tell you that it is Colonel Roess' intention to execute you, the moment he is satisfied that you have told him everything he wishes to know.' Juliette stared at her in consternation. 'And I may say,' Joanna went on, 'as I know Colonel Roess very well, that he is not likely to be satisfied by anything you have told me, and thus your execution is not likely to be quick or painless. He actually enjoys torturing people, and he enjoys torturing women more than anything else.'

'But . . . I am trying to help you catch this woman.'

'So you say. But to Colonel Roess you are merely a nuisance who can be used for his pleasure.'

'What am I to do?'

'I would say that your only hope is to get out of here and disappear. I am sure you can do that.' She smiled. 'You could join the Resistance yourself.'

'But . . .' Juliette licked her lips. 'This is Gestapo Headquarters. How can I get out of here?'

Joanna had already made a visual reconnaissance of the situation. 'Through this window behind me. It leads on to a flat roof, from which you will be able to reach the street. Once there it is up to you. But it is at least a chance. It is better than being flogged to death.' Juliette looked at her, and then at the door, and then at the window. 'Here.' Joanna opened her bag and took out the Luger. 'You will have had to over-power me. Do you know how to use this?'

'I think so.'

'Well, take it, and use it if you have to. I will pretend to have been so shocked by your getting hold of the gun and escaping that I will be unable to raise the alarm for ten minutes.'

Another lick of the lips, but Juliette took the pistol. 'Why are you doing this?'

'Let's say that I also have secrets to protect.'

Juliette looked at the door a last time, then went to the window and opened it. As she did so, Joanna screamed, 'Help! Help me!' at the top of her voice.

Juliette, having hitched up her skirt and got one leg over the sill, turned back to her, her face a mixture of outrage and anger. Lips drawing back from her teeth, she levelled the pistol and squeezed the trigger, and again as it clicked on the empty chamber. As she fired a third time, ineffectively, Joanna closed with her, having taken the knife from her bag. This she now drove into Juliette's breast, and again.

'Would you like to tell me what happened?' Roess inquired.

'Give me another glass of brandy.' Joanna was still panting as she sat in Kaufman's chair. The front of her dress was drenched in blood, and there was no doubting the genuine-ness of her agitation; but then, she had never killed someone with a knife before. Roess snapped his fingers, and one of the anxious secretaries pushed the broken door aside and hurried from the room to fetch the bottle. Kaufman also hovered, along with several of his men. Juliette's body had been taken from the window and laid on the floor; she still held the pistol. The brandy was brought, and Joanna drank deeply.

'The bitch jumped me. Took me completely by surprise. I hadn't even done anything to her yet. I was talking to her, telling what would happen if she did not fully co-operate, when she suddenly attacked me, knocked me down, took my pistol and ran to the window.'

'So you got up and went after her with your knife. But she had the gun. Why did she not shoot you?'

'Of course she shot at me. What she did not know was that

48

I always keep my gun with an empty chamber, to avoid accidents.'

'And she did not know who she was dealing with,' Kaufman said admiringly.

Roess shot him an impatient glance. 'So you obtained no information and damn near got yourself killed. You are both over-confident and incompetent.'

'Of course I obtained information,' Joanna snapped. 'She gave me a detailed description of this so-called Liane de Gruchy, and proved her entire story to be a pack of lies. She described the woman as being at least her own height. Well, she is a tall woman. I know, and so do you, Herr Colonel, that Liane is below average height.'

Roess regarded her for several seconds. Then he said, 'What else did she say of her?'

'Oh, she said that she was good-looking and had blonde hair. But these things are well known. It was obvious to me that she had never actually met Liane.'

'And the man?'

'An elderly man with a limp. Here again she betrayed herself. Jean Moulin is not an elderly man.'

'He may well appear so, after his experiences. Have you ever met him?'

'Once. Briefly. At Amalie's marriage to the Jew Burstein.'

'But you would recognize him.'

'Well, I don't know. As you say, he may well have changed after being tortured by your thugs.'

Roess gave a thin smile. 'But you are now a thug yourself, Fräulein. A veritable Kali. The evidence is before you. I think we will proceed with our plan, go to Aumont, and see what we can unearth.'

Joanna spilled some of her brandy, and hastily drank the rest. 'What for, when we know it will be a waste of time?'

'I do not agree with you. I believe something is going on there that may be well worth investigating. Now the car will take you back to the hotel so that you can change those stinking clothes. Kaufman, get rid of this carrion and have the place cleaned up. Then I will tell you what dispositions I require. Off you go, Fräulein. I will make a full report of this incident to the Reichsfuehrer.'

49

Joanna got up. I have committed murder, she thought, to no avail. She left the room.

'My darling!' Liane held James close. 'God speed.'

'And to you. If you knew how much I wish I could be coming with you . . .'

'I do know. Take care of him, Mr Brune.'

Brune, standing in the gloom beside his aircraft, took the opportunity to kiss her. 'I will do that, mademoiselle.'

James hugged Amalie and shook hands with Moulin. 'Hopefully, next time I see you I'll have an army at my back.'

A few minutes later the Lysander was soaring into the night sky. Liane stared after it until it disappeared. 'Now,' she said. 'Put out those flares, and then let us join the others. We have a long way to go tonight.'

'Do you shed not a tear for your lover?' Philipe asked.

Liane frowned at him, but he would know James had slept in her bed during his two nights at the farm. 'Did not a poet write that there is a time for everything, a time to be born and a time to die, a time to laugh and a time to cry, a time to love and a time to hate. And a time to kill. That is what we are now going to do. Jean?'

'How I also wish I could come with you. But I too will wish you God speed.'

'And you will stay at the farm until we return?'

'Well, in a couple of days time I will go into Aumont as usual, and have a drink with Jean-Pierre. It would not be a good idea to let anyone think that we are up to something.'

'I will come with you,' Gabrielle said. She also was disappointed that she was not being allowed to accompany the guerillas.

'Well, take care.' Liane hugged them both and led her people into the night.

The rest of the group were waiting for her at the rendezvous. This was the first time Liane had had the opportunity to size up her little band, for she had not worked with them before. She was actually in a unique position herself. Always before when engaging in any large-scale action, she had been accompanied by an utterly trustworthy male aide, usually her brother

Pierre, except for the two occasions she had been commanded by James himself. But Pierre was dead, cut down by Johann Roess' henchmen in the ruins of Dieppe, and James was in England.

To the men who followed her now, willingly enough because she was a legend, she was an unknown quantity in the flesh. Only Amalie and Philipe knew her personally; only Amalie had fought beside her before. She could not doubt Amalie's courage, her determination to fight, to kill Germans and, even if she had not yet seen her at work, she was prepared to believe that she had become an explosives expert, but even had James not warned her, she better than anyone knew of her sister's mental instability. It had been there even as a child, but lost in the general ambience of a wealthy, happy home. When she had met and fallen in love with Henri Burstein, she had done so with all the concentrated energy that was part of her personality.

Their parents had not approved. Although they would have denied any suggestion of anti-Semitism, however much they had to be aware that there was an undercurrent of it throughout French society, Albert de Gruchy was descended from a long line of wine growers, who over two centuries had steadily grown in wealth and prestige and social standing. While Barbara de Gruchy came, however remotely, from a family that had been at the top of the English social tree even before two members of it had made the tragic mistake of marrying King Henry VIII. Neither Barbara nor Albert felt that Henri, whose father owned a dry goods store in Dieppe, would fit into their social scene and family background, even if Henri had attended St Cyr with Amalie's elder brother Pierre, and they had been officers in the same regiment of the Motorized Cavalry. Very probably they had been right. Yet they had given way and thrown all their considerable wealth and social clout behind the wedding.

Liane knew that she had been at least partly responsible for this. Not by any arm-twisting on behalf of her little sister, and not even by expressing any great admiration for Henri – although she certainly had no prejudices – but simply because *she* had failed her parents. Not only was she their eldest child, but she was the most beautiful, the most talented, the most

51

forceful of them all. Her future had been unlimited, and carefully plotted, beginning with the Swiss finishing school, and intended to culminate in a great party in Paris at which she would be displayed to the fashionable world and hopefully be snapped up by some handsome, and rich, aristocrat and live happily ever after.

That plan had never been going to work. Liane had not liked having her life chosen for her, and she had never liked the idea of subjecting herself to one man and spending her youth in a world of nappies and aimless cocktail parties. But her mind had not been made up until she had met Joanna. At that time the concepts of sexual and bisexual behaviour, heterosexual and homosexual inclinations, had not crossed her mind. As with any collection of high-spirited teenage girls confined together there had been much exploratory horseplay, but none of it had been the least meaningful, emotionally, until the night Joanna had crawled into her bed. That had made her want more, and to the physical excitement had soon been added an emotional attachment that had lasted.

Inevitably they had been discovered and expelled. Mama and Papa had been informed and been shocked. She had been returned to the family home in Paulliac on the Gironde; Joanna had been sent back to Connecticut and her mother. Yet neither set of parents had been able to alter the course of events. Joanna's parents had been handicapped by being divorced. Her father was a Swedish diplomat, and thus she had alternate homes on both sides of the Atlantic. As she was obviously going to do her own thing, no matter what, her mother had secured her a job as a roving gossip columnist for an American newspaper, which had launched her into the European, and especially the German, social scene during the last years of the thirties, and thus had led almost directly to the bizarre situation she was now in, where her instincts had had to be submerged in Nazi masculine ideology, her very real hatred for the regime that had carelessly killed her brother so disguised as to have her called a traitor by everyone who did not know the truth – and that was only half a dozen people in the whole world. She had lived now for three years on a knife-edge. But knowing Joanna, although Liane had only

52

managed to see her on a couple of occasions since 10 May 1940, she was enjoying it to the hilt.

But when the War was over? Did she love Joanna? She thought not, in the way Joanna loved her. Because their lives, after that first separation, had taken such different courses. *Her* parents had certainly been united in their desire to change her ways, but they too had been unable to stand up to her personality. So they had surrendered, bought her a Paris flat – was it still there? – given her a generous allowance and told her to get on with her life. She had done that, losing herself in the demi-monde of would-be artists and writers and painters that thronged the Left Bank, having sex as and when she chose, with whomever she chose, male and female. She had known she was wasting her youth, her beauty and her talents but, like a drug addict, had been unable to stop.

She had been waiting for something to happen, some man to sweep her off her feet, or some event . . . The odd thing was that on the day before 10 May 1940, she had actually met such a man and seduced him with all the confident skill she had developed over the previous ten years. That James Barron had been invited to the wedding by her sister Madeleine had added spice to the occasion; Madeleine had never approved of her lifestyle. And within hours the entire world had fallen apart, and she had found what it seemed she had spent her entire life anticipating.

It had not happened immediately. First had come the traumatic events of the first few days, when she had, with her usual careless abandon at that time, volunteered to drive Pierre and Henri, and James, up to the Belgium border so that they could rejoin their units; the wedding had taken place in Chartres, just south of Paris. It had been a jolly, with Joanna at her side. And it had turned out to be a catastrophe, as on their return journey they had become caught up in the masses of refugees, had had their car destroyed, along with Joanna's half-brother, in a strafing attack, and finally when, exhausted and distraught, they had sought shelter in a deserted house, they had been found by those German deserters. Perhaps because of the life she had lived during the preceding few years she had reacted more calmly than Joanna, who had been hysterical. Yet when she had regained the safety and privacy of her Paris flat she had wanted only to shut herself away from the world. At that moment she had not even cared that France had surrendered, that for the foreseeable future she and her countrymen and women were going to have to exist as a conquered people.

Biedermann had changed that. The Gestapo officer had been one of those who had interviewed her after the rape, trying to get her to suppress her story. She had actually agreed, in her anxiety to bury the experience. But he had marked her beauty and, as he had supposed, her vulnerability, and so had come calling, once the Germans were in full control of Paris, seeking to assert the rights of the conqueror. She did not suppose anything had suddenly snapped. She had, in fact, over the preceding couple of weeks, been slowly aware of a mood creeping over her. She could not spend that foreseeable future locked in that flat, going out only to buy food. She had to *do* something, and not just to avenge what had happened to her, or for France, but to atone for the years she had wasted in meaningless hedonism. But she had had no idea what she could do, until Biedermann forced himself on her. She had submitted, because he was bigger and stronger than she. But when he was contentedly asleep, she had obtained a kitchen knife and cut his throat.

That simple act, which would have been unthinkable before the War, or even perhaps the previous day, had propelled her through life as if she had been fired from a cannon. Her first task had been to escape immediate arrest. This she had done by taking Biedermann's papers as well as his pistol and fleeing Paris. She had calculated, correctly, that Biedermann, who had been on his way home from his office, would have told none of his colleagues that he intended to visit a Frenchwoman with rape in mind, and it had been three days before his corpse had been found. By then she had been in Vichy. More importantly, she knew where she was going. For Biedermann had carelessly told her that Jean Moulin had escaped the Gestapo, by whom he had been arrested and tortured for failing publicly to condemn the original rape claim and acknowledge that the deserters had been *French,* and was reputed to be sheltering amidst the virtually impenetrable peaks and valleys and woods of the Massif Central. There she had found him, and the small band of desperate patriots who were determined to resist the Boche to the end.

She remembered with some amusement that, Jean apart, the guerillas had not actually welcomed a woman, however beautiful and however famous, in their midst. But she had soon proved more dangerously determined that any of them. And there had been a bonus she could never have expected. As they had regrouped following the disaster of Dunkirk, the British had sought help wherever they could find it, and an obvious source to tap had been those French men and women who had refused to accept defeat. The British SIS, the Secret Intelligence Service, had despatched agents to seek out possible guerilla units that they could arm and control. One of those agents had been her own brother Pierre, and his controller had been that same James Barron, with whom she had shared that unforgettable night on the eve of the invasion.

This had not been a coincidence. James and Pierre had escaped Dunkirk together, and it had seemed natural to his superiors that James, as a friend of the de Gruchys, should be Pierre's controller. James had had no idea, then, that this would involve controlling Liane as well. Out of that had come this strange, intensely intimate and yet curiously abstract relationship. They loved, desperately whenever they had been able to get together, which was about twice a year. When they were separated, they went about their business, separately and yet, as he gave the orders, always working together no matter how far they might be apart. She knew he suffered more than she did. His adoration of her was evident but, as on this occasion, he had to sit in London and wait and listen, while she risked her life; the three occasions on which they had been able to fight shoulder to shoulder had been bonuses.

Did she regret any of it? Only the death of Pierre, the anguish suffered by Amalie, who was now again her responsibility, and the deaths of the other brave men who had fought at her side. As for the life itself, did she want it ever to end? Of course she did, for the sake of France, of her surviving family – even Madeleine – and for the sake of all the thousands who were dying every day the conflict continued. But for herself? Could she ever go back to what she was before the War? Did she want to? But what was the alternative? James kept telling her he wanted to marry her, but could she ever be a normal housewife? And James, for all his charismatic personality and ruthless determination, was at heart a very conventional man. So think only of the present and the job in hand; she had, in any event, used up all of her nine lives.

Her people had assembled within a few hours of James' departure, and she looked around the faces gathered in the little wood not far from Aumont. She had met them all, but in the darkness it was difficult to identify every one of them. 'Gather round,' she said and spread the map on the ground, playing her torch beam on to the stiff paper. 'We move out now,' she told them. 'We will travel in seven groups, six of three and one of two, that is. Amalie and myself.'

'I do not think two women should travel by themselves,' Philipe objected.

'But two such women,' commented one of the other men.

'Thank you, Gaston,' Liane said. 'Just remember, all of you, that I give the orders. Now, the rendezvous is here.' She indicated the wooded area on the map. 'We meet here at dawn in five days' time. Remember, you move only by night and you take care not to be seen. You all have your rations?' They nodded. 'Then I will see you in five days' time.'

'What of the attack?' Philipe asked.

'I will give you the plan of attack when we rendezvous.' Again she looked around their faces. 'That way if any of you are captured you cannot betray us.' She smiled at them. 'But it would be better if none of you was captured.'

'What will happen if *you* are captured?' Philipe persisted.

'If I am captured, I will not be at the rendezvous. If I am not at the rendezvous by dawn on the fifth day, the mission is aborted. You will go home. And you, Philipe, will report what has happened to Monsieur Moulin and take his instructions. But as I have never been captured before, I do not see why I should be captured this time. Now go.'

She and Amalie watched them file off through the trees.

'Do you trust them?' Amalie asked.

56

'We have to trust them. But I believe they are good men. They were handpicked by Jean.'

'Even Philipe?'

'I have known Philipe for years. And he and his family have been sheltering us for six months. So he asks a lot of questions. That is because he has an active mind.'

'He is in love with you.'

'They are all in love with me.' Liane smiled. 'Even the Germans are in love with me, or the idea of me. That is the secret of my success.' She picked up her haversack. 'Let's go.'

Amalie picked up her haversack in turn. 'He is jealous of James. A jealous man is never trustworthy.'

'Who's a wise young bird, then?'

'But you will still trust him.'

'At this moment, I have no choice. *We* have no choice. It is something to be considered after this is over.'

'If anything were to happen to you, I would kill him.'

'Well, it might be a good idea to tell him that. When this is over.'

They walked until the first light, their way taking them up hills and into valleys. They passed more than one village but kept at a safe distance. Some dogs barked but because of the curfew no one ventured out to investigate. Liane had a destination in mind, and they reached it in good time; a small copse on the edge of a stream, more than a mile away from the nearest habitation. '

'Woof,' Amalie said. 'May I bathe?'

'Of course. I intend to.' The sisters stripped and entered the stream, which was deep enough to reach their waists, Amalie giving a little squeal of discomfort as the cold water got to her bruised thighs. 'How are they?' Liane asked.

'Sore. Will you look at them?'

'Yes.' Refreshed, Amalie lay on the grass while Liane inspected the broken flesh. 'They are healing. Or I should say, they *were* healing, until you did all this walking, rubbing the flesh. You should not have come. I do not understand why you are here at all.' This was the first time they had been entirely alone since Amalie's return.

'Can you not understand that I wish to be with you?'

Liane handed out bread and cheese and filled two cups with wine. 'That is very sweet of you, but if anything were to happen to you . . .'

Amalie chuckled. 'You would kill Philipe.'

'This is a serious matter, you know. I hope you have not come back simply to commit suicide in a glorious fashion.'

'I have come back to kill Germans, and to be with you. If I am to die, I want to die at your side, the way Pierre did.'

'Do you think I am happy about that? By hurling the grenade a moment before the bullet hit him he saved my life.'

'I know he would not have died any other way. Nor would I. Do you have any idea what it has been like, living in England, in the lap of luxury, knowing you were here, living like this? It was empty, so empty.'

'You were with Mama and Papa.'

'That was worse than anything. They are not the people you remember, Li.'

'Are they not well off? Papa had all those investments in England, Mama's family—'

'They are perfectly well off. But they are absolutely shattered. The months they spent in prison, then having to abandon the business and their home, and then the death of Pierre . . . It has all been too much for them. And then there is you. The Germans have put out how you are a cold-blooded murderess—'

'Mama and Papa believe that?'

'Well, aren't you?'

Liane made a moue. 'When it is necessary. For France. Can they not understand that?'

'It is not how wars were fought in their youth. They do not believe women should take part in wars, anyhow.'

'So what do they think of you?'

'I do not believe they accept me as their daughter, any more. Oh, Liane . . .' Her eyes filled with tears. 'I spend my time remembering Henri. What have I got to live for?'

'As you are here, you have France to live for. And me.'

'But afterwards . . . You will have James. And I will have nothing.'

Liane took her into her arms. 'You will have me.'

*   *   *

58

To Liane's relief, all twenty of her people arrived at the rendezvous by the appointed time. 'No one seems to have the slightest idea we are about,' Philipe said.

'Well, they will know that we are about by this time tomorrow,' Liane said and spread her more detailed map on the ground, together with the aerial photographs. 'You will see that there are woods up to within a hundred yards of the mine entrance. There is a watch tower, here, in front of the shaft, and another there, at the rear. The barracks for the guards is here, and for the miners is here, with a separate building for the mine superintendent and overseers.'

'Are these people French?' someone asked.

'The workers are believed to be Russian prisoners-of-war.'

'Who are our allies.'

'We will not shoot at them unless we have to. Going in at night, they should all be in bed, and if they have any sense they will keep their heads down.'

'And the overseers?'

'My information is that they are French.' The men exchanged glances. 'But,' Liane pointed out, 'as they are working for the Germans, they are technically traitors. If they also have the sense to keep their heads down, we will ignore them. But . . . no one can be allowed to interfere.' She looked over their faces before going on. 'Now, we have no knowledge of the guard hours of the Germans, nor of the situation within the mine. This means that we cannot carry out a hit-and-run raid. We must capture the mine and its surrounding buildings and hold it long enough for our explosive charges to be laid. I am talking of several hours.'

'Will they not be in telephone connection with their headquarters?'

'Certainly. That is why we have to seize the entire mine in a coup de main. But cutting the telephone wires comes first. Philipe, you will be responsible for that. Take two men. I will lead the assault on the barracks with nine men. Gaston, you will take the staff bungalow with three men. Louis, you will restrain the workers with the other two.'

'Will they speak French?'

'They must have picked up a word or two by now.'

'And what about the girl?' Philipe inquired.

59

'She will not take part in the assault.'

'Because she is your sister?'

'Because she is our explosives expert, and if she gets hit we may not be able to carry out the job successfully. Now it is five miles to that wood. We leave at dusk.'

Amalie took her aside. 'Are you trying to protect me?'

'I am not protecting anyone. We are in this together. But our business, your business, is to wreck that mine beyond repair, at least for a long time. That is your only business.'

Amalie gazed at her for several seconds, then nodded, 'I will blow the mine.'

The day, as such days always will, passed very slowly. The weather was good and, once the sun got up, quite warm. The men lounged around in various stages of undress, at once excited by what lay ahead of them and by the presence of the two attractive women. But mostly they sought only to sleep after their arduous march. Liane slept herself, but was awakened in mid-afternoon when Gaston sat beside her. He was a small dark man, in his middle twenties, she estimated, with pleasantly ugly features. 'You are so calm,' he said. 'You have done this often before, eh?'

'I have done it before,' she agreed.

'For me it is the first time. For all of us. The biggest thing I have ever done is let down the tires on a Boche motorbike.'

'But you know how to use your tommy-gun.'

'I think so. Will I be afraid?'

'Are you afraid now?' He held up his hand, which was trembling. 'Once you start firing your gun, you will stop being afraid.'

'Are you never afraid?'

'I do not seem ever to have had the time.'

'Will you hold my hand, mademoiselle? Just to touch you . . .'

Liane took his hand, held it for a moment, and then pressed it against her breast. Colour rushed into his cheeks. 'You will be the bravest of the brave,' she assured him.

Gaston licked his lips and got up. Liane looked past him to where Philipe was watching them, with smouldering eyes. She beckoned him. 'Do you wish encouragement also?'

60

'I wish you, mademoiselle. All of you.'

A moment of crisis? But she was as pragmatic as always. 'We will talk of it, after the attack,' she promised.

By ten o'clock they were in position at the edge of the wood, crouching in the trees and underbrush while Liane studied the mine through her binoculars, Amalie and the three unit commanders beside her. There were lights on in all the buildings, and a dull glow from the shaft. To her right she made out a pile of filled sacks, obviously ore waiting to be removed. There was no sound above a low rumble. 'That is the generator,' she told them.

'Where?' Gaston asked.

'I do not know. But all the buildings in the photographs are accounted for, so it must be situated in one of them. Probably behind the office. But remember, we do not wish it damaged; we need the pit to be illuminated, at least until after the charges are placed. Now there are two sentries at the pit head,' she said. 'I see no other movement outside.'

'What about the towers?'

'They do not appear to be manned. They think themselves secure, buried in this remote place. We will give them another hour to go to sleep.'

'Can you see the telephone wires?' Philipe asked.

'Not the wires. But the poles are visible. Make for the first one, nearest the office, and cut the wire there.' The men returned to their units and waited.

'Are you all right?' Liane asked Amalie. Although they had fought together in the past, it had been a defensive action, trying desperately to stay alive. Liane had not been there when Amalie had shot down the German officer, so she had never seen her sister in full flow, as it were. But then, Amalie had never seen Liane at work, either.

'I am all right,' Amalie said. 'But you . . . you will not get hit. Promise me.' Liane kissed her.

By eleven most of the lights were out, save for the glow from the pit head, and another in the office. The generator continued to rumble away, helpful in that it would shroud casual noise. 'You go first, Philipe,' she said. 'Cut the wire, and then fire a single shot. Then break into the office and destroy it. We will attack on your signal.'

'Wish me fortune.'

She blew him a kiss. 'I will wish you all the fortune in the world.'

He and his two men stole off, circling the wood to get behind the office. Liane kept her glasses fixed on the sentries, who were seated on a bench close to the pit head, tommy-guns on their knees, apparently oblivious to anything that might be happening around them. She lowered the glasses and then picked up a movement on the far side of the mine. She levelled the glasses again and made out a shadowy figure coming through the trees. Definitely a German soldier. So there had, after all, been a guard on the other side, who was now returning; and he was on the same side as Philipe and his companions, who were clearly unaware of his presence.

'Shit,' she muttered. 'Stand by,' she told the men. But she held her fire as well as her breath; there was still a chance.

The guard actually passed the last telegraph pole and was speaking with his two fellows. Liane couldn't hear what he was saying, but they both turned their heads. Then he suddenly checked and looked over his shoulder. Again Liane couldn't hear what had alerted him, but she knew it had to be Philipe's group; perhaps one of them had trodden on a twig.

The guard shouted, 'Who goes there?' and at the same time unslung his tommy-gun.

The reply was a single shot. The sentry staggered and then fell to his knees.

'Go!' Liane shouted, leaping to her feet and running into the clearing. The two seated guards were on their feet, initially looking to the sound of the shot but then turning back towards her. She loosed a burst of automatic fire and they both went down, although she did not suppose they were both dead. A man appeared in the doorway of the office, silhouetted against the light. She fired at him too, and he ducked back inside and slammed the door.

Lights were coming on in the bungalow as well as the barracks, and there was a great deal of noise from the work-men's barracks. Liane could hear feet pounding behind her and knew she was being supported. She ran at the garrison barracks as the door opened and two half-dressed men emerged. Both carried tommy-guns and she brought them down with another burst. Then her drum clicked empty. She had a spare in her haversack but there was no time to change them. She threw herself to the ground and rolled against the wall, while her companions sprayed the building with bullets. The garrison was awake now, and they were professional soldiers. Windows were thrown open and fire returned, and one of the guerillas went down with a shriek of pain. The rest threw themselves to the ground, but they were totally exposed and would soon be destroyed.

One of the windows was obliquely above Liane's head. She crawled to it, looked up at the rifle barrel resting on the sill. She drew a grenade from her belt, took a deep breath, pulled the pin, stood up and grasped the barrel while the soldier stared at her in consternation, and threw the grenade into the crowded room. There was a shout of alarm, but before anyone could respond it exploded. Liane had already dropped back to her knees, but even pressed against the wall she felt the enormous gush of air exploding from the window. She waited for several seconds, her ears ringing, looking at her people, who were slowly getting to their feet. She waved them down again and repeated her first manoeuvre, drawing the pin from the grenade before standing up and tossing it into the room.

Once again the response was horrific, although there were less screams than before. She changed the drum on her tommy-gun, waved her people forward and went to the door. This had been blown off its hinges; inside was suggestive of an abattoir gone wrong. There were still moans and groans from amidst the shattered bodies, but she did not suppose any of these men would ever fight again. And now flames were licking up from the floor.

'You did not need us,' one of the guerillas said admiringly. 'You destroyed them single-handed.'

'I needed you,' she assured him. 'I will always need you. Now guard the door. Shoot anyone who attempts to come out.'

'Are there many alive?'

'I do not know. But they will soon be dead. The rest of you, come with me.'

*　　*　　*

But the brief battle was already over. Having cut the telephone line, Philipe and his men had stormed the office and killed the man on duty. They had also despatched the two sentries. Louis had talked the miners into returning to bed. Gaston's group had had no difficulty in securing the surrender of the overseers, who were gathered together, four men in pyjamas and three women in nightdresses, shivering from fear and the night air. Liane was more interested in the office.

'Did he have time to make a call?' she asked.

The man lay on the floor, the telephone still held in his left hand, the receiver in his right. 'I think he tried,' Philipe said. 'But I do not think he had the time to speak to anyone.'

Liane knelt beside the corpse, took the receiver from its hand and listened. There was no sound. 'If he got through, even for a second,' she said, 'and was then cut off, it will have alerted the other end that something is wrong.'

'They could be miles away.'

'Or they could be in the next village. We must hurry.'

'I am sorry. That other guard came upon us by surprise.'

'There is nothing to be sorry about. No operation ever went entirely as planned. Now go and fetch Amalie. There is no time to lose.' She summoned Gaston. 'What are our casualties?'

'Only one. Dufour.'

'Is it bad?'

'His thigh is shattered. He cannot move and he is in severe pain. I have given him morphine.'

'But he cannot move, and we cannot carry him. I do not know enough about this man. Where does he come from?'

'He is from my village.'

'I am so sorry. Tell me of him.'

'He is twenty-four years old. Unmarried.'

'That is something. Is he an only son?'

'No. There are two other brothers.'

'Will you tell them?' Gaston nodded. 'Well, then.' She knelt beside the stricken man, illuminated by the flames from the burning barracks. He was conscious and able to focus, but was obviously in great pain; from the waist down his trousers were soaked with blood. 'You understand that we cannot carry you with us.'

'Yes,' he muttered.

'And that if the Germans capture you alive, they will torture you to death?'

Another muttered, 'Yes.'

Liane felt in her haversack and took out one of her cyanide capsules. 'This will end your pain in ten seconds. Remember that you are dying for France.'

He caught her hand. 'Will we win, mademoiselle?'

'We will win, and your name will be remembered.' She stood straight and saluted him and looked at Gaston.

'I will stay by him,' Gaston said.

She nodded and joined Louis. 'Do I shoot these bastards?' he asked.

'No. I think they are more useful to our cause alive than dead.' She went up to the frightened people. 'Do you know who I am?' she asked. They gaped at her. 'My name is Liane de Gruchy.' They gasped. 'I see you have heard of me. Well, now you have met me. When the Germans come, tell them who did this.'

Amalie had arrived, carrying her knapsack. 'I will come with you,' Philipe offered.

Liane shook her head. 'You will all stay here and make sure nothing goes wrong.'

'We need a plan of the mine,' Amalie said.

'In the office.'

They found the plan easily enough, and Amalie studied it for several minutes. Then she said, 'It is very simple. We will place the explosives here, here, here and here. These are the principal supporting timbers. When they blow, the entire mine will collapse.'

'How long will it take to dig it out again?' Liane asked.

'A few months, at least. Then,' Amalie said with a giggle, 'we will come back and blow it up again.'

It took them several days to regain the Massif, although it appeared that the clerk in the office had not been able to make any connection, and thus the assault was only discovered when one of the overseers walked to the next village, which was ten miles away. By then the guerilla band had split up and was some twenty miles away, each member making their separate ways home. Within twenty-four hours a massive hunt had been launched, with planes flying low overhead and groups of soldiers accompanied by dogs scouring the country-side.

Liane had no means of knowing how the other groups were faring, but she kept her own, which consisted of Amalie, Philipe and Gaston, under tight control, moving only at night and only after a careful reconnaissance of the country in front of them. Fortunately, as they had looted the mine's kitchens and larders before leaving, there was no necessity for them to approach any village or farm to secure sustenance, and so they needed to take no risks, and indeed spent thirty-six hours on one occasion hidden in a culvert while the Germans moved overhead and to either side.

They were naturally in a state of high exhilaration, certainly the men. Liane was indeed very glad that both Philipe and Gaston had accompanied her, because she knew of their desire for her, and they offset each other. She also remembered that she had virtually promised a sexual reward to Philipe and was happy to be able to postpone the implementation of that promise until they had regained the farm, and the calming company of his parents and Jean. After all the excesses of her youth, and even more of her recent career, she actually had no desire to have sex with any man, save James. Perhaps, she thought, I am growing old. Certainly there could be no doubt that she was on occasion very tired. As now. It was not a physical tiredness; the life she lived had made her as highly tuned as any professional athlete. It was a mental exhaustion, not caused by the planning she needed to make, the dangers in which she existed, but by the sheer horror of what she was required to do, so against her innate nature, and the ruthlessness with which she carried out those requirements. It was as if she had a split personality; one half that of a woman, the other that of an avenging angel, neither of which she could entirely control. So, she had personally destroyed upwards of twenty men, left their bodies bloody mangled messes, just as she had arrogantly displayed herself to the overseers and their wives, making sure the Germans knew who was tormenting them yet again, daring them to do their worst. And now regretted it? That was not true in real terms. She regretted the situation that was forcing her to do things like that, just as she regretted what had happened to Dufour. And always there was the threat of afterwards.

But the immediate afterwards came first. 'What happens now?' Amalie asked as they sat in a gully, having eaten the last of their food, waiting for darkness.

'We will get home tonight,' Philipe told her. 'The farm is only five kilometres away.'

'But what then?'

They all looked at Liane. 'We report the success of our mission to James and wait until he has another job for us.'

'James, always James,' Philipe sneered. 'He sends us to our deaths while he sits behind a desk in London.'

'He has fought with us,' Amalie said angrily.

'And will do so again,' Liane said quietly.

'It is time,' Gaston said. 'Will I see you again, mademoiselle?'

'Of course.'

'When the English wish you to risk you neck again,' Philipe said.

Gaston ignored him. 'I will look forward to that, mademoiselle.' He embraced her and then Amalie, shook hands with Philipe and strode off into the darkness.

'There is a brave man,' Amalie said. Philipe snorted.

'We should move as well.' Liane got up, and they followed her into the gloom. It took them two hours to see the lights of the farmhouse. Then the others would have broken into a run but Liane restrained them, and they made their approach as cautiously as they had done everything else. They had almost reached the wall before Rufus barked.

'Whist,' Philipe called, and the dog, recognizing his master's voice, rubbed against the gate and then jumped up to put his paws on the young man's chest as he pushed the gate in.

'Who is there?' Charles Chartrin called from the kitchen doorway.

'It is Philipe.'

'Philipe? Oh, thank God! Who is that with you?'

'Mademoiselle Liane and Madame Burstein.'

'May God be praised.' The farmer came into the yard to embrace them. 'I had not thought to see you again, any of you.'

67

'You worry too much,' Liane told him.

'But it has been terrible. So terrible.'

'Terrible?' Liane suddenly felt as if she had a lump of lead in her stomach. 'What has happened? Monsieur Moulin is ill?'

'Monsieur Moulin is gone,' Charles blurted out. 'He has been taken by the Gestapo.'

PART TWO

The Longest Wait

Warder – warder! Open quickly!
Man – is this a time to wait?
William Edmundstoune Aytoun

Four

The Plot

For a moment Liane could only stare at Charles in horror; Amalie and Philipe seemed equally struck dumb. Then she recovered sufficiently to ask, 'When did this happen?'

'Three days after you left. He went into Aumont as usual. And the Gestapo were waiting for him.'

'The Gestapo from Lyons?'

'Gabrielle thinks they were from Paris. Or even Berlin itself.'

'Gabrielle was there? But she was not arrested?'

'She was not actually with him when he was taken. There was no connection between them. She saw what happened and came home to tell us.'

They went inside, where Odile embraced them with stricken silence. Gabrielle was in more control of herself but even more than a week after the event was still clearly frightened. Liane took her into the parlour and sat beside her. Amalie and Philipe stood around them. 'I want to know exactly what happened. You and Monsieur Moulin went into town and . . . ?'

'I had some shopping to do for Mama. Monsieur Moulin went straight to the bar; he wished to speak with Monsieur Vlabon. When I had finished my shopping, I went to the bar. There was a crowd outside and a lot of shouting, and a lot of men in uniform. I think they were Milice Français. Then I saw Monsieur Moulin brought out—'

'Who brought him out? Plainclothes men?'

'No, no. They wore black uniforms.' Liane and Amalie gazed at each other in consternation. Gabrielle went on. 'One of them was a high-ranking officer . . . I heard one of his people address him. He called him something like Weiss.'

70

'You mean Roess?'

'That is it. Roess.'

'Roess,' Amalie muttered. 'He arrested me in Dieppe in 1940.'

'He was only a captain then,' Liane reminded her. 'Now he is a colonel. And to think I once had him at my mercy and did not kill him. What a fool I am.' Rufus rested his head on her lap. 'If someone like Roess came here to arrest Jean, then he knew where to find him.'

'They also asked after you. Well, not after you by name. Bu they knew that Monsieur Moulin was sometimes accompanied by a woman, and they asked Monsieur Vlabon if he knew who this woman was.'

'What did he say?'

'That he did not know.'

Charles poured wine and passed the glasses round. 'Who has betrayed us?' Amalie asked.

'You say this happened three days after we left?' Liane asked. 'That is nine days ago. If we had been betrayed they would have been here by now.'

'And when they torture Monsieur Moulin?' Philipe asked.

'Oh, that poor man,' Amalie said. 'After all he has been through.'

'Yes,' Liane said. 'But he will never betray us, no matter what they do to him. The question is, who betrayed *him*? Have you been into Aumont recently, Charles?'

'I was there four days ago. After Gabrielle told us what had happened, I felt I had to find out what I could.'

'Were the Gestapo still there? Or the Milice?'

'No, but there are a great many German soldiers there now, checking passes, making themselves a nuisance. But I saw no men in black uniforms.'

'And so you spoke with Vlabon. He must have had some idea of how it happened? Why it happened?'

'He does not know. But here is a strange thing. That woman he had serving behind the bar, Juliette Dugard, she has disappeared. Do you remember her, mademoiselle?'

'Yes, vaguely. You mean she was arrested too?'

'They believe so. Two men went to her lodging in the middle of the night and took her away. She has not been heard of

71

since. But this was two days before Monsieur Moulin's arrest.'

'Then she must have known who he was. But how? And how did the Germans know she knew?'

'Vlabon does not think it was she who betrayed Monsieur Moulin. He thinks it was the other woman.'

'What other woman?'

'There was a woman with the Gestapo colonel. Vlabon describes her as very tall and well built, with blonde hair and handsome features.'

Line stared at him, and then looked at Amalie again. Amalie opened her mouth, but Liane gave a quick shake of the head. 'You say this woman was with Roess? And she identified Monsieur Moulin?'

'Vlabon did not say she identified him. She was just there. But he says he is certain, from the way they looked at each other, that they knew each other.'

For a moment Liane sat still. Joanna certainly knew Jean, and he knew her, from before the War. And given Joanna's peculiar and uncertain position in Germany it was entirely possible that she might have been required to accompany Roess on this mission, but that she would ever betray the prefect was inconceivable. In fact her presence suggested a ray of hope, that she might be able to save his life as she had once saved the life of James' sidekick, Rachel Cartwright. But that could be only a dream. The reality was that the head of the Resistance was gone. They might have achieved a triumph at the mine, but that ranked as nothing compared with the catastrophe that had overtaken the movement.

'We must call London,' she said.

'Are you saying he told you nothing? Nothing at all?' Himmler was incredulous. 'What did you do to him?'

'Everything we could think of, Herr Reichsfuehrer,' Roess said.

Himmler looked at Joanna, also seated before his desk. 'Were you present?'

'Some of the time. He made me be present.'

Himmler looked at Roess. 'Fräulein Jonsson was sent as my assistant. I thought it best that she should be present.'

'It was quite sickening,' Joanna said. 'I knew this man. We

had been acquaintances before the War.'

'It is a beastly business,' Himmler said sympathetically. 'But sometimes we have to do beastly things. And you did your duty. I am proud of you. Were you present when he died?'

'No, thank God.'

'How did it happen, Roess?'

'I do not know, Herr Reichsfuehrer. I believe his heart was not as strong as the doctor who examined him said. He had been screaming in agony while we—'

Himmler held up a finger. 'I do not wish the details.'

'Very good, sir. But as I was saying, he was screaming, and then suddenly he made a choking sound and was quiet. I immediately called the doctor to examine him. But he pronounced him dead.'

'So this whole thing has turned out to be a fiasco.'

'Sir? There can be no doubt that Moulin is, was, a most important member of the Resistance. We have some evidence that he was its commander on the ground. Without him the Resistance may well crumble.'

'If you believe that, Roess, you are a fool.' Roess flushed. 'The Resistance is a self-perpetuating myth,' Himmler declared. 'It feeds on its own achievements, its own legends. The legend we wanted, the legend we must have, is Liane de Gruchy. And what was she doing while you were arresting Moulin? She was blowing up a vitally important mine. What is more, at virtually the same time six more wolfram mines were attacked throughout France. These simultaneous strikes could not have been orchestrated by Moulin, tucked away in the Massif Central. The Resistance is, and always was, controlled from London. That is an obvious fact. I can tell you that the Fuehrer is very angry. So tell me where Liane de Gruchy is now? Tell me that.'

'If I knew that, sir . . .'

'But you do not know that. You are a policeman, Roess. It is your business to know things, or to find things out. What about this woman who claimed to have seen de Gruchy with Moulin in her bar? What has she got to say for herself?'

'Madame Dugard is dead, Herr Reichsfuehrer.'

'Not another unexpected heart attack?'

Roess looked at Joanna. 'I killed her,' Joanna said quietly.

73

Himmler stared at her. 'You . . . killed her?'

'I was interrogating her and she suddenly attacked me. I had not considered her dangerous. But before I knew what was happening she had got hold of my pistol and was clearly about to shoot me, so I used my knife.'

'Good heavens! You actually stabbed her?'

'Well, what was I to do?'

'Absolutely. There was nothing else you could do. But it must have been a terrible experience for you.'

'The situation should not have arisen in the first place,' Roess remarked. 'Fräulein Jonsson insisted upon interviewing the woman alone—'

'I felt I would get more out of her as one woman to another than a lot of men brandishing whips. And I did get one very important piece of information.'

'Concerning de Gruchy?' Himmler was eager.

'Yes, sir. I got her to describe Liane for me. As a result I have no doubt that she was utterly mistaken. She described a woman who was blonde and handsome, certainly, but these facts are well known. She also said she was as tall as I and strongly built. Liane de Gruchy is five feet four inches tall and slight.'

'Good heavens! Well, it seems that we have been hoodwinked yet again. This damned woman is like a will o' the wisp. You will have to start all over again. Keep me informed.'

Roess opened his mouth and then closed it again. He glanced at Joanna, realized that she had not been dismissed, and stood up. 'Heil Hitler!'

'But that is brilliant, James,' the brigadier said. 'Great work. My best congratulations.'

'I would say that the congratulations should be directed at the guerillas.'

'Well, of course. But you set it up. There's no question that their claim is genuine?'

'If Mademoiselle de Gruchy says they destroyed the mine, then they destroyed the mine.'

'Oh. Quite. It's just that none of the other groups have reported in yet. Nor has there been any mention of any attacks on the wolfram mines in the German press.'

'Well, they would hardly publicize it, sir.'

'I suppose not. But they are certainly publicizing the arrest of Moulin. Do you suppose *that's* genuine?'

'I'm afraid it is, sir. It is confirmed by Mademoiselle de Gruchy. She is very upset. He was an old friend of her family. She has known him all her life.'

'So what does she think happened to him? How did it happen?'

'As to how, sir, he was betrayed. She does not know by whom, although I believe she intends to find out. As to what has happened to him since his arrest, she has no information on that, but we must fear the worst.'

'Will he betray his people?'

'We must hope not. In the meantime I have ordered Mademoiselle de Gruchy to undertake no further action until the position is clarified.'

'Hm. I suppose that is sensible. But they cannot be out of action for too long. You know we mean to go in next year, no matter what? That is, of course, top secret, although I am sure the Germans must realize it. We are actually going in in a couple of weeks, but the attack will be made on Sicily. There is some optimism that if we carry out a successful invasion of Sicily, Mussolini's regime may collapse with untold benefits. In any event, engaging the enemy on his southern and most vulnerable front is intended to distract him from the main business, the defence of France. Now, it goes without saying that the guerillas have an important part to play in weakening that defence.'

'You are asking them to trek across France again, to the Channel coast? The last two such ventures were catastrophic, sir, leading almost to the destruction of the group.'

'I understand that, James, and we intend to use groups closer to the coast to support the initial landings. But there is a scheme, dreamt up by de Gaulle's lot, which could play an important part in hampering the enemy on the ground. Tell me what you know of Grenoble.'

'Ah . . . I know it was the birthplace of Stendhal.'

'Who?'

'A French writer in the last century, sir. *Madame Bovary.*'

'Who was Madame Bovary?'

'His most famous heroine. Actually Stendhal was a pseu-
donym. His real name was Beyle.'

'Your erudition astounds me, James. Is this relevant?'

'You asked me what I knew of Grenoble, sir.'

'And that is the sum of your knowledge? I see. Have you
ever been there?'

'No, sir.'

'Well, I want you to get hold of a detailed map of the area
and study it. You will see that south of Grenoble there is a
large area of land, some fifty kilometres by twenty-five, called
the Vercours. It is a natural fortress, a sort of inland Gibraltar,
a mass of cliffs and ravines, caves and woods, virtually impenetrable by armour if properly defended. There is only one
approach, a road from the north, but it is estimated that this
can be held by a determined body of men.'

'Sounds interesting. What does it threaten?'

'Well, nothing. The idea is that it is a large sort of isolated
salient in the south of France, accessible and therefore support-
able by air from Algiers. Therefore the force occupying it
could not only be sustained and constantly re-armed, but additional troops could be flown in. The plans are still being drawn
up, but let us suppose that by the end of this year we are ready
to move. The occupation will be done clandestinely, of course.
By then our campaign in Sicily may well have been completed,
and it is hoped to have retaken Sardinia and Corsica as well.
From those bases we would be able to pour men and munitions into the Vercours, and before the Germans know what
is happening they'd have a whole army in their midst, waiting to strike up on the inside of their defences. What do you
think?'

'I am bound to say that it is a little fanciful, sir. This army
is to be created by drop? That will take a very long time.'

'Not by drop. We'll use transport planes.'

'You mean there is an airfield in this area? Not secured by
the Germans?'

'There is no airstrip at present. It will be the job of the
guerillas, once they occupy the territory, to lay down a strip.'

'Just like that?'

'It can be done, James, if these people are capably led.'

'You mean Liane de Gruchy?'

'Amongst others. But that lady certainly seems to have the ability to make men work for her, and fight for her.'

'And die for her,' James observed.

'If necessary. The important thing is, will she and her people take part? She will not be in overall command, of course. That will be a regular army officer, French army, naturally. Will she go along with that?'

'I see no reason why not, if the position is properly explained to her. I would have to go across. This is not something that can be done over a radio link.'

'I suppose you're right. Do you know where she is?'

'I am in contact with her, yes, sir.'

'Very good. You will have to hold it for a while. As I say, the plans are still being drawn up, and other groups have to be informed and alerted; de Gruchy's people can't do it on their own. And, of course, right now we are completely fucked up by Moulin's getting himself caught.'

'I shouldn't think he was very happy about that either, sir. Or is now.'

'Oh, well, I'm sorry for the fellow. But you can't deny it is a nuisance. Now de Gaulle's lot will have to find and establish a new man, and that is going to take a little while. So it would be best for you not even to inform de Gruchy of the plan until it is ready to be implemented.'

'But as you say, I can't just leave them in limbo, sir.'

'You can tell them that we have something big in the pipeline for which they must be ready. Have your friend recruit as many men as possible. And let me know if you hear anything concrete about Moulin.'

'Fräulein Jonsson is here, Frau,' Hilda announced.

'Oh, damn.'

'What does *she* want?' Frederick von Helsingen asked.

Madeleine squeezed his shoulder. Although she had recovered from the trauma of actually seeing the wreck that was her husband, she was still not reconciled to the fact that there were so few parts of his shattered body that she could touch without giving an involuntary shudder. Yet he was growing stronger every day, and this was confirmed by the doctors. 'Why, Frau von Helsingen,' Dr Weinhart had said only yesterday, 'We expect the colonel to be up and walking about within a month. Well, perhaps two. But it will happen. Is that not splendid news? Something to look forward to, eh?'

And then he will want sex, Madeleine had thought; his genitals were about the only part of his body that had not been torn to pieces by shrapnel. And she did not know if she would be able to respond.

'I imagine she has come to see you,' she said.

' Is she still thick with Himmler?'

'Officially she is one of his secretaries. But I think they sleep together, yes. Is it important?'

'Not in the least.' But an expression had crossed his face, a shadow she had noticed several times since his return from Russia, and which she could not identify, having never seen it before he had left for the Eastern Front. But then, she reflected, the things he must have seen and felt, quite apart from his wounds, were beyond her comprehension. She went to the door, and he said, 'Do not tell her about Kleist's visit.'

'Very well.' She opened the door and went into the lounge.

'Darling.' Joanna embraced her. She was in all the glory of a summer frock and high-heeled sandals, her hair loose, and looked quite obscenely healthy. But there were stress lines about her mouth and eyes as well. 'I hear that Freddie is back from hospital.'

'He has been back for three weeks.'

'How lovely for you. And Helen is well?'

'Very well. She is being walked by Nanny.'

'Don't tell me you're employing a nanny? You?'

Madeleine flushed. 'Well . . . I have so much to do, caring for Freddie. The nurse comes in twice a day to change his dressings, but he cannot do very much for himself, yet.'

'You poor darling. Did you have an opportunity to ask him about the front?'

'I don't think he wants to think about the front, much less talk about it. Do you wish to see him?'

'If I may.'

Madeleine opened the bedroom door. 'Joanna is here, Freddie.'

Joanna entered the room and involuntarily checked herself.

78

When she had seen him at the station he had been swathed in bandages, even his head. Now . . . She remembered a tall, handsome, virile young man. Now she looked at skull-like features, the flesh thin and wasted, the blond hair cut so short as to be almost non-existent. Presumably both flesh and hair would return, but nothing was going to replace the empty sleeve of his pyjama jacket, at least by flesh and bone. She could not stop herself looking at the limbs beneath the sheet, but there did seem to be two of them. She forced a smile.

'Freddie. How well you look.'

'Now is not the time for hypocrisy.'

She advanced to the bedside. 'I think you *are* looking well. When you think, well . . .' She kissed his forehead.

'I am alive,' he said. 'That is what matters. When thousands of my comrades are dead, uselessly slaughtered for a madman's dream.' He checked himself, flushing, and looking surprised at what he had said.

Joanna looked at Madeleine, standing on the other side of the bed. 'He is sometimes distraught,' Madeleine said.

'So I have been distraught,' Frederick said. 'Will you go scuttling back to your master and have him send his goons to take me away?'

'I only tell my "master" what I think it would be good for him to hear,' Joanna said. 'But I have heard that as soon as you are up and about you are going to be offered a position on the Fuehrer's personal staff. Will that please you?'

'I am an officer in the Wehrmacht. I go where I am sent.' But he had not looked at her as he spoke.

'I think that is very correct of you,' Joanna said. 'I can see you're tired. I'll call again.'

Madeleine accompanied her outside. 'You won't repeat any of that, will you, Joanna? Sometimes he is quite delirious, even when awake.'

Joanna sat on the settee. 'Come and sit beside me.'

'I thought you were leaving.'

'I need to talk with you first.' Madeleine hesitated then sat beside her. 'Does Freddie have a lot of visitors?'

'Well, his mother and father, of course.'

'I'm talking about other officers.'

'Oh, well, yes. Some.'

'I want you to tell me their names.'

'I can't do that.'

'Why? Is it because Freddie talks to them the way he talked to me, and perhaps they agree with him?'

'Well . . .' Madeleine's cheeks were pink.

'How senior are these officers? Have there been any generals? Come on, tell me.'

Madeleine licked her lips and muttered, 'Field Marshal von Bock.'

Joanna stared at her with her mouth open. 'Bock was here?' Madeleine nodded. 'And Freddie told him what he thought about the War?' Another nod. 'And he was not immediately arrested? How long ago was this?'

'Oh . . . ten days. Right after Freddie came home from hospital.'

'Then if he has not been arrested, he is not going to be arrested. Which must mean . . .' The two women gazed at each other. 'You must give me the other names,' Joanna said.

'It is madness. Madness. I am so afraid.'

'Listen,' Joanna said. 'You know that Germany cannot now win this war.'

'I suppose not.'

'But the Allies have said they will not negotiate with Hitler, even if he himself were prepared to negotiate, which he is not. Therefore the War is going to drag on until Germany is utterly destroyed, whether by Allied bombing or by invasion – can you imagine what it will be like if the Russians ever get in here after what you people have done in Russia? – or by the removal of Hitler.'

'Do you realize that we would all be executed if anyone even suspected what you are thinking?'

'That is why we must stick together. Listen, Franz feels the same way.'

'You have spoken with him?'

'Of course I have not spoken with him. He is in Russia. But I can tell from his letters that he is not happy with the situation.'

Madeleine's eyes were enormous. 'He has put things like that in a letter? Isn't all mail censored?'

'He is very discreet. And having a general as an uncle helps.

80

In any event, he never actually offers an opinion. He loves me, but he believes I am a firm supporter of the regime, and I cannot indicate otherwise in *my* letters. Besides, up till now I have felt that his was a lone voice wailing in the wilderness. But don't you see, if there is really a groundswell of opinion that something must be done to end the War *now*, even if it involves the removal of Hitler, well, we must give them all the support we can.'

'And wind up dangling from a noose? Groundswell? What groundswell? Half a dozen officers visiting a wounded comrade?'

'One of them a field marshal?'

'Retired. And how do we know it would do any good? That the Allies would deal with them, even if Hitler was no longer there? Anyway, Freddie is crippled. What possible part could he take in a revolution? Because you are speaking of revolution, aren't you.'

'I am speaking of the removal of Hitler from power, by whatever means may be necessary. And Freddie's importance lies in the fact that he has, or will have as soon as he is fit again, unlimited access to Hitler's presence.'

'You mean to *kill* him?' Madeleine was aghast. 'I don't think Freddie would ever go for that.'

'Why don't you ask him? And let me know.'

Joanna returned to her suite at the Hotel Albert, poured herself a cognac and discovered that her hands were shaking. Suddenly she was in possession of the biggest secret information she had ever obtained, bigger even than that Russian coup. The potential for ending the War, years – or perhaps even months – before a decision could be reached on the battlefield, with the saving of so many hundreds of thousand of lives, was breathtaking. All that these discontented and disillusioned officers needed was a guarantee of their own salvation if they took the risk of removing the Fuehrer, and only London could provide that. And there was only one person who could put London in the picture. Only one person who would be believed, at any rate. Herself.

Did she dare? But she had to dare. She might have been waiting all of her life for this piece of information. She picked up the phone and asked for the private number.

'Reichsfuehrer Himmler's office.'

'This is Fräulein Jonsson. I need to speak with the Reichsfuehrer, urgently.'

'One moment, Fräulein.'

'Joanna! Are we not lunching together?'

'Oh, Heinrich, I was so looking forward to it. But I have had a telegram from Stockholm.'

'Not bad news, I hope?'

'My father is ill. He wants to see me, as soon as possible.'

'He's not dying?'

'I hope not. But I feel I must go.'

'Of course you must. I will arrange it.'

'Oh, Heinrich, you are so kind to me.'

Rachel put her hand over the telephone mouthpiece. 'You won't believe this, but there is a policeman on the line. He wants to speak with you.'

'How can a policeman possibly have this number? What did he call me?'

'By your name. Major Barron.'

'Give me the phone.' She placed the speaker and receiver on James' desk and he picked them up. 'Major Barron.'

'Oh, major, I am sorry to disturb you at your home.' James looked at Rachel, who was listening on the extension. She waggled her eyebrows. 'Inspector Lodge here, Harwich police. We have a strange situation here, a young lady who has just arrived from Sweden.'

'Yes,' James said. Rachel sat down.

'Well, sir, the name on her passport, a Swedish passport, is Jonsson, and we were informed that a woman by that name is actually a spy working for the Germans—'

'Who gave you that information?'

'The US Embassy.'

'I see. And this lady asked you to call me?'

'She said you would vouch for her, sir.'

'She is known to me, yes. I will come down to pick her up.'

'Ah . . . The US Embassy wishes her to be held pending her arrest.'

'Inspector, as you say, the lady is travelling on a Swedish passport, which I can assure you is genuine. She may once have lived in the United States, but she has not done so for some years now, and she is a Swedish citizen. Therefore the United States have no jurisdiction over her.'

'But if she is a German spy—'

'My department will take care of it.'

There was a brief silence. 'I'm sorry, sir, but in all the circumstances, I will have to have written authority from a senior officer before I can release the lady.' His tone indicated that he did not consider a mere major to be senior enough.

'Very well. I will bring the authority with me. Thank you for calling.' He hung up. 'Get hold of the brigadier, will you, please, Rachel.'

'Yes, sir. What do you think has happened? It's been very nearly a year since we last heard from her.'

'Well, she's either running for her life, or . . .'

'She no longer officially works for us.'

'I'm not sure she understands that. Make that call.'

The police cell was small and smelt of disinfectant. Joanna lay on a cot, fully dressed, with her hands beneath her head, but she swung her legs to the floor and sat up as the door opened. 'What kept you?' she asked.

James peered at her. He had never seen her looking dishevelled before. Even her normally immaculate hair was untidy. 'There were wheels that had to be turned. Are you all right?'

Joanna stood up. 'No, I am not shitting well all right.' She glared at Inspector Lodge. 'I have been arrested by the Gestapo on more than one occasion. They were a bunch of shits, but at least they gave me a drink.'

'She has been a difficult customer, sir,' Lodge remarked. 'But perhaps you know that.'

'I do indeed. Come along, Joanna, and you'll have your drink. After we've had a little chat.'

'Bastard,' she commented.

'You'll have to sign for her, sir,' Lodge said.

'Sign for me?' Joanna demanded. 'What the fuck is that for? Am I a parcel or something?'

'You are still under arrest, madam. You are being released into the major's custody.'

Joanna looked at James. 'Let's get on with it.' He escorted

83

her from the cell into the charge room. At two o'clock in the morning this was deserted save for the constable on duty; he had been half asleep when the two officers had arrived, but now he was very wide awake.

'Are those forms ready?' Lodge inquired.

'I have them here, sir.'

'If you would sign them, major.'

James did so. 'I had a suitcase,' Joanna pointed out. Lodge held it up. 'And I suppose you've been through it.'

'That is so, madam.'

'What a bunch of shits.' She stalked outside, leaving James to bring the case.

'Important lady, is she?' Lodge suggested.

'Sometimes.' James sat beside her in the back of the car. 'London, Harry.'

'I hope we're heading for a hot bath and a cold drink,' Joanna remarked.

'I think we can arrange that. If you behave yourself.'

'Oh, I'll behave. Just get me to the Dorchester. I have a lot to tell you.'

'I imagine you do. But we aren't going to the Dorchester. You're still under arrest. Only now you are in the custody of the SIS instead of the police.'

'I hope you're joking. What am I supposed to have done?'

'What you haven't done would be a shorter list. When we terminated your employment last summer and requested you to remain at the Dorchester, under guard until your ship for New York was ready to sail, you gave your minder the slip and went to Sweden instead, thence to Germany. Why?'

'I like it there. And I felt I could still be of use to you.'

'But you surely understood that, as we had had to clear you with the State Department and inform them that you had been working for us for the previous two years, we were obliged then to inform them that you had chosen to return to Germany, without our permission. So they promptly put you on a most wanted list.'

'Well, you'll have to get them to take me back off it.'

'I don't think that is going to be possible. You're on our most wanted list as well. You don't seem to understand that this is a war, not a party game.'

84

'And my past record doesn't count for anything?'

'So you gave us some very valuable information once or twice in the past. But in a war it's tomorrow that counts, not yesterday. We gave you an out, which you declined to take. You returned to Germany. To everyone on this side of the fence that means you have chosen *your* side. And some of your recent actions don't stand up. As for coming back here, as bold as brass—'

'So what are you going to do, hang me?'

'Joanna, I do wish you'd take this seriously. It could come to that. I will do my damnedest for you—'

'Why?'

'Because I like you—'

'Gee, you sure have been pulling the wool over my eyes all these years. You sure it's not because I'm Liane's friend?'

'You aren't her friend any more. She knows about Moulin. About your part in it.'

For the first time Joanna looked concerned. 'What does she know?'

'That you were there when he was arrested. That you probably fingered him.'

'And if I deny that? Suppose I claim that I could do no more than save her life. I could do nothing for him, because the Gestapo were already on to him?'

'You saved Liane's life?'

'I persuaded Roess that the woman he was looking for wasn't Liane. And I killed the only woman who could have identified her.' James gazed at her in the gloom. But he knew she was telling the truth. 'So where is she now?' Joanna asked. 'I know she *was* there.'

'She isn't there now. She's setting up a new headquarters.'

'Where?'

'Sorry.'

'Meaning you still don't trust me.'

'Meaning it is top secret and not in your field.'

'But you are in touch with her. Will you put her in the picture?'

'I might. When I decide what I am going to do with you.'

'Meaning I'm still under arrest?' They were approaching London now, driving slowly behind dimmed headlights through deserted streets. 'Or am I being driven straight to prison?'

'You are being driven to my office, where you will be interrogated.'

'By you and Rachel? Sounds like fun.'

'This morning you will be taken to see the brigadier.'

'What a thrill. Do I have to wait until morning?'

James refused to allow her to niggle him. 'The brigadier believes in a good night's sleep.'

'And am I going to get one, too?'

'That depends. Look, Joanna, you just have to take this seriously. When you went back to Germany, against our advice and indeed against our orders, you stepped out into the cold. We have nothing going for you any more. In addition, your own people are gunning for you. Now, the brigadier signed that order for your release only on condition we find out just what you're at. No decision has been made as to what we are going to do with you. But if you don't satisfy us or, rather, him, he is very likely to hand you over to the Americans, and if that happens, you are very likely to wind up in the electric chair. Someone once said that knowing he was going to be hanged in the morning concentrates a man's mind enormously. I think you need to work on that.'

'So tell me, what do I have to do to convince you that I'm still on you side and that I have something worth telling you?'

'It would have to be something very, very big.'

'What is the biggest thing you can think of?'

'I really am not in the mood for games, Joanna.'

'Neither am I. Try me.'

'Oh, very well. The biggest thing . . . that Adolf Hitler was about to drop dead.'

'You got it,' she said. 'Well, close.'

Five

The Proposal

'Do you seriously expect me to believe you?' the brigadier asked. It was early in the morning, and he was never at his best at this hour.

'It happens to be the truth, sir,' Joanna said.

'Just like that, eh?'

'I believe it has been building for some time. Alamein, Torch and, above all, Stalingrad, the officer corps, or a large percentage of it, all those who are capable of thinking for themselves, are starting to understand that Germany cannot win this war, and that if they go on fighting to the bitter end the Fatherland will be destroyed. None of them wants that. But they also know of the Casablanca Declaration, requiring unconditional surrender. They wish to be assured that the declaration applies to Hitler and his governing circle, not to the Wehrmacht as a whole; that if Hitler were to be replaced as head of state, Churchill and Roosevelt would be prepared to deal with them on a proper historical basis.'

'And Stalin? After what they have done in Russia?'

'They believe that Communist Russia poses a greater threat to world peace than Nazi Germany ever did. In any event, they feel that if the British and the Americans agreed to a negotiated peace settlement, the Russians would have to go along with it. After all, the Russians have only managed to stay in the War, and to be now winning it, with American Lend-Lease aid.'

'You are a convincing advocate, Jonsson. And you say Bock is in this? The former commander-in-chief?'

'Yes, sir,' Joanna said, praying that she was right.

'Supposing this is true, mightn't it just be a case of sour grapes, because Hitler sacked him?'

87

'That could be so, sir. But that doesn't detract from his importance as a leader of a coup. Most of the officer corps regard him as a man who was wrongfully dismissed.'

'And just what do they want from us?'

'Simply the assurance I have outlined, sir; that if Hitler were to be removed from office, the Allies, or certainly the Western Allies, would be willing to negotiate a peace, based on the surrender of the Wehrmacht, certainly, but on the preservation of the territorial and national integrity of the Fatherland. You must understand, sir, the risk these men are prepared to take. The consequences of failure would be quite horrendous, not only for them personally, but for their families.'

'Hm. Well, obviously, even the suggestion that your information may be correct is of great importance. I will get on to the Cabinet as soon as possible and put them in the picture. But equally, the Cabinet, even Churchill himself, could not possibly act on this without the agreement of Washington. I will present your case as well as I am able, but it is possible they may wish to interview you personally.'

'Yes, sir. May I ask how long this is likely to take?'

'If they move as promptly as I should think they will, we should get some kind of answer in a week or so.'

'A *week*? Sir, I am supposed to be visiting my sick father in Stockholm. I have already been out of Germany a week. If I am not back by the end of this week, and Herr Himmler were to telephone Stockholm to find out why—'

'Are you that important to Himmler?'

Joanna flushed. 'Yes, sir, I am.'

'Good heavens! Well, I will do what I can to expedite matters. Take care of this, ah, young lady, James. Good morning.'

'Just what did he mean by that?' Joanna asked as she and James went down the stairs. 'That it's back to one of those prisons you call safe houses?'

'I don't think that will be necessary, right now. I've booked you in at the Dorchester for a week. That's your favourite hotel, isn't it?'

'It is. But James, I cannot stay a week. I told the old buzzard that.'

He nodded. 'I'm going to work on getting you out just as

rapidly as possible. But you have to play ball and sit tight until I say so. Promise?'

'Oh . . . I suppose so.'

They got into the waiting car. 'Actually,' he said. 'I would have thought that a couple of days of just lying in bed and reading a good book, with no traumas lurking at your shoulder, would do you a world of good.'

'It's an idea. But you know what would relax me more than anything? If *you* were to take a little time off and spend it with me.'

'Now, Joanna. I don't think that would be a good idea.'

'Because you don't find me sexy? Or because of Liane?'

'Any man who didn't find you sexy would have to be a eunuch.'

'Then it is Liane.'

'Amongst other things.'

'Ah, well . . . you can always send Rachel to visit me.'

Rachel drew a deep breath and tapped on the door. 'Who's there?'

'Rachel Cartwright.'

The door opened, and Joanna peered at her. 'My God! I never thought he would.'

'Would what?'

'Send you. He did send you, didn't he?'

'Actually, I volunteered. May I come in?'

'Of course.' Joanna closed the door behind her. 'I'm so happy to see you. Being cooped up here for two days . . . I've been going nuts.'

'Shall we sit down?'

'Surely.' Joanna sat on the sofa and gestured Rachel beside her.

Rachel opened her handbag and took out two envelopes. 'You're to take your pick. This one contains a reservation for a first-class cabin on a liner leaving in a convoy from Liverpool for New York the day after tomorrow. Your train ticket is included. There is also a letter from the brigadier informing the State Department that you have only just retired from working for us and have never worked for the Nazis except as a British double agent.'

89

Joanna was frowning. 'And the other?'

'Is a reservation for a first-class cabin on a Swedish steamer leaving Harwich for Gothenburg tonight, supposing you feel obliged to return to Germany.'

'Are you trying to tell me something?'

Rachel sighed. 'The War Cabinet has decided that it cannot support your proposition.'

'Just like that? What do the Americans think?'

'It has not been put to the Americans, as it is accepted that they would reject it out of hand. Their point is that the Allied position has been made clear: unconditional surrender, no matter who happens to be ruling Germany at the moment of victory.'

'The bastards! The stupid, narrow-minded bastards!'

'I'm inclined to agree with you. But . . .'

'What does James think about it?'

'He is very upset.'

'That's why he couldn't come himself, eh? Shit!'

'What are you going to do?'

'Oh, I'm going back to Germany.' She took the envelope and laid it on the coffee table.

'You don't have to,' Rachel said. 'Surely you've done your bit?'

'My bit ends when the War ends. When my brother has been avenged.'

'Oh. Well, I don't know if we'll meet again. But you saved my life, and that's not something I am ever going to forget.'

'Me neither. But you don't have to rush off. I've lots of time to get to Harwich.' She stretched out her hand and took the glasses from Rachel's nose. 'Aren't you James' stand-in?'

'That took a long time.' James didn't raise his head from the paper he was studying as the office door opened and closed. 'Took it badly, did she?'

'She wasn't happy about it.' Rachel hung her hat and coat on the hook behind the door. 'Would you sack me if I had a cigarette?'

Now James did raise his head. 'You look as if you need one. Go ahead. Was it that bad?'

Rachel struck a match and inhaled. 'What?'

'Well . . . holding her hand, or whatever.'

'Actually,' Rachel said, 'we did hold hands, briefly.'

90

'Ah . . . Good God! You don't mean . . .'

'I've never done anything like that before. Well, not since school. And then we didn't really know what we were about.'

James regarded her for several seconds. 'But she did.'

'Oh, yes. Oh, indeed.'

'And you?'

'I'm a fast learner. Don't get me wrong. It's not something I intend to take up on a permanent, or even an occasional, basis. It's just that, well, one should experience everything in life, shouldn't one? An she did *save* my life, remember?'

'Oh . . . go and have a hot bath.'

'I've just had a hot bath, sir. With Joanna.'

Madeleine stared at Joanna with her mouth open. 'You did that? Are you out of your mind?'

'I am trying to save all of our minds. And our bodies, too.'

'But if you had been caught . . .'

'I wasn't. Himmler trusts me. That's my secret; I make men trust me. Now, listen, I can't approach Freddie or any of his friends. Their instincts will be to distrust me, suppose I am Himmler's spy. You have to do it.'

'Me? I wouldn't know what to say.'

'I am going to tell you what to say. Freddie trusts you, doesn't he?'

'Well . . . yes. I think so.'

'Has he confided anything about this conspiracy to you?'

'Conspiracy? There is no conspiracy. There is just talk. Whispers.'

'Then there is a conspiracy. Has he told you any of this talk?'

'No.'

'OK. You must somehow convey to him that you know of it and want to help. Then you tell him that you have been in contact with a British agent – no names yet – who has reported to his government, who are prepared to give the plan their fullest support.'

'Is that true?'

Joanna gazed into her eyes. 'Would I be risking my life it were not?'

'No. No, I suppose not. But—'

'Yes. There is a caveat. The British cannot, they dare not,

91

publicize their support. This would not only alarm Hitler but would antagonize certain of their allies. All they can do is promise that if the coup is successfully carried out, they will deal fairly with any government that succeeds him, provided it is not headed by Goering, Himmler or Goebbels. They would prefer it to be Field Marshal von Bock, but any senior officer not tainted by Nazism would do. Can you get this across to Freddie?'

'I suppose so. But . . . he will want proof.'

'I am the proof. Once he goes for it, you can bring me in. You must do this, Madeleine. This is your chance to . . . well . . .'

'Atone for the crime of marrying a German?'

'I was going to say, silence all those people who regard you as a collaborator.'

'Will they ever know of it?'

'I will make sure they will know of it.'

'Well . . . it will take time.'

'Not too much time, Madeleine. There isn't all that much time available.'

The long message was in code, and it took Liane and Amalie some time to get it translated. Then they looked at each other in dismay. 'Vercours?' Amalie asked. 'Where is Vercours?'

'It is to the east,' Liane said. 'South of Grenoble.'

'But that is as far away from any possible fighting as it is possible to be. Who is this man Delestraint? He appears to be an idiot.'

'Delestraint is the new co-ordinator of the Resistance,' Liane explained patiently. 'And the message was sent through Pound, therefore it is our duty to obey.'

'Because you will always obey James even if, like now, you have no idea what he is really at.'

'He will tell us when he is ready,' Liane said. 'When he is able to get to us. He says so. Meanwhile he wants me to take as many people as I can, provided they are all capable of fighting. We need to be in touch with Gaston.' She looked around the anxious faces. 'I could go myself, but Pound has forbidden me to enter Aumont.'

'I will go,' Gabrielle volunteered.

'It is too dangerous,' Odile objected.

'It is not dangerous at all, Mama. I will merely go to Monsieur Vlabon's bar, and tell him . . .' she looked at Liane.

'That I need to see Gaston, here, as quickly as possible.'

'I still think it is too dangerous,' Odile said.

'How can it be dangerous, Mama? No one in Aumont save Monsieur Vlabon knows, or cares, who I am. I will go shopping, deliver the message and return here.'

'I will go,' Philipe said.

'Ah . . .' Liane said. 'I think it would be better if Gabrielle went, with respect, Odile. I do not believe that there is any risk in it.' She was too aware of Philipe's dislike for Gaston.

'Then that is settled,' Gabrielle said. 'I will go tomorrow morning.'

It was a fifteen-kilometre walk into Aumont, but Gabrielle relished the prospect. Just to get off the farm was exciting, and to go into the little town was more exciting yet, even if she could not shake off the memory of that terrifying day, over two months ago now, when she had stood outside the bar and watched Monsieur Moulin being dragged away. She had been petrified but, as everyone else in the crowd had also been petrified, she had remained just a horrified spectator; only Vlabon had known who she was, and he had not been going to betray her.

That day would remain etched in her memory for the rest of her life. But returning to Aumont had to be exciting, and her life sadly lacked excitement. Nor did she have to walk the whole way, as she had covered no more than two kilometres when she heard the rumble of wheels and a farm cart drew up beside her.

'Mademoiselle Gabrielle,' said the young driver. 'Where are you going?'

His name was Armand Dragout and he was the son of a neighbouring farmer. Gabrielle did not know him very well, as over the past couple of years there had been little socializing between the farms in the district, but he was a personable young man. 'I am going in to Aumont,' she said.

'That is a long way. Will you not accept a ride, for at least part of it?'

Gabrielle hesitated, then said, 'That would be very kind of you.'

Armand extended his hand and she grasped it to swing herself up on to the seat beside him, while he moved the axe that lay there. 'I have been chopping wood,' he explained.

She looked over her shoulder at the back of the cart, while the mule resumed its slow gait. 'It is a lot of wood.'

'Well, it will soon be winter again. One needs a lot of wood.' They drove in silence for a while, then he asked, 'Do you think the War will have ended by then?'

'I do not think so.'

'It depends on the Allies, eh? When do you think they will come?'

'It is better not to think about things like that,' Gabrielle said. 'Is this not the lane to your farm? I will get down now.'

'It is still five kilometres to Aumont. I could drive you a little further.'

'Why?'

'Because you are a pretty girl.' Gabrielle wasn't sure how to respond to that, but she made no further objection as he drove past the turn-off. 'I would like to come to see you,' he said. 'I would like to be your friend.'

'Would you like to be my friend if I were an ugly girl?'

'Well . . .'

'You have driven me far enough out of you way. I can walk the rest.'

He pulled on the rein and the mule willingly stopped. 'I have angered you.'

'Not at all. I am flattered.'

'Then can I come to call?'

'No, no. You cannot.'

'Why not? My family is as good as yours.'

'I know that. But it is not possible.' She jumped down from the seat, her satchel banging on her back, her skirts flying.

'You have another friend,' he said.

Gabrielle straightened herself. 'I have no other friend.'

'But you do not like me.'

'I like you very much.'

'But you do not wish me to call on you.'

'I have said, it is impossible.' She made sure her hat was firmly on her head and set off along the road, refusing to look back but half hoping he would come after her. Of course it

94

was not possible for him to come to the farm while Mademoiselle de Gruchy and her sister were there; as far as she knew neither Armand nor his father were members of the Resistance. But it might be possible to meet away from the farm . . . only he would have to propose that, with its suggestion of illicitness. How she would love to have an illicit boyfriend, someone with whom she could tryst, with whom she could share secrets, be exciting.

But he was turning the cart to return to his home. She sighed and trudged on.

It was late morning when she reached the town, which was crowded as it was market day. As she was very much a stranger here, no one greeted her, although one or two young men whistled at her. What did surprise her was the number of German soldiers in the town; there seemed one at every street corner. Talk about shutting the stable door after the horse has bolted, she thought. She ignored them and went straight to the bar. At least there were no soldiers in here, although it was crowded. She wriggled through the throng, again attracting admiring glances from the mainly male customers, and reached the counter. Monsieur Vlabon, a bluff, cheerful man, blinked at her.

'Gabrielle? What are you doing here?'

'I have a message for you, monsieur.'

Vlabon glanced right and left, but no one seemed very interested. 'Go into the back room.'

He lifted the flap for her, and she ducked into the bar and through the door at the rear.

'Gabrielle?' Madame Vlabon was a match of her husband. 'You should not be here. It is too dangerous.'

'No one knows who I am.'

'But did you not see the soldiers? They are everywhere. They are stopping everyone they do not know. You are fortunate they have not stopped you, yet.'

'Why are they doing this?'

Madame Vlabon shrugged. 'Because Monsieur Moulin was arrested here, and they still think Mademoiselle de Gruchy may come back. If they were to arrest you . . .'

'Why should they arrest me? I have said, they do not know who I am.' She turned to the door as it opened.

95

'This must be quick,' Vlabon said. 'I cannot be gone long.'

'I am from Mademoiselle de Gruchy. Does Gaston Ferroux come in here often?'

'He is a regular customer. He should be in today.'

'Then will you tell him that Mademoiselle de Gruchy needs to see him, urgently. He should go to the farm, by himself.'

'I will do that. What will you do now?'

'If you will give me some lunch, and a glass of wine, I will return to the farm.'

'Of course. Augustine? Now I must get back to the bar. Give Mademoiselle de Gruchy my regards.'

He bustled off, and Madame Vlabon laid out bread and cheese and a bottle of wine. 'There is something big, eh?'

'I do not know.' Gabrielle ate hungrily.

'I understand. You are a brave and loyal girl.'

Gabrielle finished her meal, embraced Madame Vlabon and was allowed to use the kitchen door. This led through the backyard, past the toilets, into an alleyway. She made her way along this and reached the main street, which ended only a hundred metres away at the road leading into the hills. She turned towards this and heard a shout: 'Hey! You!'

From the accent she knew it had to be a German and, without thinking, gathered her skirt and began to run. There were more shouts and the drumming of boots on the cobbles, then she tripped and landed on her hands and knees. Before she could recover, her arms were seized and she was pulled to her feet, to find herself between two soldiers, who looked less hostile than amused.

'Why were you running away, mademoiselle?' one asked in uncertain French.

Gabrielle had got her nerves back under control. 'My mother told me always to run away from strange men.'

'I think she has something to hide,' said the other soldier.

'I think you are right,' agreed the first.

'What can I have to hide?' Gabrielle demanded, refusing to panic. 'Look inside my satchel. There is nothing there, save a few francs.'

'It's not what's in your satchel that we want to see,' the first soldier said. 'It's what you have in here.' He squeezed the bodice of her dress.

'Oh,' she cried. No one had ever done that to her before.

'And here,' said the second soldier, squeezing her buttocks.

'Oh,' she gasped again.

'And here most of all.' The first soldier squeezed her groin.

'Bastard!' she shouted and swung the satchel, catching him a blow across the face that knocked him off his feet.

Then she tried to twist away from the other man, but he caught her round the waist. 'You have struck a German soldier, mademoiselle. Do you not realize that carries an immediate death sentence?'

Gabrielle panted and tried to kick him, but without success. The first soldier got to his feet, slowly. 'I am going to fuck you till it's coming out of your mouth,' he said and looked left and right. 'Bring her over here.'

'Wait,' Gabrielle gasped. 'Please! I am a virgin.'

'Then we'll just open you up a little.' He grasped her arm, and the other man half lifted her from the ground.

'Halt!' snapped a voice. The two soldiers released Gabrielle and stood to attention; they had not noticed the officer coming down the alley. 'You are supposed to be on duty in the market place, looking out for guerillas,' the lieutenant said. 'Not terrorizing young girls.'

'We thought she was suspicious, Herr Lieutenant.'

'You mean you thought she was an easy victim. Get back to your duty.'

The two soldiers exchanged glances then saluted. 'Heil Hitler!'

The lieutenant watched them march away, then turned back to Gabrielle. 'Are you all right, mademoiselle?'

Gabrielle had got her breath back. Now she was finding the young man rather attractive. He was not very tall but well built, had crisply pleasant features and brown hair. Of course the uniform, so smart, helped, even if it also reminded her that he was a Boche. 'They did not harm me, sir. Thanks to you.'

'It was my duty. But also my pleasure. You are from Aumont? I have not seen you before.'

'I do not live here, sir. I live on a farm.'

'In the Massif? Which farm?'

'My father's name is Chartrin.'

'Chartrin. And your name is?'

'Gabrielle.'

'Gabrielle. I like that name. How far is this farm of yours?'

'Fifteen kilometres.'

'You walked that distance to come into Aumont?'

'My mother sent me to do some shopping.'

'She is a hard woman, your mother. Come with me.'

'Sir?'

'I will drive you out to your farm. Fifteen kilometres is too far for those pretty feet.'

'I am used to it, sir.'

'Nevertheless, it will be my pleasure. And while we drive, you can explain to me why you have walked fifteen kilometres to go shopping for your mother, and are now on your way home, without buying anything.'

Gabrielle followed him back into the town, her brain tumbling. She was too afraid to think straight. Everyone had heard of the Gestapo's methods. This man was not a member of the Gestapo, but he had the power to hand her over to them. The thought made her blood run cold. But more important than what might be about to happen to her was the matter of how to get rid of him before they reached the farm. If he was to catch a sight of Liane . . .

Yet he was politeness itself as he showed her to his car, watched by everyone in the vicinity. 'You will have to tell my driver where to go,' he said, gesturing her into the back of the open tourer.

'It is the road to the west,' she said. 'It is the only one.'

'You hear that, Hans,' the lieutenant said and sat beside her. 'Is it not a nice day for a drive in the country?'

'Yes, sir.'

'You are afraid of me. You are trembling.'

But again she had her nerves under control. 'Am I not supposed to be afraid of a German officer, sir?'

'Not if you are innocent of any desire to harm the Reich.'

'I have no desire to hurt anyone, sir.' Which was perfectly true. Apart from the machinations of Liane, and these were always carried out at a distance, the only actual contact she had had with the War had been the arrest of Jean Moulin, and

98

even that had had, and retained, a sort of surrealist nightmare quality.

'Well, then,' he said. 'We shall be friends. My name is Dieter. How old are you, Gabrielle?'

'I am seventeen, sir.'

'A good age. You are no longer a child, but you are not yet a woman. Are you eager to become a woman, Gabrielle?'

'I consider myself already a woman, sir.'

'Well said. You mean you are not a virgin?'

'Sir?'

'I am being too forward. But as we are going to be friends, we can also be confidants. So tell me . . .'

Gabrielle looked left and right. They were well out of the town now, driving between low hills. There was no one in sight. She was utterly at this man's mercy, as he would certainly be supported by his driver. On the other hand, if she matched his mood, she might be able to prevent him going right out to the farm; he was obviously far more interested in her than in her family. And it would be an adventure, while he was undoubtedly an attractive man and did not look a vicious one.

'I do not wish you to take offence,' Dieter said. 'I apologize. It is merely that I find you both interesting and attractive. So I wish to know as much as possible about you.'

'I am not offended, sir. I as just surprised. Yes, I am a virgin.'

'Does not your boyfriend wish more?'

'I have no boyfriend, sir.'

'That is remarkable. Would you not like to have one?'

'Oh, yes, sir. But . . .'

'It has not happened yet. It is sad to see a beautiful young girl wasting her life on a country farm.'

'Me, beautiful?'

'Has no one ever told you that you are beautiful, Gabrielle?'

'Well . . . no, sir.'

'Then you live in an unobservant society. I would like to take care of you.'

'Sir?'

'Is the idea repulsive?'

'Oh, no, sir. But . . .'

'We have only just met? I am a man of instant decisions, and the moment I saw you I knew I had to hold you in my arms.'

'Oh, sir. But you are German.'

'Does that make so much difference?'

'Not to me, sir. But my family . . .'

'Ah. Yes. I understand. Then we shall not tell your family.'

'But if you take me home . . .'

'There is no need for me to take you right home. I can drop you off a kilometre away.'

'Oh, sir. If you would . . .'

'But first we must, how shall I put it . . . consummate our friendship. Would you like that?'

Gabrielle was just happy to have escaped the risk of having him come to the farm. 'Oh, yes, sir.'

'Well . . . that is an attractive little copse over there. Shall we explore it, you and I?'

'Oh, yes, sir, if you wish.'

'Good. Stop the car, Hans.' Hans obeyed. 'And amuse yourself for half an hour.'

'As you wish, Herr Lieutenant.'

Dieter got out and opened the boot to take out a blanket. Gabrielle stepped down, her mind tumbling. She had no idea what was going to happen to her, but she found the prospect more exciting than ever. They walked away from the car towards the trees.

'Is it not a lovely afternoon?' Dieter asked. 'One wishes that the summer could last for ever. But then one would be bored. Do you have severe winters down here?'

'They can be,' Gabrielle said. 'It is because we are high up. Were you not here last winter?'

'Last winter I was in Russia.'

'Oh. Was it very bad?'

'Let me say that it was nothing like this.' They entered the trees. 'We do not have to go very far. Just away from prying eyes.'

'There are no eyes out here.'

'You mean we could make love out on that pasture, with the sun playing on our naked bodies?'

Gabrielle gulped. Naked bodies? She had not anticipated that.

'That sounds entrancing,' Dieter said. 'We shall do it. But at the moment there is Hans. He is an inquisitive fellow. Here will do.' He spread the blanket on the ground.

Gabrielle looked at it. 'I do not know what we should do.'

'The first thing it to undress. Take off your clothes. I wish to look at you.' Gabrielle drew a deep breath and unbuttoned her dress, shrugging it from her shoulders and allowing it to fall to the ground. 'Now the petticoat.'

Gabrielle bit her lip, but she lifted the petticoat over her head and laid it on the dress, fluffing out her hair as she stood before him wearing only her drawers. 'Exquisite,' he said, standing against her to finger her breasts. 'These are so perfectly formed. Am I the first to touch them? Except yourself, of course.' Gabrielle's head bobbed up and down. 'Now the rest.'

Although she had discounted the possibility of prying eyes in this mostly lonely part of the country, Gabrielle could not resist a glance to left and right as she slid her drawers down to her ankles and stepped out of them. 'Exquisite,' he said again. 'Turn round.'

She obeyed, happy not to have to look at him for a moment, and he fondled her buttocks. 'Now lie down. On your back.'

The ground, even beneath the trees, was warm and the warmth seeped through the blanket. Gabrielle nestled into the leaves, one hand instinctively resting on her groin, the other arm across her breasts. 'You are modest,' Dieter said, unbuttoning his tunic. 'I like that. But you must look at me.'

Her attention was indeed riveted as he removed his clothes; he was wearing so much more than she. But equally she had never seen a naked man before; Philipe was a very private person, and when he used the pump in the yard to bathe she had never been allowed to be present; although she had noticed that he had no objection to Liane being around. But she was sure that Philipe could not be as large as this man. And he intended to . . . He knelt beside her, then lay, and began kissing her, while his hand roamed over her stomach and breasts. 'Open your mouth,' he said. 'I want your tongue.'

Then his hand went down to her pubes, replacing her fingers with his own. 'Oh!' she gasped.

He raised his head. 'Did I hurt you?'

'No,' she said. 'No.'

101

'Will you not hold me?' Tentatively she took him in her fingers, and he gave a sigh. Then he rolled on to his back. 'Now I wish you to suck him.'

'To do what?' That was beyond her imagination.

'Take him into your mouth and suck. Be careful not to bite.'

'But . . .' She didn't really know how to go about it.

Yet he seemed pleased. 'You are a charmer. Get on your knees and turn round.'

She obeyed, only realizing too late that in doing so she was exposing her buttocks and between her legs to his exploration, which began immediately. But by then she was lost in what she was doing, to be taken aback when he ejaculated. 'Oh!' she gasped and rolled away from him, right off the blanket.

He sat up. 'It won't harm you. And you have made me very happy. Now I must do something for you.' His lips sought her pubes.

'Papa's farm is just over the next rise,' Gabrielle said. She continued to be amazed at the calmness of her voice, the way she could address this man, a member of the conquering forces, as a total equal. But then, two people who had shared everything had to be equal.

'Thus you would like me to drop you here,' he suggested. 'Would you father beat you, if he knew of me?'

'Yes.' She didn't know if Papa would beat her or not, but the thought of what Liane might do was terrifying. Yet she could not regret what had happened. All her life she had felt that time was passing her by, and now it had suddenly caught up with her in a single bound. That this man was an enemy of her people was irrelevant. *They* were not enemies. She could not believe that any other man could be so gentle. And when, after only fifteen minutes, he had been sufficiently recovered to enter her, it had been the most heavenly experience of her life. It had not even hurt very much. When she thought of someone like Armand Dragout doing that to her . . .

'Then we must say goodbye,' he said. 'No, *au revoir*. Is that the right phrase?'

'It means we will meet again.'

'I would like that. Do you ever walk by yourself?'

'Sometimes.'

102

'Then do so, today week. At eleven in the morning, walk back towards that wood. Our wood.'

Gabrielle could think of nothing more romantic. Our wood! 'Will you be there?'

'I will be there. A week today.' He squeezed her hand and she got out. She wondered if she should say 'Heil Hitler!' but decided against it, instead waiting while Hans, who had kept a straight face throughout, made a five-point turn and drove towards Aumont. Dieter did not look back, but she did not expect him to.

When the car was out of sight, she turned and trudged up the hill, stopping at the sight of the cart waiting just over the brow. Then she resumed walking. 'What do *you* want?' she inquired coldly. 'Are you spying on me?'

'I was not. I was cutting some more wood and returning home, and I saw this car coming along the road, so I stopped to wait. There are not many cars on this road. What were you doing riding in a German car?'

'If it is any business of yours, I was walking home, and this German officer stopped and offered me a ride. So I said yes. It is a long walk, and I was tired.'

'The Boche are our enemies.'

'That does not mean I cannot ride with them.'

'What did he do to you?'

'He did nothing to me,' Gabrielle snapped. But she knew she was flushing. 'Why don't you go home and leave me alone?'

'You are a traitor, riding with the Boche.' But he poked the mule with his stick and the patient animal began its slow walk.

Gabrielle went on down the hill. The farm was now in sight, and fifteen minutes later she was at the gate and being greeted by an enthusiastic Rufus. Odile came out of the house to see what was the cause of the barking. 'You are back early,' she remarked. 'I did not expect you before dusk.'

'Well, I got two rides.' As Armand had seen her getting out of the German car, there was no point in trying to pretend it hadn't happened.

'*Two* rides? Out here?'

'Well, this morning Armand Dragout gave me a ride part of the way into town. Then, when I left town again, this German officer offered me a ride in his car.'

103

Odile frowned. 'He brought you home?'

'No. He wanted to do that, but I asked him not to, so he let me out just over the hill.'

'Why did he do that? Where was he going?'

'I do not know.'

'You had better talk to Mademoiselle de Gruchy.'

Gabrielle gulped but she knew there was nothing for it. Liane and Amalie were in the parlour, studying maps. They listened to what Gabrielle had to say with only slight apparent interest. 'Did you know this officer before?' Liane asked.

'Oh, no. I don't think he's been here long. He said he had been in Russia.'

'And he just offered you a ride?'

'Well . . . there were these two men . . . soldiers, and they . . . well, they molested me.'

'What did you say?' Odile demanded.

'They took me down an alley and said they were going to search me. It was terrifying.'

'I can imagine,' Liane said. 'And this officer intervened?'

'Yes. He sent them off.'

'And then he offered you a ride. He sounds like a gentleman. Did he tell you his name?'

'Dieter.'

'He told you his name was Dieter. Dieter who?'

'I. . .' Gabrielle bit her lip. 'He didn't say.'

'Gabrielle,' Odile said severely. 'Did this man interfere with you?'

'Oh, no, Mama. No, no. He wouldn't do a thing like that.'

Odile looked at Liane, who smiled, reassuringly. 'And you didn't let him actually discover where you live. You handled it very well. Now tell me, did you see Vlabon?'

'Oh, yes.'

'You gave him my message?'

'Oh, yes. He said he hoped to see Gaston this afternoon.'

'Then that is very satisfactory. I am very pleased with you, Gabrielle. Thank you.'

Gabrielle knew she had been dismissed, but she hesitated for a moment before leaving the room, followed by Odile, who closed the door.

'She is lying,' Amalie said.

104

'I know. Or at least, I know she is not telling us the whole truth.'

'Then . . .'

'I do not think she would betray us. Betray her family. And if she has, she would hardly have told us that the German officer brought her home.'

'Then what do you think happened?'

'I think her story is largely true. I think what she has not told us is that this German officer charmed her, and she is afraid to admit it.'

'Charmed her? A Boche!'

'Amalie, you cannot hate an entire nation because of what one or two of their people may have done to you.'

'You can say that? How many Germans have you killed?'

'I have absolutely no idea. When one is blowing up a train, one is not counting heads. But I do know that not all of them were thugs like Roess.'

'I would like you to name me one German you have met who is not a murdering bastard. And don't bring up Helsingen. You know what the Germans have done in Russia.'

'I know absolutely nothing about Helsingen, except that he is our brother-in-law. But I could offer you Franz Hoeppner.'

'Ha!'

'He saved your life.'

'As he might have driven round a cat in his car.'

'He did it because you are Madeleine's sister. I found him charming. And Joanna says she is going to marry him.'

'Joanna! She is—'

'Please don't say it, Amalie. She is my dearest friend, and she has helped our family, and especially you, more than we had any right to expect. Stop brooding on the past and think about the future. We have a lot to do when Gaston gets here. And then . . . Vercours.'

'Am I coming with you?'

'I would like us to stick together.'

'So would I. And Philipe?'

'If he wishes. We must all be volunteers.'

'Have you slept with him yet?'

'He is very faithful,' Liane said.

105

Six

The Dawn

'W ell?' the brigadier demanded, gesturing James to a chair. James sat down. 'Merry Christmas, sir.'

'Is it? Tell me about the Vercours.'

'They're there. Liane reports that there are over a thousand of them, with more coming in every day. And this fellow Colonel Huet appears to be a real live wire. He already has them levelling ground for the airstrip. What is more, Jerry doesn't seem to have any idea what is going on. Once the men and munitions start coming in from Algiers, we really will have a second front, right in the heart of southern France.'

'Delestraint has been taken,' the brigadier said.

'Oh! That's bad luck. How did it happen?'

'He was betrayed. This whole business is riddled with traitors.'

'Do you think he'll break?'

'I would have supposed so, as he is a human being. Was a human being.'

'Shit! I beg you pardon, sir. Does that mean the Germans may learn about the Vercours?'

'If they do, they'll be way ahead of anyone in London or Algiers. This entire scheme was dreamt up by Delestraint. But he does not appear to have confided it to anyone else.' James scratched his head. 'There is a report on file,' the brigadier went on. 'This was when the scheme was first mooted, back in March of last year, and I was instructed to proceed with the preliminary planning. But apparently it was then filed under F, both by us and the French Headquarters in London. It appears that no one in Algiers has ever heard of it. Well, of course, back in March of last year everyone was scrapping

106

like mad down there, and I suppose no one was really interested in a rather high-flown plan for creating an Allied base in the middle of France. But there it is.'

'You mean the plan has been aborted?' James was aghast. 'I have to tell my people to pull out after they have so carefully established themselves? I'm afraid that will have a disastrous effect upon morale. As for expecting their help when the balloon goes up—'

'Simmer down, James. Nobody is contemplating aborting. I am just explaining to you that so far there has been a colossal cock-up. However, someone has to explain to the guerillas that they can expect no help for another couple of months. Now that Italy is out of the War, and we have Corsica and Sardinia as well as Sicily, it will be possible to get *matériel* up there and then it is only a short haul to the south of France. But it can't be done overnight, certainly while the Germans are hanging on to most of the peninsula. Once we get past Rome, now . . .'

'And when will that be, sir?'

'I really cannot say. But as I say, someone has to put the guerillas into the picture, and it can't be done by radio.'

'Permission to go in, sir.'

The brigadier smiled, a rare event. 'I thought you might wish to volunteer. You understand this could be a lengthy mission. You will first of all have to go to Algiers, and both brief them and be briefed by them. This means dealing with de Gaulle personally. Then you'll be dropped into the Vercours. The trouble is, once you're in, there's no way we can get you back out, until that airstrip is completed.'

James nodded. 'As I said, they're working on it now.'

'Very good. Now there is the business of who is going to run the Pound Office while you're away.'

'Oh, Rachel can handle it, sir. She's done it before.'

'Hm. Well, if you're totally confident . . .'

'I am, sir. Besides, as practically our whole control is now in the Vercours, there won't be much for her to do.'

'That's true. Right-ho, James. I'll arrange all your passages. Oh, there's just one more thing. Have you heard anything from Jonsson, recently?'

'No, sir, I have not, and I do not expect to, after the way we snubbed her.'

'Now, James, you don't really believe there was anything in that cock-and-bull story?'

'Yes, sir, I do believe there is something going on inside Germany that could be of great value to us. And you believed it too, when she was here in this office.'

'She's a compelling young woman, I'll give you that. But considered in the cold light of day . . . It has to be absurd.'

'Yes, sir,' James said coldly. 'I hope you're right.'

'Algiers?' Rachel demanded. 'You are going to Algiers?'

'As a staging post to the Vercours. Think of it, you'll have the office all to yourself.'

'I don't want the office all to myself. For how long?'

'It could be a little while. Due to this foul-up things are way behind schedule.'

'I suppose you'll be spending all your time with Liane.'

'She is one of the people I am going to see, yes.'

'Well, you can give her some news about her girlfriend.'

'Joanna? You have heard from Joanna?'

'Of her, not from her.' She indicated the pile of papers on her desk 'A German radio transcript.'

'She hasn't been arrested?'

'Joanna? Chance would be a fine thing. Let me see . . .' She sifted through the various slips. 'Here we are: Colonel Franz Hoeppner, recently returned from the Eastern Front, was today married to Swedish socialite Joanna Jonsson.'

James sat down, 'Good God!'

Rachel continued reading. 'Colonel Hoeppner, nephew of the well-known panzer general, has served with distinction in Russia for the past eighteen months. Frau Hoeppner is the daughter of a Swedish diplomat and an American woman, and was brought up in the United States, but renounced her citizenship to work in Germany. She is currently employed as one of Reichsfuehrer Himmler's personal secretaries.' She raised her head. 'I wonder what hubby thinks of that? It goes on that the ceremony was attended by the Fuehrer and just about everyone you can think of; Goering, Goebbels, a kind of *Who's Who* of the Nazi hierarchy. And, of course, a clutch of Swedish notables, including her father, down from Stockholm for the occasion.'

108

'Trust Joanna to do things in style.'

'Doesn't this mean that she's gone over, irrevocably?'

'I don't think anything is irrevocable where Joanna is concerned.'

'I'd be very interested to know what Liane thinks about it.'

'I'll find out, I'm sure. So tell me, what do *you* think of it?'

'What has it got to do with me?' Rachel asked. James gave her an old-fashioned look and she flushed. 'It was a one-night stand. Actually it was even less than that, a one-afternoon stand. I felt she needed cheering up.'

'And I am sure you did that. Well, I have to get started on arrangements.'

'Do you wish this information sent to the brigadier? After all, she is still officially Pound Three.'

James considered briefly. 'I don't think we'll bother, Rachel. It would only increase his blood pressure.'

'Happy?' Joanna asked, stroking her toes up and down Franz's calf. They were sharing a bath in their Munich hotel after a day skiing; the same hotel where they had rendezvoused very nearly two years previously, on the night she had had to shoot the assassin sent after her by the SIS, who supposed she had betrayed their secrets to the Gestapo. That had been sorted out – at the cost of their man's life – but she could not help but wonder if the memory of that episode had played its part in their refusal to believe what she had had to tell them of the plot against Hitler.

And now . . . it could be over. It *should* be over. But if it were, surely they would have heard? On the other hand, it might have been thought prudent to keep the death of the Fuehrer secret until all the arrangements for his replacement were completed. That of course had to include the removal of Himmler from power. She felt quite breathless when she thought of that. She wondered how he would react; whether he would face his fate with undisturbed arrogance or whether he would collapse in terror. She rather suspected the latter.

But she could not discover what had happened until her return to Berlin, which would be that evening. So she could enjoy this last morning, as she had enjoyed every one of the past thirteen mornings, with this handsome, charming man. The odd thing was that Franz looked every inch the Aryan ideal, with his blond hair, his crisp features, his powerful physique and, up till now at any rate, his utter loyalty to Adolf Hitler; and yet, she knew, he personally abhorred Nazism and all the things done in its name.

Their first meetings had been frosty, because she had been working for Oskar Weber and he regarded the whole Gestapo, and even more the SD, with utter distaste. But his attitude to her had slowly changed, as he had been commanding officer of the Bordeaux area and she had been sent there time and again to take part in the search for Liane de Gruchy. Franz was no fool and it had not taken him very long to realize that, for all her apparent loyalty to Weber and all he stood for, she was in fact secretly protecting and aiding Liane to avoid capture. When she had realized that he knew this, she had anticipated immediate arrest and at best a concentration camp. Instead he had invited her into his bed, an invitation she had not felt able to refuse, and then, to her consternation, asked her to marry him.

She had been mystified until she had realized the truth: Franz was as much in love with Liane as with her. He had been captured by Liane during one of her more outrageous coups and held captive for several hours, seated against her in the back of the car she and her people had stolen. He had expected to be executed, and had perhaps spent those hours inhaling her beauty and her personality as the last things he would ever know, and then, with that romantically quixotic quirk that was one of the most attractive things about her, she had released him and permitted him to walk back to Bordeaux. Joanna had realized that that memory had remained with him ever since, that he did not *want* Liane to be captured, to be tortured by people like Johann Roess and then executed.

Thus they had shared a potentially deadly secret, and the sharing had led to love. At least on his part. She was still not one hundred per cent sure, but marriage to such a man, with such a background, promised security in this most insecure of worlds. And now . . . 'I am happy when I'm with you,' Franz said.

A cue? He knew nothing of what she and his best friend,

110

Freddie von Helsingen, were engaged in, and she had not yet dared tell him. But if it were done . . .

'You said you'd been given a post on the staff,' she said. 'That you would not have to go back to Russia.'

'Yes. I am to join General Rommel's staff. You know he has been appointed commander of our Channel defences? It appears that he requested me personally.'

'Well, isn't that a great compliment?'

'I imagine it has more to do with the fact that I commanded the Dieppe garrison for a while immediately following the defeat of France, and that therefore I should know the area better than most.'

'Well, the important thing is that you will be staying out of Russia.'

'Do you think I am happy about that?'

'Don't you want to be with me?'

'Of course I do, my dearest girl. But when I think of all those men, living and fighting in such appalling conditions, suffering . . .'

Joanna seized her opportunity. 'Like Freddie von Helsingen.'

Franz got out of the bath and towelled himself dry. 'The very thought makes me shudder. Have you seen him?'

'I call regularly. Madeleine and I are old friends.'

'Of course. I will come with you the next time.'

'He has changed,' Joanna said. 'Well, I suppose any man would change after what happened to him.'

'As I said, the idea gives me the shivers.'

Joanna also got out of the bath and faced him as she dried herself. 'Is he still your best friend?'

'I suppose so. I do not have many friends.'

'Why?'

He went into the bedroom and lay on the bed. 'I suppose . . . well . . . it is not something for you to worry your beautiful head about.'

She lay beside him. 'Is it because you have dared to criticize the way the War is being fought?'

He frowned at her. 'Are you asking that as my wife or as Himmler's secretary?'

'Do you suppose I would ever betray you?'

'Of course I do not. But . . .'

'Then would you ever betray me?'

'You mean as regards Liane? Have I ever failed you?'

'Never. But what I have to say to you now is of far greater importance than even Liane. Will you promise to listen and then judge me?'

'Tell me.' He said not a word until she had finished, staring at her all the time. Then he asked, 'Bock is in this? You are positive?'

'Yes.'

'Rommel?'

'I do not know if an approach has been made to General Rommel.'

'And the British have said they will deal with an alternative government?'

Joanna drew a deep breath. But having started this lie, she had to go on with it, even to her husband. 'Yes.'

'My God, the risks you are running. All of you.'

'Is it not, all of us?'

'I will have to talk with Freddie. And Bock, if that is possible.'

'It is too late for that now.'

He frowned. 'What do you mean?'

'The date of the coup was two days ago.'

Slowly he sat up. 'You mean, that while we have been honeymooning . . .'

'The Fuehrer has been replaced, yes.'

'And you never told me?'

'There was no point in telling you, Franz. Neither you nor I at this time can influence events or even take part in them. You have no command to rally behind you, behind the coup. And I am only of value as a messenger girl. But the time for messengers is past, until I am required by the new government of Germany.'

'You mean Himmler . . .'

'He will have gone as well. Without Hitler, he is nothing.'

'My God! Only two weeks ago they were shaking my hand. They kissed you. But . . .' He had been staring at the wall; now he turned sharply. 'But if it happened, two days ago—'

'Why are the bells not ringing? There will be a lot to be done before the fact can be made public.'

'You can speak so calmly of such an event? We must get there immediately. To Berlin.'

'We are leaving, as soon as we have breakfasted.' She caught his hand as he was about to get up. 'Franz! We are in this, together. No matter what. To the very end.'

He hesitated then squeezed her fingers 'To the very end.'

The drive took several hours, the tensest hours of even Joanna's tension-filled recent life. She had to keep up her front of absolute confidence throughout the journey, while growing increasingly uneasy. The countryside, the towns and cities through which they passed were absolutely normal or, at least, as normal as they could be in the middle of a life-and-death war. She had to keep telling herself what she had told Franz; that the news of the coup could not be released until every important post had been secured, every possible hostile leader replaced. But with every mile her uneasiness grew.

Even Berlin was as normal as she remembered; the crews of old men and boys cleaning up the debris left by a recent bombing raid had become normalcy itself. 'Where to, first?' Franz asked. As the wedding had taken place immediately on his return to the city he had not yet had the time to secure any permanent lodgings, and in any event he knew he would be on his way to France in a few days.

'The Albert first,' she decided. 'There should be a message.' But there was no message, and the staff gave her their usual enthusiastic welcome; over the past four years she had become a permanent resident.

'What are we to do?' Franz asked when they had gained the privacy of her suite. 'My orders are to report immediately to OKW on my return from honeymoon.'

'You can spare an hour to call on your oldest friend,' Joanna said.

They took a taxi to the Helsingens' apartment block and rode up in the lift. 'I feel as if I am in a dream,' Franz confessed.

'It is a little surreal,' Joanna agreed and pressed the bell.

The door opened. 'Why, Fräulein Jonsson!' Hilda said.

'No, no, Hilda. I am Frau Hoeppner now. This is my husband, Colonel Hoeppner.'

'Oh, I do apologize, Frau. Herr Colonel.'

'Is Frau von Helsingen in?'

'Oh, indeed, Frau Hoeppner. Come in, come in.'

'Who is it, Hilda?' Madeleine emerged from the lounge. 'Joanna! Oh my dear, dear Joanna.' She rushed forward to embrace her, while Joanna looked over her shoulder at her husband and waggled her eyebrows. She had never known Madeleine to be so demonstrative before, certainly not to her. But Madeleine now turned her attention to Franz. 'Franz! How well you look.' As if she had not been at the wedding a fortnight previously.

'I am well, thanks to Joanna,' he agreed.

'Well, come in, come in. Freddie will be delighted to see you. He was so disappointed not to be able to come to the wedding, but he still hasn't quite got his crutches right yet. Hilda, be a dear and make some teas, will you please?'

Again Joanna was surprised; Madeleine was not usually so gracious to her maid, a woman she both disliked and distrusted. Hilda hurried off to the kitchen, and Franz and Joanna followed Madeleine into the lounge. 'Madeleine,' Joanna said.

Madeleine gave a quick shake of the head without looking at her. 'The bedroom is down here,' she announced in a loud voice, as if Joanna did not know where the bedroom was.

'I was going to ask after Helen.'

'Oh, she is having her nap.' She led them down the corridor and opened the bedroom door. 'Joanna and Franz are here.'

'Franz!' Helsingen raised his left arm and Franz squeezed the fingers. 'It is good to see you. Joanna!'

Joanna bent over the bed to kiss him and then looked at Madeleine, who had closed the door and was leaning against it. 'Please tell us.'

Both Madeleine and Helsingen looked at Franz.

'He is with us,' Joanna said. 'We must know what has happened.'

'Nothing has happened,' Helsingen said.

'Nothing? But . . .'

'I know. It was all arranged. The bomb was in Stauffenberg's briefcase. It operated on a time system. Attached to the

114

detonator was a small phial of acid. When the phial is broken, the acid commences to eat through the metal. It can be timed to perfection; in this case it was to be fifteen minutes. Stauffenberg was to break the phial when he took out his papers, place the case close to the Fuehrer and a couple of minutes later excuse himself to go to the toilet. He would remain there until after the explosion then immediately contact us to let us know that Hitler was dead. But—'

'Wait a moment,' Franz said. 'Did you say that Stauffenberg was to do all of this? But isn't he a . . .' He flushed.

'Yes,' Helsingen said. 'He is a cripple. That is, like me, he has lost one arm and two fingers on the hand of the other. Unlike me, however, his feet are still sound. He volunteered for the task, and as he is on the Fuehrer's staff and in his condition the last man anyone would suspect of subversion, we agreed to let him go in.'

'With a bomb?' Franz looked at Joanna. 'You said he was to be deposed.' Joanna bit her lip.

'You know that is not possible,' Helsingen said. 'Hitler is not only the head of state, he is the commander-in-chief of the army. You, me, every soldier in the Wehrmacht, has taken a personal oath of loyalty to him. As long as he is alive he can command that loyalty.'

'And you are prepared—'

'Ssh,' Madeleine said as Hilda knocked and brought in the tea. 'Thank you, Hilda, that will be all.' Hilda glanced around the tense faces. Then she gave a little bob and left the room. Madeleine carefully closed the door and then poured tea.

Franz had been containing himself with difficulty. 'You do not consider assassinating him as breaking your oath?'

'I and my associates,' Helsingen said, 'understand that he must be removed for the good of the country, no matter what is involved. But we also understand that for the army to follow us, they must be relieved of the burden of that oath, and that can only happen when he is dead.'

Franz gazed at Joanna, who seized the salient point. 'But what *happened*?'

'Nothing happened,' Helsingen repeated 'Stauffenberg attended the meeting at the Fuehrer's headquarters in Rastenburg in East Prussia. He took up a position not six feet

115

away from the Fuehrer. He opened the briefcase and took out his papers. As he did so, he broke the phial and replaced his briefcase, as I said, not six feet away from where Hitler was standing. Five minutes later he excused himself and went to the toilet. He remained there for ten minutes. Then he realized that something had gone wrong, so he returned to the council chamber. The council was still going on. He took up his original position. There he was handed his briefcase by another officer, who reminded him that it was against regulations for anyone to leave his briefcase, for however short a period.'

'So what did he do?' Joanna pressed.

'He flew back to Berlin, expecting to be blown sky high at any moment, and when he regained his apartment he took the case apart and found that the acid had simply not penetrated the detonator covering, although it had made a mess of everything else in the case.'

'That was an act of God,' Franz said.

'Oh, really, Franz,' Helsingen said. 'It was a simple miscalculation, both of the strength of the covering and of the acid needed.'

'So what happens now?' Joanna asked.

Helsingen sighed. 'Obviously we must try again. But it cannot happen until Stauffenberg, or another of our group – we are all willing to undertake the task – is again summoned to appear before Hitler. And there are doubters. There are always doubters, even some like you, Franz, who feel that the Fuehrer is protected by some kind of divine power. I will tell you this; if he is protected, it is by the Devil, not God.'

'And meanwhile the risk of betrayal grows with every day,' Madeleine said.

Everyone looked at Franz. 'I will not betray you,' he said. 'But I will not assist you either. Neither will Joanna.'

Now they looked at her. 'I must do as Franz wishes,' she said. 'I have given you the support of the British Government, and I will still wish you every success.'

She kissed them both and left the room. Franz did not speak until they were outside the apartment. Then he said, 'You realize that we may have signed our death warrants.'

116

She squeezed his hand. 'I've been under sentence of death before. And I'm still here.'

James looked down at rugged peaks and sunless valleys. There were trees, and even small woods, but the terrain was certainly unsuited to any large-scale drop; he wasn't sure *he* was going to get down unscathed, certainly in the dark. But now he could see lights being waved to and fro, and they seemed just about beneath him. Then he could make out the ground, rushing at him, a providentially flat piece of country. A moment later he was down and in the midst of several pairs of hands, preventing him from falling or even stumbling.

'Welcome to the Vercours, Major Barron,' a man said. 'I am Colonel Huet, commanding.'

James freed himself of the clutching hands and saluted; on this occasion he was wearing uniform. 'Pleased to be here, sir.'

He liked what he was looking at. Not very tall, but hatchet-faced and confident, Huet also wore uniform and looked every inch a soldier. 'Now come,' he said. 'Finding safe places to drop is difficult, so it is a walk of several kilometres to my headquarters. Can you do this?'

'Certainly,' James said and fell in beside the colonel. The rest of the reception committee, some twenty men, followed. But, James established with a quick look around him, they were all men. A flicker of concern started in his brain – Liane had to have known he was on his way – but he knew he had to be cautious.

'I understand that you will be able to bring us, how do you say, up to date,' Huet remarked. 'This delay has unsettled my people.'

'I can understand that. What I have to tell you will disappoint you as much as it disappoints us.'

'I see. There has been a setback?'

'I think mainly bad luck.' James outlined recent events. 'But it is all going to happen. Much depends on the completion of your airstrip. When do you think that will be?'

'Another month,' Huet said. 'It is a matter of hewing and shifting rock with our bare hands, you understand, while concealing what we are doing from the Boche.'

117

'How many men have you?'

'There are roughly three thousand men in the Vercours.'

'That is tremendous. Virtually brigade strength,'

'We could claim that, were we properly armed. But what do we have? Rifles, some tommy-guns, a few home-made mortars . . .'

'You will have much more once the airstrip is completed,' James assured him and drew a deep breath. 'I understand you also have some women.'

Huet smiled. 'Men must have women, major. But I think you are interested in two in particular. The de Gruchy sisters.'

'Well, they were, basically still are, under my control.'

'The famous Liane. Oh, indeed. She is quite a personality. But she is not here at the moment.'

'Sir?' James could not keep the concern out of his voice.

'If she has been under your control, then you will know how difficult she is *to* control. She came to us at the end of last year, with her sister, and some fifty men. They were most welcome and worked with a will. But they were restless. Liane in particular. So they have gone off to attack the Boche.'

James was aghast. 'Attack them where?'

'Not very far. Grenoble. It is only a few kilometres away. But the moment Liane learnt that there was a munitions factory there, she became agitated.'

'You allowed her to go into Grenoble to attack a munitions factory? With respect, sir, this operation was supposed to be secret.'

'It is very difficult to maintain morale, major, when one assembles a large number of men, and women, to be sure, on the promise of aggressive action against the enemy, and then no orders come, month after month. It becomes necessary to give the more offensive spirits their heads. As for being secret . . . Do you not realize that the Boche know we are here?

'That is very probable, sir. But as yet they have done nothing about it, which must mean they are not sure of either your intention or your numbers. To attack a target in Grenoble must incur the risk of a reprisal.'

'At this moment, such attacks are going on all over France. And is that not why we are here? To draw the enemy against us?'

'With respect, sir, this was to happen after you have been properly armed and equipped, and after the Allies have invaded France. What happens elsewhere falls into a different category. This is designed as a major operation.'

'And when is the invasion going to happen, major?'

'I am not in a position to tell you that, sir.'

'I am sure you are right. But . . . they said it would happen last year and it did not. Now they are saying it will happen this year. But who is to say that it will not be postponed again, and happen next year? Your generals are perfectionists, major. They wish everything to be just right. But in war nothing is ever just right. What did Napoleon say? War is an option of difficulties. But there are also certain factors that are indisputable. And one of them, as I have said, is that to accumulate a sizeable force of men who are not trained and disciplined soldiers on the promise of aggressive action against the enemy, and then condemn them to living in the most primitive circumstances and do nothing more than build an airstrip with their bare hands, is the surest way to have such a body disintegrate, both in morale and in numbers. I authorized Mademoiselle de Gruchy's raid because I considered it necessary for the maintenance of morale until we can undertake action on a larger scale. If the enemy respond, well, we are ready for them.'

James knew his reasoning was correct. The pundits in London, and Algiers, had no real understanding of the difficulties of maintaining a large force of guerillas in the field.

'In any event,' Huet went on, 'the raid seems to have been a success. Two nights ago we heard a huge explosion. That can only have been the munitions dump in Grenoble.'

'Two days ago,' James said. 'But the assault party has not returned.'

'Well, we do not know exactly what happened. Returning will not have been easy. But I am sure they will make it. Some of them, anyway.'

'Some of them,' James muttered.

'Well, major, another inescapable fact of war is that people get killed. We must hope that the casualty list will not have been too high. Now, we are almost there. You will have a hot meal and some wine, and a good night's sleep, and tomorrow it will all look much brighter. Tomorrow I will show you our airstrip, eh?'

Once, James reflected, he would have utterly shared the colonel's point of view. It was the only point of view; no commanding officer, whether he be second lieutenant or field marshal, could ever order men into battle if he were concerned for the life of any one of them. Probably that was why women had always in the past been excluded from front-line duties. But this was a different kind of war to any fought in the past, and there could be no question that Liane, and Amalie, were as proficient fighting machines as any professional soldier. But the thought of Liane dead or, worse, captured . . . He had had to order her into battle often enough, and every occasion had been traumatic, save for the two occasions he had been able to lead her himself. But those other times had been once removed, as it were, however anxiously he had sat by the radio, waiting for news. This time was immediate, and real, and virtually unbearable.

He could do nothing but pretend the indifference of the experienced officer, accompany Huet on an inspection of the airstrip – and observe with some concern that there was indeed a great deal to be done, and a long time to go, in the absence of any mechanical aids before it could possibly be operational – and wait with increasing apprehension until two days after his arrival he was awakened by the opening of the door of the hut he had been given as a home, and there she was.

He sat up, staring at her in the dawn light behind her. As always, it might have been yesterday that he had last seen her, just before he had flown away from the Chartrin's farm; over a year ago. Sometimes he wondered if she would ever change. But then, he did not wish her ever to change. She knelt beside his cot.

'James! It is so good to see you.'

He ruffled her hair and held the nape of her neck to bring her face forward for a kiss. 'I gather you've been up to your old tricks.'

She smiled. 'Amalie's tricks. She is really very accomplished. It was a glorious bang.'

'Is she all right?'

'Oh, yes. But there were casualties. Four men. Four good men. One of them . . .' she sighed.

'Someone I know?'

'Philipe Chartrin. You remember Philipe?'

'I remember Philipe. A rather surly young man.'

'He was jealous of you. Now . . . but what is worse is that we did not see his body. He just did not join us when we assembled. He could have been captured.'

'In which case your position here is blown.'

'Philipe would never betray us, betray me. No matter what they do to him.'

James decided that it would do no good to tell her that there was no man alive, or woman, who would be able to withstand the sort of torture the Gestapo could apply; except perhaps Jean Moulin. But he had to say, 'You know you shouldn't have done it?'

She stood up and began to undress. 'It is my business to harm the enemy.'

'It is your business to obey orders. This place, this establishment, is supposed to be top secret, until the generals consider the time is right to activate it. If the Germans track you up here . . .'

Naked, she stood above him. 'Move over.' He obliged and she slid beneath the blanket beside him. 'These cots were never intended for two. I will have to get on top.' This she did. 'Oh, how I dream of this. And all you do is scold me.'

He put his arms round her to hug her. 'Don't you think I dream of this too? But . . .'

She kissed him. 'You worry. My business is to harm the Germans, your business is to worry about it. We were a group of twenty. That is not giving away any secrets. I always operate with groups of that size. So I have shifted my position away from the Massif. That is understandable. Since poor Jean was taken the Boche have established a permanent presence in and about Aumont. But they will have expected me to turn up somewhere else. Now they have to start looking for me all over again.'

'Hold it a moment. You are speaking as if you think they will know you were responsible for the destruction of that arms dump.'

121

'Well, of course they do.'

'How?'

'We did not kill all the guards. I let the survivors see me, and I told them who I was.'

'Why did you do that?'

'Because I am the symbol of the Resistance. As long as I am known to be in the field, carrying out my attacks, so will every other Resistance group. Now we have been serious for too long . . .' She worked her body on his, left him incapable of coherent speech for several minutes, while she sighed her way to orgasm after orgasm. Then she lay with her lips against his neck while they both regained their breaths.

'You will make me think you have not had a man since last we were together.'

'Or that you have not had a woman,' she riposted and giggled. 'I have not even had any Germans to seduce.'

'And none of these three thousand blokes have had aspirations?'

'I think they are all afraid of me.'

'Even your own people who came with you from the Massif? You said there were fifty of them.'

'There were. But they are more afraid of me than any of the others.'

He was frowning. 'These fifty men, just disappearing from their homes . . . Won't they be missed? I mean by the Germans. If they are really in strength around Aumont.'

'They are used to sudden disappearances. Just about every man who thinks he is about to be called up for forced labour in Germany disappears.'

'But this chap Philipe; he would be exempt from any labour conscription, wouldn't he? If he is needed to work the farm.'

'Yes. But that being so, they wouldn't even bother to look for him. Anyway, the Chartrins are virtually under German protection at the moment.'

'Say again?'

'The daughter, Gabrielle . . . Surely you remember Gabrielle?'

'I do indeed. A pretty girl.'

'Well, she has a German beau.'

'Good God! How did she do that?'

'I have no real idea. But she does. An officer, no less. Amalie and I would have had to leave the farm anyway, even without your orders. But as long as he goes calling, the Chartrins are safe.'

'Li, darling, we are going to win this war, you know.'

'I have never doubted that.'

'And it is going to happen quite soon. Perhaps this year. When it does, there is going to be an awful lot of settling of old scores, of reckoning with people who have collaborated with the enemy.'

'Shit! I never thought of that. Those people are some of the most faithful I know.'

'But only you know that. And you're not likely to be there when the Germans finally surrender or are even driven out of the south of France. Do they still have the radio?' She nodded. 'Then as soon as they get me out of here, I'll be in touch with them to warn them.'

'You've just arrived and you want to leave again.'

He kissed her. 'Well, I am going to be here at least until you have completed the airstrip; there is no other way I can leave. I gather from Huet that we could be talking in terms of at least a month.'

'At least,' she said. 'Oh, it will be heavenly, having you here for a whole month. We have only once had that, before, and then—'

'I was too badly wounded for you to be able to do much more than change my dressings and give me a quick flick from time to time.'

'This time will be different. When you say the War will be over this year, do you mean the Allies are actually going to invade this year? After so many promises? I cannot believe it.'

'That is what this place is being set up for. To come to life, constantly replenished with troops and munitions, to stab the enemy in the back once the invasion is under way. That is why we do not want the Germans to become interested in us here until we are ready.'

'I am in deep shit. You should hang me.'

'I prefer the good old British Army method of confining you to barracks, this barracks, for a prolonged period. But the

War could be over even before the invasion. Joanna has been in touch.'

She rose on her knees, still straddling him, and threw off the blanket. 'She's all right?'

'At the moment, as far as I know. You know she's married Hoeppner?'

'Has she? What a hoot. He was a really nice fellow. But . . . won't that make her even more of a collaborator than Gabrielle?'

'Not if, when the roof finally falls, she can get to us before a lynch mob can get to her. But it's what she got in touch about that matters.'

'Tell me.'

He did so, and she listened with rapt attention.

'What a coup that would be,' she said when he had finished. 'But you say your government wouldn't support it?'

'Sadly, no.'

'They are cretins.'

'I agree with you, at least part of the time.'

'But you think she'll go ahead with it?'

'I believe she will continue to encourage the conspiracy, yes.'

'God, if she could bring it off . . . but the risk.'

'You do realize that if Helsingen is involved, then Madeleine is too. And the way the Nazis react to conspiracies against them . . . The niece you've never seen, either.'

'Hitler's god-daughter,' she said thoughtfully. 'How soon will it happen, do you think?'

'I would say it has to be soon.'

Joanna got out of the car in the forecourt of Gestapo Headquarters in Berlin and entered that so familiar doorway. It was a damp early June day, the sixth, but the weather appeared to be bad all over Europe. The weather was in keeping with her mood. She had enjoyed the past two months, living as a housewife, and on the Channel coast as well, even if she had been surrounded by a mixture of anticipatory elation and equally anticipatory apprehension, and not only because of the vast forces everyone knew were gathering just across the Channel, waiting to strike.

She and Franz had had their own apprehensions. To her great relief, his adoration of her had proved greater than any hostile consideration of her treachery, as most Germans officers would have considered it. But then, he knew all her secrets, or he thought he did. If he had no idea that she was, and always had been, an SIS agent, and fully accepted her explanation that she approached James Barron with her story because he had been an old friend from before the War, he knew that she had always secretly supported Liane and therefore the Resistance. But he had a sufficiently male ego to be certain that now she was married to him those days were in the past. For all the tensions that surrounded them, the fathomless uncertainty of the future, whether the plot against Hitler succeeded or not, they had been happy these past couple of months.

She had even enjoyed meeting Erwin Rommel again; an older, sadder, grimmer Rommel, so different to the totally confident, debonair young brigadier general she remembered from 1940. She had been surprised to discover that he remembered her as well, although, sadly, he remembered Liane more. But that figured. No man who had ever met Liane was likely to forget her, even without her name constantly being headlined in the German press.

But now the honeymoon was definitely over. Himmler had never actually allowed her to retire from his service, merely given her prolonged leave of absence. Now he had summoned her back. Franz had been furious. 'You are not to go on any more missions for him,' he had declared. 'Those days are finished.'

'I don't see what mission he can possibly have in mind,' she had pointed out. 'But I must go.'

'And if he simply wants to sleep with you?'

'Are you going to be jealous of that limp rag?'

'God, it makes me so angry that a man like that can have such power. But there is another point. Suppose he has found out about the conspiracy, and your part in it, and intends to hand you over to someone like Roess for interrogation?'

'I think if he had found out about the conspiracy, he would have sent a warrant for my arrest, rather than a mere request for me to go to him.'

'You are so calm. Don't you have any nerves at all?'

'I think they all got burned up, long ago.'

Which was a lie, she thought, as she walked along that unforgettable corridor. Sentries stood to attention, secretaries smiled at her; they all knew who she was. But no one could enter this building without a sense of apprehension, except perhaps Himmler himself. And if one happened to have a guilty conscience it could be quite terrifying.

She went up the stairs and was greeted by another secretary. 'Frau Hoeppner. The Reichsfuehrer is waiting for you.'

The double doors were opened for her, and she entered the office. 'Heil Hitler!'

'Heil!' Himmler came round his desk to embrace her. 'You are looking splendid. Marriage agrees with you. Don't you think so, Roess?'

Joanna turned her head sharply and Roess grinned at her. 'Indeed, Herr Reichsfuehrer.'

What was he doing here? Could her nightmare be about to come true? Himmler looked genial enough, but she knew how two-faced he was. 'Well, sit down, sit down,' he said. 'Now tell me, Joanna, How is life in Boulogne?'

'Tense. On a clear day we can see England.'

'Do you know, I have never seen England?' Himmler sounded almost wistful. 'But I am sure Field Marshal Rommel has things under control.'

'He has certainly done wonders since taking command, sir. But I do not think he is content. He could do with more men and more resources.'

'More men and more resources. That has been the cry of every commanding general since time began. Rommel was always complaining in Africa about shortage of men and *matériel*. Well . . .' He glanced at their faces, daring either of them to point out that Rommel had been defeated in North Africa, at least partly because he had run out of men and *matériel*. 'In any event, I have brought you here to deal with a more serious matter. Have you seen these reports? I have had a list made up. March 26, the Phillips radio factory at Brive-la-Gaillarde, blown up. April 4, sabotage halts production at Broonzavia aircraft components plant outside Paris. April 6, sabotage halts production at Timken ball-bearing factory, also near Paris. April 28, several tanks blown up and some cars stolen – stolen! – from the Renault works outside Paris. April 29, Dunlop factory at Montlucon crippled; repairs had only just been completed after an RAF raid. May 2, steel works at Aubert and Duval completely shut down. May 3, 100,000 litres of acetone set on fire at Lambiotte plant in Premery. May 13, production halted at SP gun factory of Lorraine-Dietrich, Bagnieres-de-Bigorre. May 17, attack carried out on CAM ball-bearing plant at Ivry-sur-Seine. May 22, hydroelectric station at Bussy blown up. May 25, production of artillery pieces halted at Arsensal National, Tarbes. May 26, hydroelectric station supplying Tulle badly damaged. May 30, Decazeville colliery attacked.

'The Fuehrer is absolutely furious. He wishes this so-called Resistance stamped out, and before the Allies can launch any kind of invasion.'

'Hostages,' Roess said. 'If we take sufficient hostages and start shooting them—'

'That has not produced any results in the past,' Joanna pointed out. 'Why should it now, when they are almost daily expecting the invasion?'

'Joanna is right,' Himmler said. 'We must strike at their leaders.'

'Well, Herr Reichsfuehrer, we have done this, successfully, whenever we have been able to identify them. Moulin, Delestraint . . .'

'But not de Gruchy.'

'With respect, sir, de Gruchy is not a national leader. She has a following of at most thirty—'

'You think so.'

'And in addition, we have heard nothing of her for some months now. Indeed, not since the capture of Moulin, and her raid on the wolfram mine. It is my belief that she was thoroughly scared by that, and that we shall hear little more of her.'

'You believe,' Himmler said scathingly. 'You should read this.' He threw the sheet of paper across the desk.

Roess picked it up cautiously. 'A munitions factory? Grenoble?'

'I assume you know where Grenoble is?'

'Indeed, sir. It is not a place in which de Gruchy has ever operated before.'

'But she was there.'

'Is this identification positive?'

'I believe it is. Not only did she play her usual trick of making herself known, but one of her people was captured and he has admitted that she was the leader of the attack. And you say she commands not more than thirty men? This man has told us that more and more men have been assembling in the area south of Grenoble known as the Vercours. Do you know of it?'

'Ah . . .'

'It is a large area of very wild country, a mass of hills and ravines and woods and natural obstacles. There are only a few minor roads through it and a couple of villages. It is an obvious place for outlaws to accumulate.'

'And no one has reported it?'

'Hitherto it has not seemed very important; the local commander in Grenoble seems to have assumed that most of the people fleeing there were attempting to escape the labour draft. But they were causing no trouble, and he knew that to flush them out would take at least a brigade of front-line troops. His superiors agreed with him. Now the situation has changed. These people are being led by Liane de Gruchy. And do you know how many men she may have at her command? Not thirty, Roess. Not even three hundred. Bittner estimates, from the information given him by this prisoner, that the figure could be as high as a thousand.'

'With respect, sir, I find that impossible to accept.'

'Well, colonel, I am going to give you the opportunity to verify those figures. This is an opportunity we have not had before. We now know where de Gruchy is. And we can be pretty sure that she is going to stay there, using the Vercours as a base from which to mount raids on the surrounding country, just as she did from the Massif Central in the early days of the War. We also know that she does not abandon her people. If they are attacked, she will stay and fight with them to the end. It will be your privilege to see to that end, colonel. With Joanna's assistance.'

'Me?' Joanna cried.

'Yes, you. I am sorry to inflict this upon you in the early days of your marriage, my dear, but it is necessary for the good of the Reich. We all know how de Gruchy is so skilful at disguising herself. As with the last time we attempted to capture her, I want a positive identification of the body by someone who knows her well. The difference between this time and the last time is that we *know* she is there.'

'I am sure Colonel Roess knows her well enough to identify her, sir.'

'As I understand it, when Roess had, shall I say, an acquaintance with the lady, that is . . .' He smiled at the discomfited colonel, 'before she put him in hospital with a blow on the head, she was wearing one of her disguises, so he has never actually seen her as she really is. Is that not correct, colonel?'

'I believe so, sir,' Roess muttered.

'Even if, no doubt, she was still beautiful. In any event, the last time you two worked in tandem you turned up Moulin. I am sure you will be similarly successful again.'

Roess and Joanna gazed at each other. While he did not look displeased at the prospect, her brain was as usual doing handsprings. Last year had been a small-scale operation, in which she had been able to influence events, even at the cost of committing murder. But if this were to be a large-scale military operation . . .

Roess was obviously thinking the same thing. 'How many men will I command, sir?'

'Bittner has a division at his disposal. That is more than ten thousand men, in the general area. He is a general and will obviously command in the field. You will be an observer for the Gestapo and will take charge of any prisoners. However, you will also inform General Bittner that if he requires any additional forces or the services of the Luftwaffe, he can apply for them, through you, to me and I will see that he gets them. These vermin must be utterly destroyed. Do not come back until that is done. Either of you.'

'Yes, sir. I should imagine that ten thousand professional soldiers should be sufficient to deal with a thousand guerrillas.'

'Just remember that it is very rough country, and that these are not front-line troops.'

'Yes, sir. I still am certain that they will be sufficient, with

129

a little careful preparation. This prisoner who was taken after the attack on Grenoble, is he still available?'

'You will have to ask General Bittner. He may well have been executed by now.'

'That would be a pity. However . . .' Roess stood up. 'We shall leave tomorrow. Heil Hitler!'

Joanna also stood up. 'Am I allowed to inform my husband where I am going? Or, at least, why I will not be returning for a few weeks?'

'My office will inform Colonel Hoeppner. And I sincerely hope you will be back at his side a lot sooner than in a few weeks.'

'Thank you, Herr Reichsfuehrer.'

They turned to the door, which suddenly burst open, to admit a panting uniformed secretary.

'What the devil—?' Himmler demanded.

'Herr Reichsfuehrer,' the girl gasped. 'The invasion . . . Normandy . . . the Allies . . .'

'Pull yourself together, woman. What is it you are trying to say?'

The girl stood to attention, gulping air into her lungs. 'It has just been reported, Herr Reichsfuehrer, that at dawn this morning the Americans and the English landed in Normandy in great strength.'

PART THREE

The Brightest Day

But westward, look, the land is bright.

Seven

The Traitor

'Have you lost your senses?' Himmler demanded. 'Normandy? That is about the furthest part of northern France from England. Of course they would not invade there. It must be a raid.'

'But the report, Herr Reichsfuehrer . . . Thousands and thousands of men, thousands of ships, thousands of aircraft . . .'

'That sounds like some hysterical junior officer losing his nerve.' Himmler glared at Joanna, as if wondering if Hoeppner could be the culprit. 'Has the Fuehrer been informed?'

'I believe the Fuehrer is still asleep, sir.'

'Well, no doubt he will deal with the situation when he wakes up. Meanwhile, get confirmation of those absurd numbers, if they can be confirmed.'

'Yes, Herr Reichsfuehrer.' The girl hurried from the room.

Himmler looked at Roess and Joanna. 'The material one has to work with . . . One despairs. What are you waiting for?'

'I was wondering if this new situation requires any change in our plans?' Roess asked.

'This new situation? It is a raid, nothing more. It can only be a raid. Normandy? Rubbish. You have your orders, Colonel. Carry them out.'

'I shall do that, Herr Reichsfuehrer.'

'With respect, sir,' Joanna said. 'If there is fighting in Normandy—'

'Your husband will be involved. So will Frau Rommel's husband and thousands of other wives throughout Germany. Believe me, your husband will do a much better job without you there to distract him. Heil Hitler!'

*　　*　　*

Joanna and Roess went down the stairs together. 'Do you believe it is just a raid?' she asked.

'That depends on how accurate those figures are.' He glanced at her. 'Are you frightened?'

'Why should I be frightened? I am concerned for my husband's life.'

'Do you not realize that if this is the invasion, we my well be looking at the defeat of Germany?'

'Can you dare say that?'

'Oh, come now, Joanna. You know very well that we cannot defeat the Allies if they get a foothold in France. Look at what is happening in Italy. Do you know that Rome has fallen?'

'I did not know that.'

'It happened yesterday. So they are steadily working their way up from the south, the Russians are steadily working their way in from the east and if the Allies are now going to start working *their* way in from the west . . .'

'Don't you believe in all these secret weapons we are developing?'

'A few rockets are not going to make a jot of difference, supposing they work. But you can be sure that one of the first things the Americans will do when they get to Berlin will be to hang you.'

'What an intriguing thought. Perhaps they will hang you beside me.'

'They will have to catch me first. And before they do, I am going to have the satisfaction of hanging that bitch Liane de Gruchy, slowly.'

Over my dead body, Joanna thought. But she was realizing that it could well come to that.

It was two days before they got out of Berlin, as it turned out that the Allied landings were not merely a raid after all. But OKW remained convinced that while the attack appeared to be a genuine attempt at invasion, it was still a diversionary attempt to draw Germany's attention and troops, especially panzers, away from the Pas de Calais, where logic dictated that the real invasion would take place. This was certainly Hitler's point of view, and he refused to release his armour. In the uncertainty and confusion the railways were the most confused of all, with some trains being cancelled entirely on the authority of the local stationmaster and others being diverted to move troops. The confusion was even greater in France, where a large part of the railway network had in any event been disrupted by RAF bombing.

It was therefore Thursday June 8 before they finally left Berlin to begin the journey south by train. Joanna had actually disobeyed Himmler and tried on her own to get through to Franz, but it had been impossible to locate him. 'He could be dead already,' Roess remarked. He was in a thoroughly disagreeable mood at the delay, and Joanna decided the best thing to do was ignore him. Franz could not possibly be dead, she told herself. 'If he *is* dead,' Roess pointed out, 'you will be left without a man. I suspect that Himmler is tired of you.'

'Surely that is my business?' She spoke as coldly as she could.

'I mention it because, in the circumstances, I might take you on.'

Joann stared at him. 'I would sooner lie down with a snake.'

He retired behind a wall of hostility; his mood had not improved by the following morning when, just after breakfast, the train suddenly ground to a halt. He looked out of the window. 'This is not Limoges.'

'Which is, I am sure, a place you remember very well,' Joanna suggested.

The conductor appeared at the door of the compartment. 'I am sorry, Herr Colonel, but our journey will be delayed.'

'Here? Where are we?'

'The nearest village is called Oradour.'

'Oradour?' Joanna asked. 'Isn't that where the woman Dugard claimed to have seen Liane de Gruchy?'

'Which you say was a lie.'

'It was. My point is that it is only a dozen kilometres north of Limoges.'

'That is correct, Fräulein,' the conductor said. 'But we will not be able to get there today. The line has been torn up.'

'What?' Roess shouted. 'Torn up by whom?'

'The Resistance, Herr Colonel. They are very strong in this area. Our people are working on the line, but it will take time.'

134

'How much time can it possibly take to re-lay a track?'
Roess demanded.

'It is not a difficult job in normal circumstances, sir. But
there are men in the woods, shooting at our people.'

In fact they could hear the distant pop-pop. 'That is outrageous.'

'I agree, sir. We have radioed Limoges for assistance, and
I understand there is an SS regiment stationed there, which
should be with us at any moment.'

The SS company arrived two hours later and after a brief skir-
mish drove off the guerillas. Then having been informed of
who was travelling on the train, Captain Hoffmann came to
the compartment. By then Roess was in one of his furies.
Joanna had always doubted his sanity, since Liane had delivered that crushing blow to his head; now she half expected
him to start foaming at the mouth.

'This is an intolerable situation,' he shouted at the captain.

'It is aggravating, I agree, Herr Colonel,' Hoffmann
conceded. 'But we will soon have you moving again.'

'And when you have gone, they will destroy the line again.'

'I'm afraid that is very likely, sir. We simply do not have
the men to patrol the entire line, certainly not now that a large
proportion of our people are being sent to the west to deal
with the trouble in Normandy.'

'But the people who dug up this line, they were shooting
at the workmen only an hour ago. They can't be far.'

'I am sure they are not, sir. In fact, I am fairly sure that they
are people from Oradour. We have had trouble there before.'

'If you are sure they come from there, why do you not go
in and get them?'

'It's not as easy as that, sir. We have conducted searches
before, but everyone appears to be a simple farmer or shop-
keeper, and we have never found any concealed weapons. They
are very clever.'

'Too clever for the SS? I think it is necessary to make an
example of these people, Captain. Obviously they have been
emboldened by this Allied raid, and they will get bolder yet
if they are not taught a lesson. Now. You are certain these
terrorists come from this village Oradour?'

135

'Most of them, yes.'

'Very good. You will, first of all, send to Limoges for additional troops. Then you will surround the village and place every male over the age of twelve under arrest. You will assemble these male terrorists in the centre of the town and you will execute them all by gunfire.'

Hoffmann gulped. 'But, Herr Colonel, some of them will be innocent.'

'I am sure they are all guilty of giving aid and comfort to the enemy, which is a capital offence.'

'The women and children . . . There will be a terrible scene.'

'Shut all the women and children up in the church before you commence the executions. Let them have their scene in there.'

'Yes, Herr Colonel. Ah . . . you will put this order in writing?'

'I have given you an order,' Roess said. 'Carry it out. Heil Hitler!' The captain saluted.

'Roess,' Joanna said. 'You cannot be serious.'

'It is time these people were properly dealt with. If I had been in general command, this problem would have been solved the moment it arose.'

Joanna was on the verge of an explosion. But she managed to keep her temper. 'You understand that I will make a full report of this business to Reichsfuehrer Himmler.'

'I would be grateful if you would do that, Fräulein. I am sure that the Reichsfuehrer will commend me.' Sadly, Joanna had to agree with him.

There followed the worst twenty-four hours of Joanna's life, at least to that moment. The rest of the SS battalion arrived that evening, while the work of repairing the line went on throughout the night. The next morning at dawn Oradour was surrounded. Joanna remained in her compartment but she could not shut her ears to the sounds of gunfire, which went on for nearly an hour. The conductor appeared, looking visibly shaken. 'The line is repaired, Fräulein.'

'Then why do we not leave this place?'

'We must wait for the colonel.'

Joanna looked out of the window and saw only trees. Then

she saw smoke rising behind them, which soon became quite dense. A few minutes later Roess appeared, pulling off his gloves. 'That is done. You may proceed, Conductor.'

'Immediately, Herr Colonel.' The conductor bustled off, and a few minutes later the train began to move.

'So, how many men do you reckon you have murdered?' Joanna asked.

'About three hundred men have been executed.'

'And you are now burning their remains.'

He looked out of the window at the smoke, now falling behind them. 'That is the church. The rest of the village will be set alight afterwards.'

'You mean that in addition to murdering those women's husbands, you intend to destroy their homes.'

'I have given orders that the village is to be obliterated, yes. As for the women and children, I do not suppose they are any longer very interested.'

Joanna stared at him, then looked back at the smoke, then looked at him again, while icy fingers seemed to be wrapping themselves around her heart. 'You could not,' she whispered. 'You would not dare!'

'They were all guilty,' he said. 'Had they been left alive, they would only have joined some other guerilla band.' Joanna continued to stare at him for several minutes, then she got up and went to the door. 'Where are you going?' he asked.

'Anywhere but here,' she said.

She felt physically sick. She knew, of course, of the destruction of the village of Lidice in Czechoslovakia as a reprisal for the murder of Reinhard Heydrich in 1942 but that *had* been an act of reprisal, and the women and children had not been murdered outright but had been sent to concentration camps; a more slow and horrible end for most, perhaps, but at least with a chance of survival for the few. The people of Oradour, if indeed it had been them – there was no proof – had done no more than delay a train by forty-eight hours . . . and had suffered to the last babe in arms. And there was nothing she could do about it. Save remember. There would be a judgement day. But in the meantime, the Vercours . . . and Liane. My God, if Roess were to be the victor there . . .

'It will be very difficult,' General Bittner said. 'You have

137

not seen the terrain. I have flown over it. It is quite impenetrable to large bodies of troops.'

'We were told that there are roads into it,' Roess said.

'A couple and they are hardly more than tracks leading to the few villages in the area. And they are easily blocked by the guerillas. I have sent detachments to try to force their way through, and they have been repelled with heavy casualties.'

'What sort of casualties?'

'Ten men killed and more than thirty wounded.'

Roess snorted contemptuously. 'Those are heavy casualties? Reichsfuehrer Himmler's orders are that the entire area is to be reduced, regardless of casualties.' Bittner gulped. Like most regular army officers he felt uneasy in the presence of the Gestapo, and when he was also in the presence of such a striking woman . . . 'However,' Roess went on reassuringly, 'we shall reduce the problem by reducing the guerillas first. Have these villages been bombed?'

'More than once. It does not seem to have had much effect.'

'Well, let us be logical. You estimate there could be more than a thousand men in those hills. This has to have taken several months to happen. And yet in all those months there has been this one attack in this vicinity. Why? Why are these men gathered there, doing nothing?'

'I have no idea. Down to this recent outrage I have been content that they should be there, because I knew where they were and they were causing no trouble.'

'They are there to cause trouble, Herr General. This prisoner you took. Have you still got him?'

'Of course I still have him.'

'And is he still capable of answering questions?' Joanna asked.

Bittner shot her a nervous glance. 'He has answered all of my questions.'

'But you do not seem to have asked him the important ones, Herr General,' Roess said. 'We will interrogate this fellow.'

'Interrogate? You mean . . .' Bittner swallowed. 'He has been entirely co-operative.'

'And I am sure he will continue to be so. Has he been seen by the Gestapo?'

138

'Seen? Ah, no. They wished to have him, but I refused their request.'

'Why did you do that?'

'I regard him as a prisoner-of-war.'

'With respect, Herr General, how can a guerilla – which means by definition that he is an outlaw and an enemy of the Reich, and who, in addition, has been captured in an act of destruction against the Reich – be considered a prisoner of war? On the authority given to me by Reichsfuehrer Himmler, I wish this man delivered to the local Gestapo Headquarters immediately. My colleague and I will interview him there.'

Bittner swallowed. 'When am I to move against the Vercours?'

'When we have heard what this man has to say. But you may start making your preparations now. How many men do you command?'

'I have a brigade here in Grenoble; say three thousand men.'

'I was told you had a division.'

'I do. But that is to control the whole area.'

'Well, the garrison here should be sufficient to deal with a thousand terrorists. But I will confirm this after I have spoken with this man.' Roess stood up. 'Heil Hitler!'

Bittner acknowledged the salute. 'May I ask, what is the estimation of the Reichsfuehrer of this large-scale raid by the Allies in Normandy?'

'That it is a large-scale raid, which will be dealt with.'

'That man is not fit to command,' Roess remarked as he and Joanna were driven to Gestapo Headquarters.

'But he has you to stiffen his back,' Joanna pointed out.

He glanced at her, correctly suspecting sarcasm. 'Are you looking forward to interrogating this man.'

'No.'

'Because you have not the stomach for *that*.'

'That is quite correct, Herr Colonel. I am not ashamed to admit it. Rather I would be ashamed to admit that, like you, I enjoyed it.'

'But you will be present. That is an order.'

Joanna sighed. 'I will be present, Herr Colonel.'

It was a short drive to the small building occupied by the

local Gestapo, but even so they could see the devastation caused by the exploding munitions dump. 'Must have been some bang,' Joanna remarked.

'It is criminal, placing a munitions dump within a city,' Roess grumbled.

The car stopped and he stamped into the building, saluted by the usual group of secretaries, all highly nervous at this unexpected visit by their most famous commander.

'Herr Colonel,' said Captain List. 'Welcome to Grenoble.' He looked at Joanna, eyebrows arched.

'My assistant, Fräulein Jonsson. Has the prisoner arrived yet?'

'Not as yet, Herr Colonel.'

'Well, telephone Wehrmacht Headquarters and find out where he is. You have an interrogation room?'

'Of course, Herr Colonel.'

'Show it to us. And make that phone call.'

Philipe arrived a few minutes later. By then Roess had thoroughly inspected the underground chamber, grunting his disapproval. Joanna sat in a chair. Having been forced to watch his interrogation of Moulin, she knew she was in for a thoroughly unpleasant time. She would have to shut her mind to what she was going to see and hear, and hope that the man would not scream too loudly.

She remained far more concerned about Liane. There could be no doubt that she was within a few miles of her, having taken refuge in an apparently impenetrable part of the country. Like Roess, she wanted to know why. If, Liane having established herself there, it seemed logical for her to have raided Grenoble, that still did not indicate any reason for her being there in the first place; there was no other possible target in the vicinity. While now she appeared to be cornered, supposing the Germans could bring sufficient forces to bear, and they seemed determined to do that.

Supposing they *could* bring sufficient forces to bear. If this landing in Normandy were the invasion at last . . . She was no strategist, but she did know that while both Franz and his boss, Rommel, had beefed up the defences in Normandy, they had concentrated most of their efforts in the Pas de Calais, where only twenty miles separated France from England.

140

Franz had told her that Rommel's calculations were that any invasion could not possibly gain a toe-hold, much less create a bridgehead, with less than two hundred thousand men, who would first of all have to be ferried across the water and then maintained, and not only with food and munitions, but with all the requirements of modern warfare, principally fuel for their tanks and vehicles. They had considered that might just be possible over a twenty-mile stretch of water; if the Allies felt that it could be done over three times that distance, the implications for their overwhelming strength were startling.

And frightening? Only to the supporters of Nazidom. What was frightening was that those who did not support the regime, but were obliged to fight for it, would have to suffer and die in a vain attempt to prevent the Allied victory. If ever there were a time for the conspirators to act, it had to be now. And she could do nothing either to encourage them or to help them; she was stuck down here having to supervise the destruction of her dearest friend!

Feet clattered in the corridor, and the prisoner was marched in by two uniformed agents. To Joanna's relief she did not recognize him – there was always the risk of some old acquaintance showing up – but he was unfortunately attractive as a man, tall and thin, with a not unhandsome hatchet face, lank black hair and lively dark eyes. He was dressed in shirt and trousers and moved without any visible handicap, as might have resulted from a severe beating.

Nor was he at this moment particularly afraid, even when confronted by Roess; he obviously had no idea who the little man was.

'Your name?' Roess asked.

'Philipe Chartrin.'

'You are a member of the terrorist band that recently attacked this city?'

'Yes.' He continued to speak boldly.

'You understand that you have committed a capital offence?'

'I was fighting for France.'

'You were committing an act of terror, for which you are going to be hanged.'

Philipe's cheeks paled. 'I must be tried.'

'You must be nothing that I do not decree. You will be

141

hanged, slowly. There will be no trapdoor, no drop. You will be hoisted from the floor by your neck, while your bowels open and your prick stands up straight.' Philipe licked his lips and glanced at Joanna. 'But you may even enjoy it,' Roess said. 'Because before that happens, we are going to make you hate the day you were born. The Fräulein will make you do that. She is good at making men hate the day they were born. It is her hobby.'

Philipe opened his mouth as if he would have spoken, and then closed it again. Roess went behind the desk and sat down.

'However,' he said, 'it may be possible for you to avoid all of that. If you tell us everything that we wish to know, it could come down to a single shot in the back of the head, and you would know nothing more. No pain, no fear. I would think carefully about this.'

Philipe drew a deep breath. 'I will tell you anything you wish to know.'

'That is very sensible of you. Now, Philipe Chartrin, where do you come from?'

'I . . .' The question had taken him by surprise. 'I come from the south-west.'

'You will need to be more accurate than that. Would it be from the Massif Central?' Philipe stared at him, clearly trying to decide whether to lie or not. 'You know,' Roess said, 'for a man who has just promised to tell me anything I wish to know, you are not being very co-operative. Put him on the frame.'

The guards grasped Philipe's arms and he gasped. 'I am sorry. For a moment I could not think. Yes, I come from the Massif.'

Roess jerked his head and the guards pulled Philipe to the wooden X frame set against the wall and extended his arms outwards and upwards, securing his wrists to the shackles that hung there. 'I am telling the truth,' he shouted.

'I know that you are telling the truth,' Roess agreed. 'But you need to be a little more prompt.' Another nod, and Philipe's legs were pulled apart to allow his ankles also to be shackled, to the lower arms of the X frame. 'What do you do there?' Roess asked.

'I am a farmer.'

'Are you, now? How old are you?'

'I am twenty-three.'

'That is too young to own a farm.'

'Well, my—' he bit his lip.

'I see. Your father owns the farm. His name?'

'Charles Chartrin.'

'Make a note of that, Joanna.' Joanna wrote the name in her notebook. 'And of course you have a mother. What is her name?'

'Odile.' Joanna wrote it down.

'And the names of your brothers and sisters?'

'I have no brothers.'

'But you have a sister. What is her name?'

'Gabrielle.' Joanna wrote it down.

'Gabrielle,' Roess said. 'What a pretty name. Is she a pretty girl?'

'I think so.'

'How nice. Well, Philipe, I am going to hang her as well, together with your mother and father.'

'But you said—'

'I said nothing, except that it might be possible to mitigate your execution. But the same thing might be possible for your parents and your pretty sister. So you came all the way from the Massif to join the terrorists in the Vercours. You were recruited. Was this by Liane de Gruchy?' Philipe stared at him. 'Very well,' Roess said. 'Remove his trousers.'

'Yes,' Philipe gasped. 'I was recruited by Liane.'

One of the guards removed his belt, tore open his flies and then ripped the trousers to drag them down to his knees, then did the same to his pants. 'How many of you were there?'

Philipe panted, afraid to look at Joanna as he reacted to his situation. 'There were forty of us.'

'All to go to the Vercours. Where you linked up with . . . how many others?'

'I do not know. There are a lot of us.'

'More than a thousand?'

'I think so.'

'More than two thousand? Three?'

'Yes. I think so.'

'And these are all commanded by Liane de Gruchy?'

143

'No, no. She only commands her own action group.'

'Then who is in command?'

'Colonel Huet.'

Roess looked at Joanna, who considered for a moment, then shook her head. She had genuinely never heard the name before. 'It sounds like a military rank,' she suggested.

'Yes, it does. So, we have what could be a regular officer commanding a force of as much as three thousand men, only a few miles away. This could turn out to be a serious business. But the question is why? These men have voluntarily bottled themselves up in this remote area. The only way they can move in any numbers, or receive adequate supplies, is via the roads leading out to the north. That is on our doorstep. They may be able to block those roads to prevent us getting through in any strength, but we can surely block them to prevent them from getting *out* in any strength. So what are they doing there? You are going to have to tell us that, my friend, or I am going to burn your prick right off.' He lit a cigarette.

'I will tell you,' Philipe gabbled. 'It is to attack you, in great strength, the moment the invasion starts.'

Roess and Joanna exchanged glances. 'The guerillas are going to attack us, in great strength,' Roess said. 'Three thousand men?'

'No, no,' Philipe said. 'Once the airstrip is completed—'

'What did you say? They have an airstrip?'

'They are building one. That is why they are there in such numbers. To build the strip and then defend it, while men and munitions are flown in from Corsica.'

'My God!' Roess said. Joanna felt like putting down her notebook to clap her hands. 'You are lying,' Roess said. 'Our planes have overflown that area regularly and have seen no sign of an airstrip.'

'They work all night and then camouflage what they have done.'

Roess stared at him for several seconds. Then he said, 'And when will this airstrip be completed?'

'Any day now. They are just about finished. They are only waiting for the Allies to invade.'

'And you know where it is situated?'

'Oh, yes. I have worked on it.'

Roess took a map of the area from his briefcase. 'Show me.'

The guards released Philipe, who hastily dragged up his pants as he was thrust at the desk. He leant over the map. 'It is here.'

Roess gave him a pencil. 'Mark it.' Philipe did so. 'Thank you,' Roess said. 'Well, I think you have given us all the information we need. He has been very co-operative. Take him outside and shoot him.' He picked up the telephone on the desk. 'Give me General Bittner.'

'Wait!' Philipe screamed as he was dragged to the door. 'Listen. There is a secret way in. It is the way we used to get out and attack Grenoble. It is a path not marked on the map.'

Again Roess stared at him. 'It can be used by tanks?'

'I do not think so. But a body of men could traverse it.'

'Is it not guarded?'

'Yes. But only by one, or at most two, men at a time. I will lead you and get you past them.'

Another long stare. Then Roess said, 'Put him in a cell until we need him.' He turned back to the phone. 'Herr General? Roess. It appears that this situation may be more serious than we first supposed. I would like you to make arrangements for an immediate assault on the Vercours with all available men.'

'My dear Roess, that is quite impossible. These things take time to organize. I have to call in replacements for the garrison and make up a tactical plan, and—'

'How long will you need?'

'I would say a week.'

'A *week*? My God! Very well, Herr General. The very moment you can move.' He thumbed the phone. 'Put me through to Berlin. A person-to-person call to Reichsfuehrer Himmler.'

The guerilla captains crowded round the radio. 'Can it be true?' Amalie asked. 'Can it really be true?'

'The code is correct,' Huet said. 'It has to be true.'

'Then where are the reinforcements from Algiers?' Gaston asked. Everyone looked at James.

'They know the strip is complete,' Liane said.

145

'I'll get on the radio again,' James said. 'Perhaps they are also waiting to be sure the news from Normandy is correct.'

'Oh, to be there!' Amalie said. 'Killing the Boche!'

'You'll have your chance,' Huet assured her. The colonel had grown quite fond of the over-emotional young woman during the past months.

James got on the radio to Algiers. 'Yes, the news is correct,' he was told. 'The Allies have landed in force in the Bay of the Seine and have established a large bridgehead. There is heavy fighting going on and the situation is still unclear, but it is not expected that there will be any withdrawal.'

'Then surely now is the time for us to strike, here in the heart of France?'

'That would be desirable,' the impersonal voice said. 'Unfortunately, there has been a problem with the planning, and the matter has had to be put back. Only briefly, it is hoped. We are sending you a large drop of munitions and some technicians to prepare the airstrip for the arrival of heavy forces. It should not be long now. Over and out.'

James regarded the set with frustration.

'What does that gobbledegook mean?' Liane asked.

'It means that some other general has got a bee in his bonnet and has persuaded Giraud and de Gaulle that his plan is more viable than this one.'

'Then we are wasting our time.'

'Not if I can help it. I'm going to get on to the brigadier and see what strings he can pull. But it does mean that we are on our own for the next couple of weeks.'

'Well,' she said, '"we have been on our own for the past six months. And if they really are sending us a big drop—'

They both sprang up as there was the blast of a bugle. 'What the shit—'

'That is the alarm call,' James snapped.

A man burst into the hut. 'Quick, quick!' he shouted. 'The Boche! They are in the Vercours!'

Liane and James looked at each other. 'That cannot be possible,' she said.

They picked up their tommy-guns and went outside to find men assembling from every part of the encampment. 'They seem to have got up the secret path,' Huet said.

'But how? No one knows of that path, save—' Liane bit her lip.

'Yes,' he agreed grimly. 'We have been betrayed. But we are not done yet. It would seem that only a company or so came up that path, overpowering the sentries. Now they have turned back to attack the villages and open the roads for their main body. But the garrison there are still holding out, and we must relieve them and retake the path. Liane, you and James take your people and do that. I will relieve the village. Captain Didrich, just in case they break through, you must hold the airstrip. James, did you get though to Algiers?'

'I did. There has been a delay. But they are sending us a drop and some technicians.'

'I am sure they will be most helpful,' Huet remarked sarcastically. 'What sort of a delay?'

'A matter of weeks, it seems.'

'Are we fighting on the same side? Jules, use the radio and inform Algiers what is happening. Now we must make haste.'

Liane's group, now reinforced to sixty men, was already assembled. They had only tommy-guns and rifles, which had been taken with an ample supply of ammunition from the munitions dump in Grenoble before it was destroyed. They could thus travel fairly quickly, but it was several kilometres to the head of the path, and the morning was well advanced before they reached a position overlooking their objective.

They had spoken little on the march, every one being preoccupied with their own thoughts, principally about their betrayal. Now Liane asked, 'What is our plan?'

'We must close that track.'

Liane levelled the binoculars. 'There is steady movement.'

'And there is a post,' Amalie added.

James studied the position. The path dipped steeply into a ravine between sheltering walls of rock, so that only the head was visible. It was also very narrow and allowed only two men abreast to come up at a time, which meant that it could be controlled by a handful of men, if adequately armed and sufficiently resolute. Apart from the fact that no one outside of the Vercours was supposed to know of the path's existence,

147

the fact that the guard seemed to have been overcome so easily again indicated treachery.

But however difficult and limited of access, the Germans had used it well. From the west there came the rattle of small-arms fire, with some deeper booms to suggest mortars, while below them, as Liane and Amalie had pointed out, not only was there a steady stream of men emerging, being formed in a company before being marched off, but also a machine-gun post established amidst the rocks.

James surveyed the assembling company. There were some eighty men, now being marshalled by a couple of officers and NCOs.

'We must seal it,' Liane said.

'After that lot have left.'

'But there are more coming up all the time.'

'Two at a time. The odds will still be better in ten minutes. Right now we're up against two to one and they are better armed. We mustn't sacrifice our people unnecessarily.' Liane made a face but would not question his estimation of the situation. 'However,' he said, 'take twenty men and work round to the east. Try not to make any noise. And remember, no shots are to be fired until I shoot. Then open up on the path head. And move in. But carefully.' She nodded and crawled off to collect her command. 'You'd better go with her,' he told Amalie.

'I would rather stay with you.'

He considered; but it was his intention to lead the main assault, with the risk of the highest casualties. 'You will go with Lucien.'

'Where? Why? You're trying to protect me.'

'I am making what I consider the best disposition of my forces, and you will obey orders. Now, Lucien, take twenty men and Amalie and work round to the west. Your orders are the same as Liane's. Your target is to support my group, but once the machine-guns are silenced you move on to seal the path. Again, remember, there is to be no firing until I give the signal.'

Lucian nodded and went to his men, followed by Amalie. The remaining twenty clustered behind James, who continued to study the machine-gun post and the ground before it. Like almost everywhere else in the Vercours it was broken, with trees and shrubs offering concealment, but it was a good hundred yards to the post and they would not make it unnoticed in broad daylight; yet it had to be done. And the time was now. The company was marching off and already another dozen soldiers had emerged on to the upper ground. 'Start moving,' he told his men. 'We advance without shooting until we are noticed. When that happens, we rush it. Use your grenades first.'

He glanced around at their faces; they all looked determined enough, even if they must know that casualties were going to be high. 'Let's go.'

He crawled forward, moving from cover to cover. More men slowly emerged from the path, but there were still no more than twenty. The squad had covered half the distance when one of the machine-gunners suddenly shouted and pointed. But he was not looking at him, James realized.

'Go!' he yelled, rising to his feet and drawing the pin from his first grenade. At fifty yards there was no point in waiting the required four seconds. He hurled the bomb and followed it immediately with another, then charged forward, his men behind him, still seeking what shelter they could from the trees without allowing them to impede their progress.

Now the machine-guns opened up, as did the rifles of those men outside the path, and there were several shrieks from either side. But now too both Liane's and Lucien's squads went into action, charging forward behind flying grenades and chattering tommy-guns. To James' alarm the standing soldiers turned away and rushed at Lucien's people, who were between them and regaining the hopeful safety of the path. But he could do nothing to help them; the machine-guns continue to fire, but now the Germans realized that they were virtually surrounded and were moving their weapons to and fro.

James covered the remaining fifty yards in under ten seconds and was up to the hastily erected earthworks surrounding the post when he tripped and landed on his hands and knees. He supposed that saved his life, for he looked up at the barrel of a machine-gun immediately above his head as it swung back towards where he had been. The gunner looked down at him, realized that he could not sufficiently depress his weapon, and released it to draw his pistol. James pulled the pin from his last grenade and threw it. There was no time to count, but it struck the German in the face and he fell backwards, clutching at the bomb; before he could regain his balance it exploded, blowing off both his arms and most of his head.

James swallowed, scrambled to his feet and leapt over the earthwork wall, tommy-gun levelled. But the defenders were all dead or too badly wounded to continue. His own people were assembling beside him, but there were only twelve out of the original twenty. He looked at the path head and saw fluttering blonde hair to his great relief. Liane's people were still firing down the ravine, so the Germans had not given up their intention of gaining the plateau. But Lucien's squad had disintegrated, scattered by the fury of the German charge, and it seemed certain that several of the enemy had reached safety. Hastily he checked the machine-guns. One had been hit by an exploding grenade and was inoperable but the other, the one he had assaulted, was still in working order. 'Carry that to the head of the path,' he said. Lucien arrived. 'Casualties?'

'Three men hit. None dead.'

'I have had several. Find them all and tend their wounds.'

Lucian hurried off and James followed the machine-gun to the head of the path, where Liane and her men were still firing into the ravine. 'They are keeping their heads down now,' Liane said. 'Have we gained a victory?'

'Here we have, certainly,' he agreed. 'Place the gun here,' he told his men. 'How many people will you need to hold this?'

'With that machine-gun?' Liane asked. 'Is there ammunition?'

'Enough for a couple of hours, if they rush you.' Three of the men were bringing the various spare belts, taken from the second gun as well.

'Leave me my twenty. And you?'

'The rest of us had better get over to the main battle.' There were still sounds of gunfire from the west.

She nodded. 'Just be careful. And leave Amalie with me.'

'Amalie!' He looked over his shoulder.

150

'Here I am,' Amalie said, emerging from the trees. 'We beat the hell out of them, didn't we?'

'This time,' Liane said. 'But they'll be back.'

Lucien arrived. 'Four are dead, five are wounded, two seriously.'

'And the Germans?'

'Twenty dead.'

'And wounded?'

He gave a crooked smile. 'There are no wounded. But there is another dead body, over there. Philipe Chartrin.'

Both Liane and James swung to face him and spoke together. 'Philipe?'

Lucien led them to where the body lay, in the wood to the left of the path head. Philipe was on his back, and he had his face blown away. But there was no weapon to be seen. 'He was fighting for the Germans?' James asked.

'No, no, Major. He was with the Germans, but he was not fighting for them.' Lucien dug his toe in the dead ribs and rolled him over. 'A single shot in the back of the head. I think he showed them this path, and he must have distracted the guard, to allow the Boche to overcome them. Then, as he was no more use to them, they shot him.'

'You mean he betrayed us?' Liane asked, speaking very quietly. 'He is responsible for this?'

'I think that is so, mademoiselle.'

Liane also used her toe to roll Philipe on to his back again. Then she drew her pistol and shot him twice in the groin.

Eight

The Battle

Joanna stood at the window of Gestapo Headquarters beside Roess to watch the soldiers stumble back into the city. It was the first time she had actually seen beaten men returning from battle, and she was surprised at how shattered they looked, in such strong comparison to the smart, efficient and, above all, totally confident men who had marched out a few hours previously. These men shambled and their heads drooped. Even their officers looked shaken. 'What in the name of God can have happened?' Roess demanded.

'Looks like they got a bloody nose,' Joanna said and added mischievously. 'I think you should have gone with them, Herr Colonel. Shown them how to fight.'

He glared at her, then snapped his fingers. 'Fetch my car,' he told the waiting orderly. 'We must get over to headquarters immediately.' The orderly hurried from the room. 'And you,' Roess barked at a woman secretary. 'Get me Berlin. Put the call through to General Bittner's office.'

'What can Berlin do about it?' Joanna inquired. 'Don't you think they have their hands full with this Normandy business?'

'Bah. Himmler promised me whatever I needed to finish this job. Well, I know what I need. A division of the Waffen SS and a squadron of heavy bombers. These Wehrmacht people have no stomach for a fight.'

'You don't know what actually happened up there,' Joanna pointed out.

'I have eyes, haven't I? We sent five thousand professional soldiers into the Vercours. And they couldn't do the job. Bittner will have to explain why.'

'I told you we did not have sufficient men,' General Bittner complained.

'You outnumbered the terrorists by virtually two to one. You had mortars and heavy machine-guns—'

'But they controlled the roads. One determined man with a rifle, concealed and protected, can always stop ten in the open, however well armed they are. A hundred well-led men can stop a thousand.'

'I did not come here for a mathematics lesson, Herr General. You had the means to get behind the defenders. Or did that swine Chartrin betray you?'

'No, no. He took my people up the path and then distracted the sentries so that they could be overrun. But one at least got away. We had got about two hundred men up the path, then there was a counter-attack and the ravine was sealed.'

'Just like that?'

'These people are organized. They were led by a British army officer, and by that blonde-haired devil Liane de Gruchy.'

'A British army officer?' Roess looked at Joanna.

James, she thought. It has to be James! Fighting alongside Liane! Oh to be with them. 'He must be someone parachuted in to take command,' she suggested.

'What a fuck-up. Where is Chartrin now?'

''Dead,' Bittner said.

'They shot him?'

'Not the guerillas, although I suppose they would have had they captured him. No, once the field commander realized he was being attacked in force and would have to withdraw, he shot him.'

'*What* a fuck-up. Well . . .'

'I have Reichsfuehrer Himmler on the line, sir,' the secretary said. 'For Colonel Roess.'

'Now,' Roess said, 'we shall get something done.'

'Well, say, Colonel,' said Major Lewis, 'you guys sure have made a swell job of this.'

There were actually eight Americans disembarking from the Dakota on to the new airstrip. The aircraft was being feverishly unloaded by the guerillas, as it had to be off again before it could be spotted by a roving German machine, but not all the new arrivals were looking as pleased as their commanding officer.

'It is kind of you to say so,' Huet acknowledged. 'May I present my second-in-command, Major Barron of the British SIS.'

Lewis shook hands. 'I heard you guys were involved. Say, that's easy on the eye.'

'That is Mademoiselle Liane de Gruchy,' Huet explained and waited expectantly. But the American had obviously never heard of the legend or even of Gruchy wine.

'She working with you?' Liane was out of earshot, superintending the unloading.

'You could put it that way, yes.'

'And there's another one!'

'Mademoiselle de Gruchy's sister, Amalie.'

'Well, I have to say, Colonel, you guys sure know how to fight a war. Any chance of an intro?'

Huet looked at James, eyebrows arched. 'If you play your cards right, Major,' James said. 'But it had better keep. Liane doesn't like being interrupted.'

It was Lewis' turn to raise his eyebrows. 'If you gentlemen will come with me,' Huet said, 'I'll show you to your quarters.' The encampment of huts was situated some distance from the airstrip, in a sheltered gully to protect it from air strikes.

'Come on, guys,' Lewis said, and his men picked up their knapsacks. 'And maybe you'll put us in the picture. There don't seem too much Kraut activity.'

'There has not been much activity for three weeks,' Huet told him. 'Reconnaissance flyovers, some bombing . . . nothing big. I expect this is because there is so much going on elsewhere.'

'But they did try to get at you back in June, right?'

Huet nodded. 'And damn near got in. But we held them. We expected them to come again, but they haven't.'

'So you can bring us up to date on what's happening,' James suggested.

'Well, you guys have finally taken Caen, so it looks as if we're at last gonna get out of Normandy. It's been one hell of a slog. Those guys can fight.'

154

'Tell us about it. So what exactly are you chaps here to do?'

'Well, your situation is that the plans are being drawn up to get you going.'

'Weren't those plans made months ago?'

'Sure, so they say. But you know what it's like when the brass starts to tinker. It's change this, cut that, increase that . . . they'll get around to it.'

'When, do you suppose?'

'Well, heck, it'll have to be soon, or the shooting will be done before you guys get any action. Right?'

Huet winked at James and opened the door of the hut. 'This will be your quarters. The latrines are just down the road and there is a shower available.'

'Sounds great. Tell me, those two little chicks got one of these?'

'They have accommodation, yes.'

'And are they . . . well . . . do they date? When they're not working?'

Again Huet looked at James, allowing him to handle it. 'There is a question I need to ask you, Major,' James said. 'How many men have you killed in this war? I mean personally.'

'Well, shit, killing people isn't my business, buster.'

'Then why are you here?'

'To advise you guys on guerilla procedures, defence—' Now Huet laughed. 'I say something funny?' Lewis inquired.

'I'm sure you didn't intend to be funny, Major,' James said. 'But just to put you in the picture, and so you don't make any mistakes, those two "chicks" you find so attractive have, between them, killed over a thousand German soldiers. That includes something like fifty in what might be termed eyeball-to-eyeball conflict.'

'You're putting me on.'

'Well, don't say you haven't been warned.'

'Those Americans spent the entire evening staring at me,' Liane said as they undressed after dinner.

'Well, you're worth staring at, wouldn't you agree?'

'I don't think it was lust.'

155

'By no means. I would describe it as sheer fright.'

She slid beneath the blanket beside him. 'What is he doing here, anyway?'

'You will not believe this, but he has come to teach us how to wage guerilla warfare.'

'Big joke. Does he know when the reinforcements will arrive?'

'That's the bad news. He thinks it may be a few weeks yet.'

'God,' she said. 'What is keeping them? We have been here for eight months doing fuck-all.'

'Well, I wouldn't altogether agree with that. Blowing up an ammunition dump, repelling a German attack—'

'But now they have decided to ignore us and we are doing nothing, while the biggest battle of all is raging. Suppose they just leave us here to rot?'

James kissed her. 'Somehow, my dearest girl, I don't think they are going to do that.'

'At last,' Johann Roess said. 'What do you think of this, Fräulein?'

Joanna got up from the breakfast table to join him at the window. They had spent so much time together over the preceding three weeks that they had almost become friends. Almost. He could be quite pleasant company, if she could avoid his eyes, which roamed over her face and body with such desperate longing; and the longing was not for any response from her, but for the possession of her, and not in any normally lustful sense, she knew. His idea of possession was that of the chain and the whip, his idea of pleasure that of a woman screaming in agony.

And then there was Oradour! She would never forget Oradour. And she intended to see that the world never forgot it, either, whenever this madhouse into which she had voluntarily plunged was finally destroyed. That was coming closer every day now. As long as the invading Allies had been pinned down in Normandy, the Germans could have had some hopes of hurling them back into the sea. But now that Caen had finally fallen, the road to the interior of France, to Paris, had been prised open. And Franz was there, somewhere, trying to keep that door closed. Of course, he was on the staff and would not be exposed to

156

actual fighting, but his mood had to be one of despair as he saw everything he considered of value ripped apart.

That made what she was looking at over Roess' shoulder the more incomprehensible. For she was watching dozens of trucks rolling through the streets of Grenoble, to come to a halt in the square beneath them, and out of every truck there was debouching a mass of men, the smartest troops she had ever seen, in perfectly fitting black uniforms and black boots, black helmets, even black bayonets hanging on their hips to fit on to their black rifles when required to do so. Other trucks were unloading heavy machine-guns and others had artillery pieces bouncing along behind them.

'The Heinrich Himmler Division of the Fighting SS,' Roess said, his tone reverential.

Clearly the people of Grenoble had never seen anything like it either. They lined the streets, at a safe distance from the trucks, to gape at the troops and mutter to each other. 'Shouldn't they be in Normandy?' Joanna asked.

'Oh, they will go to Normandy when they have completed this job. It will not take them more than a few days. And then, why, you may be reunited with your old friend, Fräulein, and my greatest ambition will be fulfilled. I am afraid it will only be a temporary reunion, of course, but I will allow you to watch her die.'

Joanna almost drew the Luger automatic pistol she carried in her handbag and shot him on the spot. But what would that accomplish, other than her own death? She had to believe that Liane would somehow survive. Because Liane always survived. And James would be fighting, and if necessary dying, beside her. Her mouth twisted, because she knew that that was how Liane would wish to go.

'The general,' Roess said urgently. 'Look smart.' They hurried downstairs to where the SS commander, having been greeted by Bittner, was just entering the building. 'Welcome to Grenoble, General Kirschner,' Roess said.

'Ah, Roess,' Kirschner remarked disparagingly. He was a stockily built man with heavy features. 'I understand this is your idea.'

'The Reichsfuehrer instructed me to reduce these people, Herr General.'

157

'And you estimated it would take a division of the Waffen SS to do this.'

'They are very strongly entrenched, Herr General. General Bittner's opinion coincides with mine.'

Kirschner gave Bittner an even more disparaging glance, then looked at Joanna. 'Frau Hoeppner,' Roess hastily explained. 'The Reichsfuehrer's personal assistant. She is here to interrogate the prisoners.'

'Prisoners,' Kirschner remarked, more disparagingly yet. 'I did not come here to take prisoners. We have met, Frau Hoeppner.'

'Yes, Herr General. At a reception at the Chancellory in 1939.'

'You have a good memory. You were Fräulein Jonsson then. And now you are married to Colonel Hoeppner. A good officer. I hope he is well?'

'I hope so too, Herr General.' Kirschner raised his eyebrows. 'He is on Field Marshal Rommel's staff,' she explained.

'Ah. Well, perhaps I shall have the pleasure of meeting him, when this business has been completed. You have an office, Roess?'

'Just up here, Herr General.' Roess led the way into the office, where Kirschner sat behind the desk, the other three, including Bittner, being left standing in front of him.

'Now then,' Kirschner said. 'My instructions are to liquidate the guerilla base said to be established in the Vercours as quickly and completely as possible and to render it impossible to be reoccupied at any future time. This will, of course, necessitate the destruction of all dwellings or places of refuge, and of all inhabitants of the area who may be considered capable of assisting guerillas in the future.'

'You mean total annihilation,' Joanna said in a low voice.

'It may well come to that, Frau Hoeppner. If you have no stomach for it, I suggest you remain in Grenoble.' Joanna gulped.

'Ah . . . with respect, Herr General,' Roess said. 'It would be useful to take *some* prisoners for the information they may be able to give us on other guerilla groups.'

Kirschner shrugged. 'If they are unwise enough to surrender, Colonel, you are welcome to them. Now, the operation commences at dawn tomorrow morning, when the bombers go in. I estimate this will take about three days.'

'I do not think that is going to be very effective,' Bittner objected. 'We have been bombing them, on and off, for months, with no result. The country is so split up with narrow valleys and precipitous cliffs that it is impossible to pinpoint any targets.'

'As you say, on and off. But I am not seeking individual targets. This will be blanket bombing designed to crush their morale.'

'And of course, if we can knock out the airstrip they have built,' Roess said eagerly, 'we can prevent them receiving any help from Algiers.'

'The airstrip will not be touched,' Kirschner said. 'I have instructed the Luftwaffe commander regarding this. We need the use of it. Now, as soon as the bombing is completed, my people will commence an artillery bombardment of the approach roads, following which my infantry will advance. I will require you people to follow, General Bittner, to consolidate our gains.'

'A frontal assault, even supported by artillery, will be very expensive,' Bittner remarked. 'The ravine we used to attack them has been entirely blocked.'

'My people are not concerned with casualties, General. In any event, I am told there are at most three thousand guerillas. With our combined forces we will deploy fifteen thousand men; fifteen thousand German soldiers, highly trained and heavily armed. Do you really think we are going to be stopped by a handful of ill-equipped peasants?' He looked from face to face, daring anyone to argue. 'Very good. Assembly will be a three a.m., when the bombers go in, so I suggest you get a good night's sleep. However, Frau Hoeppner, perhaps you will join me for dinner?'

Taken by surprise, Joanna for a moment did not know what to say.

'May I ask, Herr General, what is our role in this campaign?' Roess inquired.

'As you are a policeman, you will follow the troops and see if you can find any of these prisoners you seem to regard as so important. Frau Hoeppner?'

159

Joanna had got her breath back. 'It will be my pleasure, Herr General.'

Kirschner had appropriated the *hôtel de ville* as his headquarters, and the meal was served in a private dining room. 'I have never really been able to appreciate French cooking,' he admitted. 'I suppose that is because I am only a simple peasant at heart.' Once again Joanna was left without words or, at least, any she dared utter. 'But you,' he said. 'The so sophisticated American who has opted for Germany instead of her own country . . .' He paused inquiringly.

'I am half Swedish, Herr General.'

'Ah. Yes, there is a point. And now you are Reichsfuehrer Himmler's confidante.' Again there was an expectant pause.

'That is correct, Herr General.'

'As well as Franz Hoeppner's wife. The Reichsfuehrer must be a generous man.'

'When he wishes to be, Herr General. Do you know him?'

'We have met once or twice. He takes great pride in the Waffen SS.'

'With reason, I am sure.' Joanna finished her wine. They were approaching the crunch.

'I have also met Franz Hoeppner,' Kirschner went on. 'A good soldier. He should go far.'

'Is there any longer far to go, Herr General?'

He studied her for several seconds. Then he asked, 'Do you say things like that to the Reichsfuehrer?'

'From time to time.'

'And what is his response? Some people might call what you have just said treason.'

'I think he finds me refreshing. In private.'

'Ah. Yes. I am sure he does. You and I are in private now. Would you care to refresh me?'

Joanna smiled. 'Have I not just done so, Herr General?'

'Touché, as the French say. I was thinking of refreshment in a more positive manner.'

It was tempting; she might be able to find out his actual plans; she was sure he had not outlined them that afternoon. It was even more tempting to consider than she might be able to murder him. But again that would be to die for no purpose. The

160

assault might be delayed but only until another general arrived. It would not help Liane, or James, in the long run. So she said, 'I'm afraid, sir, that I am a happily married woman. And besides, did you not say that we should all get a good night's sleep?'

'I do not think that applies to you, Joanna. Or to me. The troops will not be going in for three days.'

'I must still decline, Herr General. I have to obtain the Reichsfuehrer's permission before I sleep with any man, apart from him. Or my husband, of course.'

Another appraising look, then he said, 'We will resume this conversation when this campaign is over. But you will accompany me when we go in. I am sure the Reichsfuehrer would wish you to do that.'

Joanna drank some more wine.

Liane dug James in the ribs. 'Bombers.'

He listened to the drone and the explosions. 'So what's new? They can't get at us in this gully.'

'This is different. It is only just dawn and there are more of them than usual.'

He sat up. The noise was certainly very loud. 'Maybe we'd better have a look.'

They dressed and went outside to find most of the encampment also peering up at the sky. 'They're going for the airstrip,' Huet said. 'That has to be it.'

James frowned. Although the noise was tremendous, it was all relatively distant; the strip was only a quarter of a mile away. 'They don't know it's there,' he said. 'How can they?'

'Then what the hell are they at?' Lewis demanded.

'I would say they're softening us up for another assault.'

'They wouldn't try the ravine again, surely?' Huet objected.

'Not as long as it's adequately defended. Then they'll be coming up the road.'

'We can slaughter them like flies.'

'Maybe. But in the meantime they are slaughtering the villages like flies. We had better get down there.'

'I will assemble all our people,' Huet said. 'Major Lewis, would you get on the radio to Algiers and tell them that we are about to be attacked in considerable force and that we need assistance now.'

'Will do.' Lewis hurried off to the radio hut.

'I'm coming too,' Amalie said.

'Just be careful,' Liane warned.

The bombing continued for the next three days, scouring the entire area, destroying most of the few villages, driving the inhabitants out to shelter in the woods and ravines and yet, because of the terrain, there was surprisingly little loss of life; nor, in the continuing warm weather, was there any great discomfort in being out of doors, although the women and children, and a good number of the guerillas, never having experienced anything like this before, were clearly shaken. Huet and James, Liane and Gaston went amongst them to lift their spirits and they had good news to impart as well. Lewis had been in touch with his headquarters and a massive drop of arms and ammunition had been promised, with troops to follow later.

'I think we could be going to gain a great victory,' Amalie said, 'But you are not so optimistic, eh, James?'

'James is never optimistic,' Liane said.

'I cannot understand why they have not touched the airstrip.'

'Because they do not know it is there,' Amalie insisted.

'Maybe. But they have bombed every other piece of flat land in the whole area, save just for that.'

'So they are not as good as they think they are.'

'Are you really worried?' Liane asked as they lay together that night.

'Let's say that I have a high regard for the efficiency of German planning.'

She hugged him. 'I wish they would come and get it over with. You have so much on your mind you are no good in bed.'

That night the call came from Algiers that the drop would be made at dawn with, hopefully, the airlift of reinforcements to follow twenty-four hours later. 'The strip must be cleared tomorrow night,' Huet told his people.

Before dawn the bombing stopped. 'That's very odd,' James remarked.

'Their reconnaissance aircraft have told them our boys are

162

coming,' Lewis pointed out. 'And they don't have any fighters to put up.'

The continued, somewhat irrational, confidence all around him James found irritating, but the skies were certainly clear as the American aircraft came over in great waves protected by fighters and the parachutes filled the sky as they drifted down.

'Bazookas!' Lewis shouted.

'Aren't they meant for use against tanks?' Liane asked.

'Sure. The Krauts will have tanks.'

Liane scratched her head; she had traversed that road up from the north, and she couldn't see it standing up to tanks, while once they left the road . . .

That afternoon it was misty; as the wind dropped the temperature fell. As there was no sign of any German planes, the people began to drift back to what was left of their homes. But just before dusk the advanced positions overlooking the approach road reported the sounds of a considerable number of motor vehicles in the valley beneath them.

Huet's dispositions were already made. It was simply a matter of taking up positions. He himself commanded the centre group of a thousand men, directly blocking the road. James was on the left with five hundred, Liane on the right with another five hundred; Amalie was with her. Gaston commanded a reserve of three hundred, to be used to plug any gaps that might occur. Lewis remained at the airstrip with the last hundred effectives; they had more than two hundred men too sick or wounded to fight. His orders were to clear the strip of its camouflage as soon as it were dark.

'Remember,' Huet told his commanders as they prepared to march off. 'All we have to do is hold them for tonight, and our reinforcements will be here.'

James' position lay just in front of one of the villages, which was again full of people despite the fact that only half the houses were still intact. They cheered and clapped as the guerillas filed by. 'You will give the Boche a hiding, monsieur,' said the priest, standing in front of his as yet undamaged church.

'We'll try,' James agreed, endeavouring to disengage

163

himself from the crowd of small boys and girls who were marching to either side and in front of him. To his relief, they were persuaded to retire when the position was reached, although he suspected that quite a few were still hiding in the trees behind, waiting to see the battle.

Lucien was his second-in-command and, having distributed their people, they crouched together to look down at the valley. The pickets had been called in. They had actually seen nothing, but they were adamant about the noise, and now it could clearly be heard.

'Are those tanks?' Lucien asked. They had been given two of the bazookas and he was anxious to use one. But he had never actually seen, or heard, a tank in action.

'Trucks,' James told him. 'And . . .' He frowned. 'That sounds like self-propelled artillery.'

'They'll never get anything like that up here,' Lucien said.

Certainly the road beneath them was quite steep, but James knew that they would have caterpillar tracks. On the other hand . . . 'I don't think they mean to try,' he said, as the mist was suddenly starred with red gleams and the shells screamed over their heads into the trees and the village. From behind them there came shouts of alarm and screams of pain and distress. The guerillas, over-conscious of the children, moved restlessly. 'Easy,' James told them. 'They'll be coming soon.' As he spoke, the guns ceased firing.

The night was quiet, but when in the first light James levelled his binoculars and peered into the mist he could see movement; as the men down there came into view he caught his breath. Black uniforms!

Lucien had seen them too. 'Those are SS!'

'Those are Waffen SS, the fighting branch. They are probably the best trained and most fanatical fighting troops in the world.'

Lucien gulped. 'What do we do?'

'We fight. They are flesh and blood, like us. When they are shot, they die. Tell our men to hold their fire.'

Lucien hurried off, while James continued to study the slowly advancing troops through his glasses. For all his brave words to Lucien, his heart was pounding quite painfully. He

164

knew this was the supreme crisis of his life. Of all of their lives. Everything would depend on how many of the SS were being deployed. He was looking at no more than a few dozen, but these were clearly skirmishers, their cautious advance intended to discover in what strength the approach was held. He glanced along his line of men, crouching in the bushes and behind rocks. They looked grim but determined. They would obey his orders, he was sure. Of course the German advance had to be stopped, but when it was it would mean revealing their position to the gunners behind, supposing even one of the advance guards survived to get back to the main body, 'Hold it,' he said. 'Hold it. You'll get your—'

A shot rang out, and then another, followed by a volley and the chatter of machine-guns. 'Damnation,' he muttered. It had not been his men who had opened fire, far too soon, in his opinion, but those further to the right. But there was no point in recriminating now. 'Fire!' he shouted.

His men responded with a will, and his own machine-guns started chattering. But the range was too great, and the black-clad soldiers simply disappeared behind their own rocks and bushes. He supposed one or two had been hit, but not more, while the guerillas continued to blaze away for several minutes before they could be brought to cease firing, both wasting ammunition and amply revealing their positions. 'What happens now?' Lucien asked, crawling back to him.

'All hell is going to break loose.'

The artillery bombardment recommenced a few minutes later; the advance party was obviously in radio contact with their support. Shells burst amongst the trees and penetrated the rocks, and men shrieked in pain as they were hit. 'We must withdraw,' Lucien said.

'That is just what they want us to do. We have to stick it out.' Lucien gulped and nestled deeper into his rocks.

The artillery bombardment was again maintained for five minutes, then it ceased and the Germans probed again. Once more they were halted by the sustained fire of the defenders, but by now there had been casualties amongst the guerillas, caused mainly by the shells exploding amidst them. James had to be concerned for Liane and Amalie, but the main part of the shooting was directed straight up the hill and, as his casualties were light, he had to presume they were similarly light on the far side of the valley.

As the evening closed in, so did the mist. 'This is the time they will come at us in force,' James told his men.

But surprisingly they didn't, and as darkness fell even the guns were silent, although shots were fired up the hill at regular intervals. 'What do you think they are doing?' Lucian asked.

'Waiting for tomorrow,' James suggested. 'They'll have something planned. What they don't know is that tomorrow our reinforcements arrive. So sleep easy.'

He saw that the men had their dinner, prepared by the villagers behind them, organized a watch system, told the sentries not to waste their ammunition in replying to the German sniping, then settled down for the night. It was a great temptation to leave Lucien in command and make his way round the defensive perimeter to find out if Liane was all right, but it had to be resisted. Were the Germans to launch a surprise attack in the darkness, and he not be here, it would be disastrous. Besides, as she had proved over and over again, Liane had a gift for survival.

He was equally concerned about the weather, for as the night progressed the mist developed into fog. This was common enough. The question was, how soon would it burn off in the morning, to allow the American planes to get down? He slept and was awakened by Lucien's fingers on his arm. He sat up, instinctively looking down the hill, but being unable to see more than fifty yards because of the fog.

'Listen,' Lucien said.

There was certainly a great deal of noise. 'Aircraft!' Were the bombers back?

'They are flying very low,' Lucien said. 'It has to be the Americans. Do you think they will be able to land in this?'

Hallelujah, James thought. 'Major Lewis will have lit flares,' he said. 'They'll get down.'

'Then we have won,' Lucien said.

'Well, at least we know we aren't going to lose.'

There was not a sound from the valley beneath, as the sky slowly lightened, revealing the yellow mist wall only a few yards away. Obviously the Germans had heard the drone of the planes as well and were waiting to see what would be the result. Was it possible to hope that they might withdraw altogether?

The noise of the aircraft dwindled and then swelled again. 'They are putting their people down and taking off,' James said.

'What do we do, Major?' someone asked.

'We wait, and hold, until they join us,' James said.

The morning drifted on in almost uncanny calm. Th sun rose higher, and the mist began to fade. It was ten o'clock when they suddenly heard a burst of firing from *behind* them. 'What the shit?' Lucien asked.

James was trying to think. The only possibility was that a small party of Germans had got through the perimeter somewhere but, if they had, they had done so without a shot being fired against them, at least until now. And he realized that this could not be a small party, for the firing was now general and widespread. A man stumbled through the trees. 'Orders from Colonel Huet, Major. You must withdraw.'

'Withdraw? We are to hold this opposition until relieved by the Americans.'

'That is no longer possible, Major. The Boche are behind us in great strength.'

'But those planes—' Lucien protested.

'They were German transports, monsieur. They have landed on the airstrip and put down several thousand men.'

'Aided by our flares,' James said bitterly and turned back to the valley. Because suddenly it was astir, as through the now-thinning mist he could make out the ranks of black-clad infantrymen advancing up the road. The temptation to disobey orders and engage was enormous; they could undoubtedly inflict tremendous casualties, but they would be committing suicide themselves, if there were substantial enemy forces behind them. On the other hand . . .

'Where are we to retreat to?' he asked.

'We must recapture the airstrip,' the messenger said. 'If we do not do that immediately, we are destroyed. Colonel Huet requires all our forces to concentrate on that objective.'

James nodded. 'Tell the colonel we are on our way.'

The messenger saluted and hurried off. 'Are we not destroyed anyway?' Lucien asked.

'Let's get on with it,' James said. 'Move out the machine-guns. We will need a rearguard. Fifty men. I will command it personally, but you hold it for the time being.'

'I will do so. What about our wounded?'

The greatest problem in any lost battle. 'Those who can walk will come with us. Those who are too seriously hurt to walk we must leave in the village. I will arrange this now.' He went to see the priest. 'We have been ordered to retreat, Monsieur l'Abbé. But we must leave our seriously wounded.'

The priest nodded. 'We will care for them.'

'You understand that these are SS troops who will be coming up here.'

'They are men, Major. And they will obey the laws of war.'

'Ah . . . well, we must believe that.' He shook hands. 'I will see you when we return. When we have secured the airstrip and our allies have joined us.' He had a quick word with the men he was leaving behind, encouraging them also to believe that theirs was a temporary separation from their comrades, and then joined Lucien and the fifty men of the rearguard. The Germans were still advancing very cautiously, taking cover whenever the guerillas returned fire. But from behind them the noise of battle was becoming ever louder.

'Let's go,' he told his men.

The heavy weapons had been taken away, and they were down to their tommy-guns. Thus they were able to move at the double, passing through the village, watched by the sombre eyes of the women and the still-excited claps of the children. Beyond were woods through which the trail led, over uneven country but ground they knew well. James kept looking for signs of the other guerilla units but saw none, although he quickly enough caught up with his own people. They paused for a rest and a consideration of the situation, while he checked his map. They seemed to be surrounded by firing on every side, although not in combat themselves.

'The airstrip is south-east of us,' he said. 'But the heaviest gunfire is due east.'

'Then that is where we are most needed,' Lucien said.

'We will obey our orders,' James said. 'The strip is only half a dozen kilometres away now. If it is only lightly held at this minute, we may be able to retake it on our own.'

168

'Look there,' someone said. They looked back to the north, at the plumes of smoke rising into the still morning air.

'The village,' Lucien said. 'They have fired the village.'

The guerillas looked at each other, remembering their comrades, the cheering children. 'We must go back,' someone said.

'We have our orders, and will obey them,' James told them. 'Move out.'

They followed him obediently enough, but he sensed that he was losing them. They were not professional soldiers, simply a mixture of fugitives and desperate men, with a considerable criminal element in their midst. Most of them were certainly patriotic, but equally a large number of them found the life they had lived for the past few years, essentially outside the law but with the blessing of their countrymen, however tacit, at once stimulating and exciting. But none of them had ever fought a pitched battle before, and they were all intelligent enough to know that this battle was lost; they had never been taught the discipline that would keep them standing shoulder-to-shoulder to the bitter end. They needed to fight, and they needed to win, rapidly.

And suddenly the moment was upon them. 'Enemy,' someone shouted.

'Take cover,' James replied. 'Hold your fire.' They were only two kilometres from the airstrip, and there was a chance these might be Lewis' people. But then he saw the black uniforms. 'Open fire!' he bawled.

The guerillas responded but their shooting was wild, their nerves, already in shreds, destroyed by this sudden confrontation. The Germans were not halted but ran forward behind a wall of fire that had men tumbling to and fro whether they were hurt or not. The majority dashed for the hoped security of the trees and ravines, pursued by the victorious enemy. For a moment James almost rose to his feet, to at least die with honour, then he remembered that he did not yet know if Liane were alive or dead, and as long as there were a chance that she might have survived . . . He saw and heard booted feet smashing the undergrowth in front of him, behind a burst of automatic fire. Desperately he rolled to his left, clutching his tommy-gun to his chest, and the ground disappeared

For some seconds he had no idea where he was, stunned and winded by the fall. Then he realized that he had gone down some twelve feet into one of the narrow ravines that cut across the surface of the plateau. And the sound of firing had moved away. His command was destroyed. Now his only business was survival, until he could link up with some as yet unde-feated guerillas . . . or Liane. He sat up and felt himself. He did not appear to have broken anything and, if he had lost his tommy-gun, he still had his revolver in its button-down holster. Painfully he got to his feet and made his way along the ravine to where it was practical to climb out.

Still the firing was all around him, but he did not feel that there was much point in trying either to rally any of his men or to continue towards the airstrip, so he set off to the east, where he could hope to encounter some of the other retreat-ing guerillas. He had to dodge several groups of marauding Germans, who seemed to be all over the plateau, but contin-ued on his way until he encountered a group of men hiding in a hollow, looking thoroughly scared and, distressingly, having discarded most of their weapons.

'Who is your commander?' he asked.

'We have no commander.'

He could not afford to be irritated. 'Then who *was* your commander.'

'Mademoiselle de Gruchy.'

James heartbeat quickened. 'Where is she?'

'I do not know, monsieur. We were retreating, and we encountered Germans and broke up.'

Exactly what had happened to him, James thought. 'But Mademoiselle de Gruchy, did she survive?'

'We did not know, monsieur. It was all so confusing.'

The thought of Liane captured, after so many years, was unbearable. 'Where did this encounter take place?' They pointed to the north-east. 'How far?'

'About two kilometres.'

James left them and made his way through the bushes, until he came upon several dead bodies. They were all guerillas, and there was no sign of any Germans. Indeed even the firing had died down, except for the occasional shot. The victory had been complete. But at least there was no dead woman to be seen. On the other hand, they would certainly have wanted to claim Liane alive if it were possible.

His brain was spinning under a combination of so many emotions he could easily have supposed himself mad. Certainly it was just about impossible to make a decision on what to do next. He was wearing uniform, and therefore technically he could surrender, although he doubted it would do him much good, as he had clearly been fighting with the guerillas. But he had no intention of surrendering, unless that was the only way of regaining contact with Liane. To watch her tortured and then hanged? He took a step to the north, as if he would go after her, then heard a sound and swung round, revolver thrust forward. And there she was.

A moment later she was in his arms. 'James!' she said. 'Oh, James!'

She was weeping. He kissed her lips and then her eyes. 'They massacred us,' she said. 'All my people. Amalie . . .'

'Amalie is dead?'

'I don't know. Oh, James, I don't know. We were separated when we tried to retreat, and then we were overrun. I think I heard her voice, shouting, and them . . . James, we must find her.'

'Where did this happen?'

She gestured to the north. 'Soon after we began to withdraw. I wanted to go back, but Gaston made me stay with my men. As he said, they were my men. I brought them here. I could not abandon them.'

'Where is Gaston?'

'Dead. I saw him go down. But Amalie . . .'

'Is almost certainly dead also.'

'I must *know*.'

'And die yourself?'

'What have I got to live for, James? All these brave men, who followed me so willingly . . . they were betrayed. I was betrayed. You were betrayed. Algiers said they would arm us and reinforce us. That we would be an army. So they sent us a few machine-guns. Now my sister is dead. As is my brother. I am done. The Resistance is done.'

He held her shoulders and gave her a gentle shake. 'You cannot be done. And as long as you are not done, the

171

Resistance cannot be done. You are Liane de Gruchy. The Germans will certainly claim you are dead and the world will mourn. But when you appear again, alive and well and killing Germans, think what a blow that will be to the Reich, what a triumph that will be for the Resistance.'

'I have no followers.'

'You have me.'

'Oh, James.' She hugged him.

'What is more, we cannot possibly be the only survivors. We will find them or they will find us.'

'And then what will we do?'

'We will leave this place and strike at the Germans.'

'Oh, James, you are a romantic. How can we leave this place?'

'We will, somehow. Because you are Liane de Gruchy.'

The command car had climbed the steep, rutted road in low gear and now the radiator was boiling. 'Well, stop the thing,' General Kirschner said. 'And find some water. There must be some in that village.'

The houses were still burning, as was the church. Dead bodies littered the street. Joanna, seated beside the general, swallowed; she felt sick. 'Those are children.'

'Some of them, yes,' Kirschner agreed. 'Children are always a nuisance when one is trying to fight a battle.'

Joanna opened her mouth and then closed it again, watching another command car bouncing towards them. It stopped and a colonel got out.

'Ah, Mintner,' Kirschner said. 'Report.'

'The victory has been complete, Herr General. The enemy has suffered very heavy casualties and the survivors have been scattered.'

'How many survivors?'

'There cannot be more than fifty.'

'But,' Joanna said, 'it was estimated there were more than three thousand guerillas.'

'I believe that was so, Fräulein. As I said, they have suffered very heavy casualties. They are not all dead, of course. We have some prisoners . . .' He paused to look at the general.

'Oh, give them to Bittner,' Kirschner said. 'It is time he did something to earn his pay. He can also take over the eliminating of the rest of these rats. Our business is to be out of here as soon as possible. We are required in Normandy. See to it, Mintner. I wish us to be on our way by dawn tomorrow.'

Mintner saluted. 'I will attend to it, Herr General. Heil Hitler.'

'Is there anything else you wish to see, Fräulein?'

Joanna looked at the dead children a last time. 'No, Herr General. I have seen enough.'

'Then we will return to Grenoble. I trust you will report the success of my operation to Reichsfuehrer Himmler?'

'I will do that, Herr General. Down to the last murdered child.'

He glared at her and she smiled at him. But she knew her words would be empty as far as Himmler was concerned.

'She has not been found,' Roess said, walking up and down the Gestapo office. He had just returned from a brief tour of the Vercours, taking care to keep well away from any potentially dangerous places. 'But she must be there somewhere.'

'She is almost certainly dead,' Captain List asserted. 'Lying in a ditch or a ravine, somewhere.'

'Then she must be found.'

'There are still pockets of resistance. As soon as they are all reduced—'

'For God's sake, List, it is three days since General Kirschner smashed these vermin and took away his men. He estimated that there were not more than fifty left alive. And we have been unable to complete the job?' He glared at General Bittner.

'My men are doing the best they can,' Bittner protested. 'It is very difficult country. Small groups of men hiding in those caves and ravines are very difficult to locate, much less winkle out. General Kirschner had the easy part, meeting them on open ground.'

'He also had the Waffen SS, which you do not.'

'Isn't it possible that General Kirschner underestimated the number of survivors?' Joanna asked, quietly. There had been no report of a British officer's body being found either. Could it possibly be that Liane and James might both have survived?

'What a fuck-up.'

'On the other hand,' Bittner said, 'the SS took several prisoners, who they turned over to my people. They might be able to shed some light on the situation, tell us where the survivors are most likely to be hiding.'

Roess snapped his fingers. 'Excellent. Kirschner promised to give them to me. Have them brought—'

'I have Reichsfuehrer Himmler on the line, Herr General.' The secretary hovered in the doorway. 'He wishes to speak with Colonel Roess.'

Roess took the phone. 'Herr Reichsfuehrer!'

'Roess? Roess?' Himmler shouted down the line. 'Where are you? I have been trying to get you all day.'

'I am in Grenoble, Herr Reichsfuehrer, where I have been for the past month. However, I am at last able to report a complete victory. Thanks to the efforts of General Kirschner and the Waffen SS, the guerillas have been entirely destroyed.'

Bittner and Joanna exchanged glances. They could still hear Himmler's voice, as he was still speaking very loudly. 'I can't be bothered with that now, Roess. Tell me when you see me. I want you back in Berlin now. This very minute. Bring Jonsson with you.'

'Sir? But—'

'The most terrible thing has happened, Roess. There has been an attempt on the life of the Fuehrer!'

Nine

The Flight

Roess stared at the receiver for some seconds, as did Joanna, who had overheard what was being said. Her mind was whirling. But Himmler had said 'attempt'. She couldn't believe that it had gone wrong again. And this time it had been discovered! Roess had also picked up on the word 'attempt'. 'Is he all right, Herr Reichsfuehrer? The Fuehrer?'

'He is better than can be expected in a man who has just been blown up.'

'Blown up?'

'Oh, yes. Some treacherous dog carried a bomb into the council chamber at Rastenberg. We think it is Stauffenberg. But he is clearly only the delivery boy.'

'But you say this bomb went off?'

'The briefcase containing it was placed on the floor within a few feet of the Fuehrer. However, someone moved it to the other side of a thick wooden upright, and this made the main force of the blast go the other way, while protecting the Fuehrer from any worse effects than concussion and some cuts and bruises.'

'What an amazing thing.'

'Oh, yes, the hand of God. He is convinced of it.'

'And the conspirators have been arrested?'

'Not all of them. It is apparently a vast plot, stretching throughout the Wehrmacht.'

'But then—'

'Oh, the immediate conspiracy is under control. Stauffenberg returned to Berlin, apparently believing that Hitler was dead, and issued a call to arms. Fortunately the garrison commander telephoned Rastenberg for confirmation

175

and actually spoke with the Fuehrer himself. He then contacted Dr Goebbels and myself. Stauffenberg was arrested and the city put under martial law. But, as I say, the conspiracy is clearly widespread. It must be rooted out, down to the last man or woman. This is your immediate task.'

'Yes, sir. I assume Stauffenberg will be able to name his associates?'

'Unfortunately, the cretin who arrested him had him shot before interrogation.'

'Ah . . . is that not suspicious?'

'It is very suspicious. It will be your job to discover who these people are.'

'I am on my way. sir. But the situation here—'

'I said tell me about it when you get here. And don't forget to bring Joanna with you.'

'Of course, sir.' He replaced the receiver and grinned at Joanna. 'So it is back to our travels. You will have to put this business on hold, Herr General, until I have spoken with the Reichsfuehrer and obtained his decision on how to handle it.'

Bittner was gasping for breath. 'Can it be true? An attempt on the life of the Fuehrer? Who would do such a thing?'

'That,' Roess said, 'is what I am going to find out.'

'You understand,' Roess said, as the train sped north, 'that we can leave no stone unturned. There is no one who can be considered above suspicion.'

'I understand that,' Joanna said. She wished he would shut up; she needed to think. Because this was now a matter of life and death. Himmler had said that Stauffenberg had been shot before he could be interrogated but that there had been other arrests. Finding out who those others were was *her* first priority, because she had no idea how many people knew of her part in it, how many people Helsingen might have felt it necessary to tell, to urge them into action.

Or had he told anyone? It was getting on for a year since she had promised the conspirators British support, and in all that time they had done nothing. Undoubtedly it was the invasion – that it was the invasion and not just a raid could no longer be argued – that had sparked this latest attempt. But that did not mean that at some stage someone under interrogation

176

was not going to bring up her name. She should get out now, while she could. And she could, even if Himmler would not let her go. With her contacts and the fact that she was well known in the Baltic seaports, she could be in Sweden before she was even missed in Berlin. Of course she would never be able to return, at least before the War ended . . . but surely she had done her bit now?

But that would mean abandoning Franz. If she were to be implicated, he certainly would be too. It would also mean abandoning Madeleine, who was most certainly implicated. It was easy to say that Madeleine had willingly involved herself in the looming tragedy that was the Third Reich when she had married Helsingen back in 1940. She had done her best to redress matters since, mainly because of *her* arm-twisting. To abandon her . . . that was what a true agent, cold-blooded, ruthless and amoral, would do. Joanna was prepared to accept that she was amoral, and that she had, too often, been utterly ruthless and cold-blooded . . . but she had never abandoned a friend, or even a fellow agent like Rachel Cartwright – when they had been no more than acquaintances – no matter what the risk involved. Madeleine would at least have to be warned, as would Franz. And then . . . she would make up her mind when those two essentials had been dealt with.

Berlin was totally quiet, certainly as quiet as a city could be, both under constant bombardment and aware that Germany was now fighting for its very existence; that there were soldiers on virtually every street corner would indicate only to those in the know that an incipient coup had just been put down.

They were driven straight to Gestapo Headquarters and shown to Himmler's office. The Reichsfuehrer was clearly agitated. 'You will get to work immediately,' he told them. 'The Fuehrer wants blood. A great deal of blood.'

'He will have it,' Roess said. 'May I ask what have we got so far?'

Himmler handed him a sheet of paper containing a list of names. 'The ones that are ticked have already been arrested and await interrogation. The others were supplied by various agents, but I awaited your return before acting on them.'

177

Roess scanned the list while Joanna held her breath. Then she asked, 'May I see it, sir?'

'Certainly,' Himmler said.

Roess gave her the list and she felt an almost sick sense of relief as she could find neither the name Helsingen nor Hoeppner. But her relief was premature. Roess said, 'There are some names that should be added.'

'Then add them. Who did you have in mind?'

'Colonel and Frau von Helsingen, for a start.'

Himmler frowned. 'I hope you're not serious. Frederick von Helsingen is the son of one of the Fuehrer's closest friends, as well as being a decorated war hero.'

'I am aware of that, sir. But my department has had its suspicions of Frau von Helsingen for some considerable time.'

'Because she is French? And a de Gruchy?'

'Because of her activities in the past. I may say, sir, that Colonel Weber also had his doubts about her from an early stage in the War, but was prevented from doing anything about it by General Heydrich for the same reasons you have just given. But he kept a file on her, which is now in my possession.' Himmler took off his glasses and polished them. 'You did say, Herr Reichsfuehrer,' Roess pressed, 'that our investigations should include everyone of whom there could be the slightest suspicion, regardless of rank or position.'

Himmler looked at Joanna. 'Frau von Helsingen is a friend of yours, is she not?'

'She is Liane de Gruchy's sister,' Roess said.

'I knew her before the War,' Joanna said. 'And I visit her from time to time. My husband was her husband's best man.'

'Your husband,' Himmler said, half to himself, and Joanna's heart constricted; could Franz already have been arrested? 'Yes,' he went on. 'Perhaps you are right, Roess. Frau von Helsingen should be investigated. But it must be done with the greatest tact. I put this in your care, Joanna.'

'Sir?' Roess was outraged.

'We want none of your bull in the china shop methods until we have proof of her guilt. Joanna will handle it, will you not, Joanna?'

'If you wish me to, sir.' Joanna could hardly dare believe the reprieve – for both of them.

'With respect, sir,' Roess said. 'In view of Frau Hoeppner's long and close friendship with Frau von Helsingen I feel that this investigation should be handled by someone else.'

'Are you suggesting that Frau Hoeppner would suppress or conceal evidence that might convict Frau von Helsingen of treason?' Himmler looked at Joanna as he spoke, but she was well practised in keeping her features immobile.

'Yes, sir,' Roess said. 'I do think that is possible.'

'Oh, go to work, Roess. Just tell me first, what went wrong in the Vercours?'

'The guerillas were in much greater strength than we were told, Herr Reichsfuehrer. There were perhaps as many as five thousand, with artillery.' Joanna stared at him with her mouth open, but he did not look at her. 'They were also commanded by British officers, and there were very probably British soldiers serving with them. They also possessed an airstrip, which enabled them to receive a constant stream of reinforcements and supplies. However, General Kirschner attacked with the utmost determination, and they were utterly defeated. I was in the middle of co-ordinating the mopping-up operation when you summoned me back here.'

'I am sure Bittner can complete the job. I congratulate you.'

'We have not yet found Liane de Gruchy's body.'

'But she *is* dead?'

'Oh, undoubtedly. However—'

'Even Liane de Gruchy must be put aside until this investigation has been completed. We will discuss the situation when that is done. Probably by then Bittner will have found her, or what is left of her. Heil Hitler!'

Roess stood to attention. 'Heil Hitler.'

Joanna also got up.

'I would like you to remain for a few minutes, Joanna,' Himmler said.

'Yes, Herr Reichsfuehrer.' She sat down again.

Roess gave her a suspicious glance and left the room. 'He hates you,' Himmler remarked. 'Because he wants you. Has he ever made advances?'

'Repeatedly.'

'And you have always refused him?'

'Always.'

'You are very strong minded. Now it will be necessary for you to be even stronger minded. When last did you hear from your husband?'

Oh, my God! Joanna thought. Here it comes. 'I have not heard from him since the invasion, Herr Reichsfuehrer. Before then, before you summoned me here to go down to Grenoble, I was able to be with him.'

'Yes, of course. War is a dreadful business, is it not? Joanna . . . Colonel Franz Hoeppner has been reported missing, believed killed.' Joanna stared at him. 'He died most gallantly, if recklessly,' Himmler said. 'As a staff officer he should not have been engaged in combat. But he was present, as an observer, when a counter-attack was launched on a British position outside Caen. As the attack was about to begin, the commanding officer was hit by shrapnel from an exploding shell and killed. His men were wavering. So Franz went forward and himself led them into action. Sadly the attack failed; the British position was too strong. Colonel Hoeppner was seen to fall while trying to rally his men. He did not return with them.' He paused. Joanna continued to stare at him. 'I am most terribly sorry,' he added.

Joanna drew a deep breath. 'When did this happen, Herr Reichsfuehrer?'

'Three days ago. I did not send the news to Grenoble because I had already instructed you to return here, and I preferred to tell you myself.'

'Thank you, sir.'

'Would you like to take a few days off? There is no rush about this Helsingen investigation. I am quite sure that Roess is barking up the wrong tree there.'

Joanna was collecting her thoughts. If Franz was indeed dead, one of the links binding her to Germany was broken. Only Madeleine remained. Once she was warned, her duty would be done. It might even be possible for them to escape Germany together. 'I would rather proceed with the investigation now, sir.'

'Do you know, I had no doubt you would say that? Duty above everything, eh? Very good, Joanna. You will make your report, supposing you find anything to report, direct to me.'

'Yes, sir.' She stood up. 'Heil Hitler.'

'Is there anything you need?'

'Ah . . .' She appeared to think. 'I think I may need a carte blanche, signed by you, authorizing me to do whatever is necessary, for the good of the Reich. The Helsingens have many powerful friends.'

He considered for a moment, then nodded. 'You are probably right.' He drew a block of his headed notepaper to him and began to write.

Joanna went first of all to the Albert, where she received her usual warm welcome from the staff. She went up to her suite, poured herself a cognac, and then a hot bath, in which she soaked while sipping her drink. She reminded herself that she should be grief-stricken. But she wasn't. She had never known Franz well enough.

They had begun by sharing a secret; his knowledge that she had lied about Liane's death, her knowledge that for all his apparently enthusiastic pursuit of Liane, he did not wish her to be caught and executed because he loved her too much, without ever having known her at all, and certainly not in the biblical sense.

Sharing such a secret, *they* had inevitably gravitated into a biblical relationship. She had found him such a relief after Oskar Weber, with whom she had had to sleep to maintain her position in the heart of the Gestapo. Franz, unable to obtain Liane, had found in her voluptuous beauty, in such strong contrast to Liane's delicacy, a satisfying substitute. But had they ever loved each other? He undoubtedly had regarded her as a prize; she supposed love could well follow; it had been showing signs of appearing during their honeymoon. She had always told herself that she was *going* to love him, as soon as she could stop betraying him . . . or, at least, the regime that he so reluctantly served. Now she would never have the opportunity. And there was a great deal to be done. She got out of the bath and towelled herself dry.

'Frau Hoeppner!' Hilda said. 'You see, Frau, I remembered.'

'That is very good of you, Hilda,' Joanna said, not for the first time wondering at the transformation that had overtaken this previously dour little woman. But perhaps she was just happy to have her employer back, however shattered; her change of demeanour had first been observable after Frederick's return. 'Is Frau von Helsingen in?'

'Oh, yes, Frau. She will be pleased to see you.'

She stepped back, and Joanna entered the lobby, then went into the lounge. Hilda hurried down the corridor to the bedrooms, and a moment later Madeleine appeared. She was as elegantly handsome as ever, her long brown hair tied back in a loose ribbon, but there were stress lines at her eyes and she found it difficult to smile. 'Joanna,' she said and was in her arms. 'Oh, Joanna. It was in the *Gazette*.'

Joanna kissed her. 'Himmler has just told me.' She led her to the settee and sat beside her.

'Are you . . . ?'

'I will mourn him. When I have the time.' She lowered her voice. 'You know what happened?'

'Of course I do. Stauffenberg telephoned Freddie.'

'He did *what*?'

Madeleine licked her lips and glanced at the open door. 'He was so confident. He even told us to contact you so that you could inform your people.'

Joanna stared at her in horrified consternation, then turned her head sharply, as there was a noise from the lobby. 'What was that?'

'I imagine Hilda going out. She often does about this time.'

'This does not bother you?'

'Well, it's a free country. Well . . .' She flushed.

'Madeleine,' Joanna said as earnestly as she could. 'You do realize that you are in extreme danger?'

'Stauffenberg would never betray Freddie. Anyway, he is dead.'

'Madeleine, he betrayed you the moment he telephoned you. And me.'

'But he telephoned several people. To tell them we had succeeded. He was so confident of it. He heard the bang before he left Rastenberg . . . we still don't know how Hitler survived.'

'Just about all of those people he telephoned have already been arrested or are about to be arrested. I have seen the list.' Madeleine's face paled. 'You are just fortunate that, because of your connections, Himmler has given me the job of invest-

182

igating you, rather than Roess.' She gave a quick smile. 'He feels I will handle you more sympathetically.'

Breath rushed through Madeleine's nostrils. 'Then we are safe. You will protect us.'

'I cannot protect you here in Berlin. I believe you that Stauffenberg would never have betrayed you. But one of the others now under arrest will certainly do so. How many people know of my involvement?'

'I don't think any, really. Freddie merely told them that he had been contacted by a British agent who had promised London's support in the event of a successful coup.'

'Well, that is something.'

'You mean you are just going to abandon us?'

'Not if you do as I say. But you cannot remain here. Now listen, I can get you out of Berlin, out of Germany, if you act promptly enough. Where is Helen?'

'I sent her to stay with her grandparents until this is over.'

'Shit!'

'I can get her back.'

'You have no time for that. You will have to leave her.'

'But—'

'Surely the senior Helsingens are not involved?'

'I don't think so.'

'Then Helen will be safe. It is you we have to worry about. You must pack a bag. A small bag.'

'What about Freddie?'

'Where is he?'

'In bed, asleep. He spends a lot of time under sedation.'

'Can he walk?'

'Well . . . he is learning to use his sticks, but it is very diffi-cult.'

'Then I'm afraid . . . '

'You cannot ask me to abandon my husband.'

'I am sure if you asked him he would tell you to get out while you can.'

'Of course he would. He's a gentleman.'

'Well, then . . .'

'I am not going to desert him.'

Joanna sighed. 'You do realize what will happen to you if you are taken into custody by the Gestapo?'

'One hears rumours. But there is never any proof. Freddie has always said it is just propaganda.'

'Madeleine, I have seen these people at work. Have you ever met Johann Roess?'

'Who?'

'He is the current head of the SD. But you have met Oskar Weber.'

'Your lover,' Madeleine said contemptuously. 'A detestable man.'

'I couldn't agree with you more. But Roess is ten times more vicious. Would you like to find yourself in his hands?'

'I am sure I should hate it. But I m not going to find myself in his hands. I know exactly what I am going to do. I will appeal to the Fuehrer. He is my friend, and he is the godfather of my daughter.'

'I don't think ...' Joanna said.

There was a crash from the lobby. Both women started to their feet as there was another crash from the lounge door-way, and it too was ripped from its hinges by the four men who burst into the room.

'What are you *doing*?' Madeleine shouted.

'Frau von Helsingen, you are under arrest,' said the leader. 'Klaus.'

The man called Klaus produced a pair of handcuffs.

'You have no authority for this,' Joanna said.

The leader turned towards her. 'You are also under arrest, Frau Hoeppner.'

'Are you out of your mind? I am Reichsfuehrer Himmler's personal assistant.'

'Then no doubt the Reichsfuehrer will attend to the matter. I have my orders.'

'Given to you by whom?'

'By Colonel Roess.'

Joanna knew she had to think very quickly and very accurately. She had no doubt that something had happened in the few hours since she had left Himmler's office, but she had no idea what. On the other hand, she knew Gestapo methods very well. If they might be afraid to harm her personally, they would certainly keep her incommunicado until they had had a chance to interrogate Madeleine, and Madeleine would certainly not be able to withstand what they would do to her. As for justification, they undoubtedly had that incriminating phone call. Roess must have had this telephone tapped for months; he had always been suspicious of Madeleine. Therefore her decision was made for her, even if it were not as she had planned it.

The Gestapo agent was extending a pair of handcuffs; Klaus had already turned Madeleine round to clip her wrists behind her back. For the moment at least Madeleine was speechless. Joanna opened her handbag and put her hand inside. The agent, who clearly had no idea of what she was capable, did not react, and in that moment he died, Joanna firing through the material to hit him in the chest. Then she did draw the Luger, firing left and right with deadly precision. Only one of the Gestapo agents managed to draw his gun out and he died before he could use it.

The bodies fell to and fro while Madeleine stared in horror, her mouth slowly opening. 'Don't scream,' Joanna warned.

'But . . . you . . . my God! Are they all dead?'

Joanna realized that Madeleine would never have seen a dead body in her life before. She stooped over the corpses. One man was still gasping for breath, but from the amount of blood he was losing she knew he would not survive more than a few minutes. 'They all will be, soon enough,' she said.

'But . . . just like that. . .'

'I was trained to it,' Joanna explained. 'By the British.' She went to the door. There was no sound from downstairs; the Luger actually made very little noise. But then from behind her there was a shout and a bump. She swung round.

'Freddie!' Madeleine gasped, tugging vainly at her handcuffs. 'He's woken up.'

'I'll see to him.' Joanna replaced the pistol in her bag and hurried down the corridor to the bedroom. Helsingen had fallen out of bed and was trying to pull himself to his feet, difficult with only one arm.

'Joanna,' he asked. 'What . . .?'

Joanna dragged him up and laid him on the bed. 'Madeleine will explain in a minute,' she promised. 'Please just lie there.'

She went back into the lounge, where Madeleine was

185

walking to and fro, carefully stepping around the dead bodies, still tugging at her wrists. 'Is he all right?'

'He's agitated.' Joanna knelt beside the man Klaus, avoiding the blood that had gathered beside him, felt in his pockets and found the key to release the handcuffs.

'God!' Madeleine said. 'These bodies . . . I am going to be sick.'

'Take deep breaths. Now listen—'

'They will cut off your head.'

'Will you listen, God damn it! How many other people live in this building?'

'There are five families. But at this time of day they will all be out.'

'That is why there has been no reaction. Excellent.'

'I must go to Freddie. What am I going to tell him?'

'Will you listen? There is no time to pack anything. If we leave now, we can be far away before these bodies are even discovered.'

'Leave? How can I leave Freddie?'

Joanna hesitated. But there was no longer any time to argue. 'All right,' she said. 'Come into the bedroom, and I will do the best I can for you.'

'What?'

'Just do as I tell you.' Joanna exchanged her empty Luger for one of the agents' full weapons.

Madeleine was holding Frederick in her arms and weeping. 'Now,' Joanna said. 'There is a faint chance that nothing has been proved against you yet, that Roess was acting entirely on his own initiative and against Himmler's orders. Either way, you must tell them that I came here to persuade you to leave, that you refused, that the Gestapo men broke in, and that I shot and killed them all. You see, I am not asking you to lie. Then I tied you both up so that you could not raise the alarm, and left.'

'Tied us up? But—'

'That is what I am going to do now,' Joanna explained. 'Help me tear the sheets into strips.'

Himmler himself went to the Helsingen apartment to look at the shambles. By then it was five o'clock – Hilda had not dared return for several hours – and the building was buzzing. But the Helsingen apartment was sealed off by the Gestapo.

'My God!' he remarked. 'Joanna did this?'

'That is what the Helsingens claim, Herr Reichsfuehrer,' Roess said. 'And in this instance I believe them.'

'But . . . four men . . . She must have been hit herself.'

'Not one of my people's pistols has been fired. One has been taken, in exchange for hers.'

'Four armed men, killed, before any one of them could reply? The woman is a monster. And to think she has shared my bed.' He glanced at Roess and flushed.

'I would say you were lucky, Herr Reichsfuehrer.'

'But what made her do such a thing? She must have come here to pursue her investigation . . . Do you think she suddenly had a mental breakdown, went berserk?'

'I'm afraid that is not the case, sir. I have evidence that Frau Hoeppner, or Fräulein Jonsson as she was, has been a British agent from the summer of 1940, that throughout that time she has been working hand-in-glove not only with the SIS, but also with the de Gruchy family, and especially Liane de Gruchy, her old schoolmate and lover. I have tried to make this point on several occasions but have always been prevented.'

'But . . . she worked for Weber. She was one of his most trusted agents.'

'I'm afraid Colonel Weber was rather easily hoodwinked by a pair of large tits.' Roess gulped as he realized what he had just implied, but Himmler was too agitated to notice.

'What is this evidence?'

'Well, sir, I have routinely tapped the telephones of everyone I suspected of working against the regime. The Helsingens, or Frau von Helsingen, certainly, has been under suspicion for some time, as I have explained. Colonel von Helsingen was one of the first people Stauffenberg telephoned when he returned from Rastenberg, when he announced the success of his mission, as he then assumed. He distinctly said, "You must inform Joanna immediately so that she can contact her people and remind them of their promise to us."'

'She cannot be the only woman in Germany named Joanna.'

'Who is so friendly with the Helsingens that she is included

187

in their conspiracy, and who could be connected to outside forces waiting to take over the Reich? Would that not be stretching coincidence too far?'

'I suppose it would.' Himmler was looking quite upset.

'I have also for a long time had the Helsingen maid, Hilda, on my payroll. She has supplied me with the names of all the officers who have called regularly to see Helsingen. All worried about his health, apparently. So when, this afternoon, as a matter of routine she left the apartment and telephoned to say that Frau Hoeppner was in the flat and deep in conversation with Frau von Helsingen, I instructed my men to move in and arrest the pair of them. I had no idea it would turn into a massacre.'

Himmler nodded. 'You had no idea what a monster we have been sheltering in our bosom. Neither did I. She must be arrested immediately. Where is she?'

'I have put out an All Points Bulletin on her, but nothing has come in as yet. On the other hand, she is not a woman who can hide in a crowd. We will get her.'

'See that you do.'

'And then, sir?'

'I wish her brought to me. I will interrogate her personally.'

Roess was not disappointed; he had expected that. 'But you will let me have her afterwards, I hope?'

'Oh, you may have her.'

'And the Helsingens?'

'Where are they?'

'I have them under arrest.'

'But they have not yet been interrogated?'

'No, sir. I thought I should wait on you authority.'

Himmler nodded. 'I shall have to check with the Fuehrer. However, I do not have much doubt of what he will wish done.'

'Yes, sir.' Roess' eyes gleamed. He had long dreamed of having the right to interrogate Madeleine von Helsingen.

'And have these bodies removed and this place cleaned up. It makes me sick to my stomach.' He turned at the knock, colour draining from his cheeks as if he thought it might be Joanna, returned to commit some more mayhem.

But it was a Gestapo agent, looking somewhat apprehensive. 'We have news of Frau Hoeppner, Herr Reichsfuehrer.'

'Excellent. Where is she?'

'Well, sir, she apparently visited one of our garages this afternoon, demanded the use of a car and drove away.'

'They gave her a car, just like that? With a driver?' Roess demanded.

'No, sir. She drove herself.'

'They gave this woman a car, without any authority—'

The agent looked more embarrassed yet. 'She had written authority, Herr Colonel.'

'How in the name of God did she get that?'

'Ahem,' Himmler said. Roess turned to him, open-mouthed. 'She felt she needed a blanket authority to enable her to deal with the Helsingens without having to worry about interference from above,' Himmler explained. 'I had no idea that she was a member of the conspiracy. Or that she was an English spy.' His tone indicated that he considered his lack of information on both those subjects was someone else's fault.

'Yes, sir,' Roess agreed.

'Anyway,' Himmler said confidently, 'she can't get far. I assume we have both the make and the number of the car?' Again his tone indicated that if they did not, someone was in trouble.

'Yes, sir,' the agent said. 'But . . .' He looked at Roess for support.

'She has had a two-hour start, Herr Reichsfuehrer,' Roess said. 'Berlin is only about two hours' drive from the Baltic Coast.'

Himmler stared at him for several seconds. Then he said, 'Then close the Baltic Coast. Now.'

It was half-past five when Joanna drove into Lubeck. The journey had been trouble free – the Gestapo car and her carte blanche had seen to that – but she knew she had to expect the telephone lines to start buzzing any moment now. She drove straight to the ferry docks, parked the car and went into the Departures hall. There was a ship alongside and some activity.

'Why, Fräulein Jonsson,' said the ticket clerk. 'What a pleasant surprise.'

Joanna did not trouble to correct him. 'I am in a hurry, Pieter,' she said. 'When does the ferry leave?'

'At half-past six, Fräulein.'

Just under an hour. But there was no alternative. 'Very well. I will have a ticket.'

He made out a return ticket, as he always did, and she paid him. He peered over the counter. 'You have no luggage, Fräulein?'

'This trip came up rather suddenly. Not to worry. I have a wardrobe full of clothes in Stockholm. When can I go on board?'

'Passengers board at six o'clock, Fräulein.'

'Thank you, Pieter.' She went into the Departures lounge and straight to the bar for a cognac; she needed it. Then she bought a magazine and sat in a corner; she had no intention of reading anything, but the magazine provided a useful cover for her face if anyone she knew came in.

There was a large clock on the wall opposite, with a ticking second hand. She tried not to look at it too often, but it seemed to be moving very slowly. Other passengers came in, casting curious glances at the handsome blonde woman before seating themselves. Five to six. In a moment . . . The door opened again and a man entered. Joanna caught her breath. He was a very ordinary looking man, wearing a somewhat shabby suit, but she knew him. His name was Fischer, and he was the local Gestapo commander. They had crossed swords two years before when he had attempted to interfere with her regular comings and goings, and she had had to refer him to Oskar Weber, from whom he had received a stinging rebuke for hampering the activities of his private spy. Since then he had been unfailingly polite, although that he loathed her could not be doubted.

As he was obviously looking for her, there was no point in attempting to hide behind the magazine. He came towards her and sat beside her.

'Fräulein Jonsson. But it is Frau Hoeppner now, is it not?'

'My husband is dead.'

'After such a brief marriage? I am so sorry. And now you are returning to Sweden?'

'There is nothing left for me here.'

190

'I can appreciate that. Sadly, your departure will have to be delayed.'

Joanna allowed no flicker of alarm to cross her features. 'Why is that?'

'I have received orders to close the port.'

'You have done this? The ferry sails in half an hour.' People were already filing from the room, revealing no great interest in the couple seated in the corner, speaking in low tones.

'Actually,' Fischer said, 'I have not done it yet, because the reason I have been told to close the port is in order to make sure a certain Frau Hoeppner does not leave the country. But as I am sitting next to Frau Hoeppner at this moment, it seems to me to be unnecessary to disrupt the life of the port. Do you not agree?'

'So what happens now?' Joanna asked, feeling the tension of impending action slowly creeping over her.

The last of the waiting passengers had left the room, and in their place another man had entered and stood by the door. 'You will come with me to my office,' Fischer said. 'And you will wait there while I telephone Berlin and inform them that I have you, and receive their instructions as to what is to be done with you. So if you do not mind, Frau . . .'

He stood up, and Joanna did also. He was another unfortunate who had no idea who he was dealing with, assuming that she was no more than a courier who travelled for the Reich and had somehow blotted her copybook. She almost felt sorry for him as she stepped past him and went to the door, which the other man opened for her. 'You know where to go,' Fischer said. 'Please do not make any trouble.'

'Do I ever?' Joanna turned down the corridor and went to the Gestapo office, the two men at her shoulder. The poor doomed fools had not even tried to take her handbag. But then, on their previous meetings, she had never been armed.

She went inside and stood beside the desk. The two men came in and the door was closed. The agent stood against it and Fischer sat behind the desk and picked up the phone.

'Wouldn't it be nice,' he said, 'if I am given permission to search you? I have always wanted to do that.'

'Then I had better show you what I have,' Joanna suggested and opened her handbag. The two men could only gape at her

191

in consternation as the Luger exploded four times before either of them could draw his own weapon. Joanna ascertained that they were both dead, then listened for a moment. But there was no sound, because the office was sound-proofed to prevent the screams of anyone undergoing interrogation inside from being heard outside. She thought that was rather quaint.

She placed the Luger on the table, as she did not want to risk any trouble with Swedish customs, and went outside. Only the ticket clerk remained at his window in the main hall. 'No trouble, I hope, Fräulein?' he inquired.

'No, no. Just a message from Berlin. *Auf wiedersehen*, Pieter.'

'Oh, indeed, Fräulein.'

She went on to the dock, where the ferry crew were about to take up the gangplank. 'Wait for me,' she said, hurrying up the slope.

'Miss Jonsson,' said the officer on the deck. 'You left that late.'

'Yes, I did, didn't I?' She showed him her ticket, then moved along the deck to watch the mooring warps being cast off.

Beneath her feet the diesel engines were already rumbling, and the ship was slowly moving away from the dock. She kept watching the land, almost expecting to see men running towards her, calling for the ferry to put back. She remained where she was until the ship cleared the pier heads. Then she went inside to the bar and ordered a cognac. She took the drink to a corner table and sat there while she sipped it. In a couple of hours' time she would be in Sweden, and the great adventure would be over. She had hoped to see it out, actually to be in Berlin when the Allies marched into the city. Well, she supposed, nothing ever works out exactly as it should.

So now, what? A great deal of emptiness. After the lies she had told to the conspirators, she could not even claim a medal. She had sent a good many gallant men to their deaths in an attempt to bring off one final coup. And at least one woman, who had never really understood what it was all about. Oh, Madeleine.

But then, oh, Liane. Survive Liane, she thought. Oh, please survive.

Ten

The Last Betrayal

'Time to move,' James said.

Slowly Liane uncoiled herself. Although it was high summer, at this altitude the nights were cold and made more so by the persistent fog. She checked her haversack. 'There is half a sausage left.'

'So we may have to go hungry for a few hours. We are almost there.' He had followed his map for the past two days and was certain that they were just about at the western edge of the plateau. Progress had been slow because the entire Vercours was crawling with troops, but these at least were not members of the SS and were more intent on going through the motions of searching for any remaining guerillas than in actually finding them. But they still had to be avoided, which meant long hours crouching in the bushes or in gullies while the troops had tramped by, while every so often they would hear a burst of gunfire to suggest that the Germans had either found someone or were extremely trigger-happy. And if they had managed to avoid meeting any Germans, they still had to get down the outer slopes of the plateau.

'What happened, James?' Liane had asked. 'Were we betrayed?'

'I don't think we were betrayed deliberately,' James said. 'We were just too low on the list of priorities. If Delestraint had survived to push his pet project . . .'

'But they said they were coming. And they didn't.'

'I think they probably tried and were put off by the fog. They must have thought they had time, as if they couldn't get in, no one else could.'

'But the Germans did.'

'They have a somewhat more ruthless approach to human life, including that of their own people.' They had passed by the airstrip in their escape and seen the several wrecked aircraft.

'So they always win,' Liane said bitterly.

'So they always lose,' James insisted. 'There is a greater force in the world than pragmatism.' She had accepted his dogma, but now it was a matter of putting it to the test. They left their hiding place and made their way west. 'Will we find friends down there?' he asked.

'I have no doubt of it.'

'So all we have to do is climb down. Just take your time and follow me.' They reached the first steep decline. There was no way of telling whether it was an outer wall or merely another ravine. They clambered down and up the other side. 'False alarm,' he said. 'You OK?'

'I'm OK.'

But as she spoke there was a challenge. 'Who is there?'

The words were spoken in French, but the accent was not. Without hesitation Liane brought up her tommy-gun and fired a burst into the mist. There were screams of pain and alarm. The pair of them went to ground as fire was returned, over their heads.

'Shit,' Liane said. 'My drum is empty.'

James had already drawn his revolver. 'Then we must wait for them to come to us.'

'We cannot,' she said, as they listened to the whistles being blown.

'Well, then, to the left.' They crawled through the undergrowth, listening to answering whistles and some more shots. But clearly the soldiers were not sure where their enemies were. A few minutes later they reached another steep downward slope. James peered into the mist. He could see nothing beyond fifty feet, but fifty feet could mean a wide ravine or . . .

'We're going down,' he whispered.

'Who is there?' a voice called from very close at hand.

Liane rolled on her back, her Luger thrust forward.

'No,' James said urgently. The rest of the patrol had to be close at hand.

194

Liane looked at him but was prepared to obey. The sound of feet came closer until they could see boots. 'You will surrender, eh?' the man said, peering down at them behind his rifle.

James scythed his feet sideways, catching the soldier on the ankle. In the same movement he got up, his revolver replaced by his knife . . . but the soldier had gone, into space, with a despairing scream. Liane was also on her feet. But James seized her arm and dragged her down again. 'Not a sound,' he whispered.

'Joseph?' a voice called. 'Joseph?'

'Be careful,' someone else said in German. 'He has gone over.'

'Down there?' the first man asked.

'We must get after him.'

'He is gone. It is a drop of several hundred feet.'

'But he was speaking to someone. Challenging someone.'

'Do you hear anyone?'

'There was no reply.'

'Then there was no one there. Let us get away from here, before we fall over as well. This place gives me the creeps. And we have reached the end of our sweep.'

'Poor Joseph,' the first man said. 'That is a terrible way to die.'

'It is better than a bullet in the gut.' The voices faded.

'Several hundred feet,' James said. 'You game?'

'As the man said,' Liane responded, 'it is better than a bullet in the gut. Or a Gestapo torture chamber.'

'You are from the Vercours,' the patron said as he served cheese and bread and wine.

'What makes you say that?' Liane asked.

'Your clothes. You are filthy. Besides, you are Liane de Gruchy. I have heard much about you.'

Both James and Liane rustled as they sought their weapons. 'What are you going to do about that?' Liane asked in her softest voice.

'I will tell my grandchildren that I once served Liane de Gruchy.'

'And where are your grandchildren?'

'They are not born yet, mademoiselle.'

'Ah.'

'We heard the shooting, the bombing, the noise . . . It was terrible. I do not know how you got out.'

'Mademoiselle de Gruchy always gets out,' James said. 'Is she not immortal?'

'I wish to believe that, monsieur. Without her, we are a defeated nation.'

'Well, then, will you help us?'

'Tell me what you wish.'

'We need a bed to sleep,' Liane said. 'After we have had a hot bath.'

'Of course, mademoiselle. And a change of clothes, certainly for the gentleman. He will not get very far in an English uniform.'

'Are there many Germans about?'

'Too many. But I believe they will soon be pulling out. They have already sent off their prisoners.'

'Prisoners?' James asked. 'They have taken prisoners?'

'Oh, yes, monsieur. There were several prisoners. I saw them being marched to the railway station. They were an unhappy lot. Especially that poor girl. She looked so sad.'

Liane put down her wine glass. 'Did you say girl?'

'Well . . . a young woman, mademoiselle.'

'And she was a prisoner. Was she hurt?'

'Well . . . there was blood on her clothes. But she moved freely, not as if she were badly hurt.'

'And what was going to happen to her?'

'As I understood what was being said, they were being sent to Paris. For interrogation by the Gestapo.'

'There are no Gestapo in Grenoble?'

'Oh, there is an office. And there was a bigwig down from Berlin to oversee the attack, but he had to hurry back. Have you not heard the news? Hitler has been blown up.'

It was James' turn to put down his glass. 'Hitler is dead?'

'I do not believe so, monsieur. But a bomb was set off close to where he was standing. He was certainly injured. All Germany is in turmoil.'

James stared at Liane. Joanna? Certainly she must have been telling the truth, regardless of how long it took. But Liane did not know about Joanna's coup; he had never told her, nor did she care what had happened to Hitler. Her mind was else-where. 'You say this man took the prisoners with him?'

'No, no. He was in great haste. From what I heard the soldiers saying, it was General Bittner's decision to send them to Paris.'

'For interrogation,' Liane said softly. 'How long ago was this?'

'The day before yesterday, mademoiselle. As to when they will get there, or if they will get there at all . . . This country is also in turmoil.'

'I know,' Liane said. 'You were going to draw us a bath.'

'I do not think there will be sufficient hot water for two.'

'That is not important. We will share.' The patron rolled his eyes but hurried off.

'You do not know that it was Amalie,' James said.

'Of course it was Amalie. She was the only other woman fighting with us.'

'Well, if it were . . . what can we do?'

'I am going to Paris.'

'Now, my darling girl, how are you going to get there? The country is alive with German troops—'

'I can get there.'

'And then?'

'I have friends.'

'And you think these friends will help you get Amalie out of a Gestapo cell? That is, supposing she is still alive?'

'She is still alive. I feel it in my bones.' She rested her hand on his. 'Will you come with me? Or do you feel you should report back to Pound and take their orders?'

'That is what I *should* do, certainly. But if I do they'll pull me out for the rest of the War. And what the hell, they almost certainly think I'm dead, anyway.'

'They will be sad. Rachel will be sad.' He gazed at her with his mouth open. She squeezed his hand. 'I am not a fool, James. So, would you rather live with Rachel, or die with me?' He squeezed her hand back.

Feet, in the corridor. Madeleine sat up, straightening her dress and smoothing her hair. She was not used to sleeping in her clothes, to being unable to clean her teeth or wash her face.

197

The last couple of days had been the most ghastly of her life, made bearable by the fact that no one had actually touched her as yet, save from handcuffing her to bring her here. But the cuffs had been taken off, and she had been left alone, visited only by the two female warders, who had brought her meals. They had not spoken to her. They were afraid to do anything until they had heard from the very top. But now her deliverance was at hand. Oh, Adolf would be very upset at what had happened. He was probably very angry. But he had never been angry with her, and he was Helen's godfather. He might well banish Freddie and her from Berlin for the rest of the War, but she thought she would rather welcome that.

The door opened to admit Roess. Madeleine had not seen him since the moment of her arrest, two days before. Now he smiled at her, and if the smile was rather that of a cat regarding a captive mouse, she reminded herself that he always smiled like that. 'And how are you today, Frau von Helsingen?' he inquired.

'I am looking forward to getting home and having a hot bath.'

'Ah, yes. A bath. Do you know, that is what we are about to give you, a bath. Sadly, it will have to be a cold bath. But that is better than nothing, eh? And while you are bathing, you and I will talk.'

Madeleine stared at him. 'What are you saying? Do you think I am going to allow you to be present while I am bathing?'

'My dear Madeleine ... you do not mind if I call you Madeleine? I feel we are going to become so intimate over the next few days. What you must understand is that you are no longer in a position to allow, or to disallow, anything. You are absolutely in my power.' He stepped up to her, held her chin and turned her head to and fro. 'Do you know for how long I have looked forward to this moment? I have always known it would come.'

Angrily Madeleine jerked her head away from his grasp. She was panting but still unable to accept what was happening. 'The Fuehrer—'

'Ah, the Fuehrer. Do you know, I have just come from the Fuehrer. He gave me, Johann Roess, a personal interview. That is a measure of how seriously he is taking this business, taking your part in it, your relationship with the woman Jonsson.'

'Joanna? You have arrested Joanna?'

'She has got away.' Roess' voice was suddenly harsh. 'Having killed four of my agents in your sitting room, she killed two more in Lubeck, presumably when they tried to stop her leaving the country. The woman is an absolute monster.'

'But she got away,' Madeleine said. 'She wanted me to go with her. And I refused.'

'That was silly of you. Her escape has angered the Fuehrer even more. Do you know what he told me? He said, Johann – he called me Johann! – Johann, he said, make that bitch squeal. Wring every last moan from her body before you hang her. And I wish a photograph for every moment of her torment. So, you see,' he snapped his fingers, and the photographer brought his equipment into the cell, 'we will begin now, when you are sitting here, fully dressed, a little scruffy, perhaps, but obviously unharmed and in the best of health. Then we will take you along to the bathroom and remove your clothes. You will be photographed again while this is happening.'

This *cannot* be happening, Madeleine thought. I am having a nightmare.

'When you are naked,' Roess went on, his voice caressing now, 'we will photograph you again, several times, I think, from various angles, to illustrate your finer points, shall I say. Then we shall place you in the bath. The water will be ice cold and it will drive the air from your lungs. While you are in that situation, we will hold your head under the water until you think you are about to drown. Then we will take you out and revive you. That will almost certainly have to be by mouth-to-mouth resuscitation, or by punching and squeezing of the chest to force the water from your lungs. The Fuehrer will enjoy those photographs. And then—'

'Stop it!' Madeleine shouted. 'What is it you wish to know? Ask me, and I will tell you.'

'Why, we require names. The names of everyone who has visited your apartment since your husband's return from the Eastern Front.'

'How am I supposed to remember them all?'

'I am sure you will do so, Frau, as we encourage you.'

'Has my husband not given you names?'

'Sadly, Madeleine, your husband is dead.'

'What?' Madeleine shouted.

'Or,' Roess said, looking at his watch, 'he should be. In view of his wounds, and his past services to the Reich, and the fact that he is the son of an old friend of the Fuehrer's, he was offered the option of taking poison rather than being hanged. I imagine he has done so by now. But do not worry, Madeleine. You will be hanged when I have finished with you.' Madeleine screamed.

'Come in, Roess,' Himmler invited. 'Sit down. What is the news of Jonsson?'

'There is no news, Herr Reichsfuehrer. We know she landed in Sweden but then she disappeared.'

'Surely she has gone to her father?'

'One would assume so. But I have had our agents watching Herr Jonsson's house, and there has been no sign of her. I think she may have gone on to England.'

'That would be a pity.'

'Would you like me to mount a raid on Jonsson's house? That way we would know for sure if she is there or not.'

'I absolutely forbid it. With things as they are, well . . . the Swedes may be very useful to us. We certainly do not wish to antagonize them. As a matter of fact, I have called you here today because . . .' He paused. 'I assume that other business has been completed.'

'Yes.' Roess' tone was bitter.

'Good. When is Frau von Helsingen to be hanged?'

'She will not be hanged, Herr Reichsfuehrer.'

Himmler raised his eyebrows. 'Indeed? Why not?'

'Because she is already dead.'

'You allowed her to commit suicide? That was careless of you.'

'I do not know if she committed suicide. We were using the cold water treatment, and the fools held her under a moment too long. Perhaps she deliberately inhaled, although I would not have said she had that much courage. In any event, she could not be revived.'

'Did you get anything at all out of her?'

'No. But that is not relevant. We have enough to go on with. The Fuehrer wanted her to suffer, and I had such plans for her. She really had a superb figure.' He sighed.

'Water under the bridge,' Himmler said. 'Or over the body, eh? Ha ha. But you would have had to give her up to some-body else, anyway. You have more important things to do. I want you in Paris just as quickly as you can get there.'

'Paris?'

'You served there for a couple of years. You know it well.'

'Yes, I do. But—'

Himmler leant forward. 'Listen to me, Roess. Things are not going well. The Russian advance is slowing, but we have not actually checked it. But it is in France that the situation is more serious. The Allies have now broken out of Normandy and the situation there is calamitous. And now this landing on the Riviera . . . If we are not careful we could lose the entire country. Thus the Fuehrer has decided that we must create a strong point that must be held to the last man. The obvious strong point is Paris. It is a huge city and if the Allies get bogged down in trying to take it, street by street, they will expend thousand, tens of thousands, hundreds of thousands of men. We know they will never try to bomb or shell it out of existence; we saw that in their approach to Rome. But most importantly, it will cost them time. Time for us to complete the development of our secret weapons.'

'Yes, sir,' Roess said doubtfully, both on account of the secret weapons, in which he had no faith, and of this holding to the last man idea. 'But I am not a soldier, Herr Reichsfuehrer. I am a policeman.'

'That is exactly it. We are sending a new commanding general, Choltitz. As I have said, his orders will be to defend Paris to the last man, and I may tell you in confidence that he also has secret orders that when he is down *to* the last man, he will destroy the city by means of previously placed explo-sives, so that only a burnt-out shell will eventually fall to the Allies. But frankly, I personally have no great faith in Choltitz's strength of mind. I am sending you back, as Gestapo overlord, with two objectives. Firstly, we know that Paris is riddled with the Resistance. This must be stamped out before they can mount a rising. I give you carte blanche. Deal with them as you dealt with the people in the Vercours. Shoot anyone you have to, as many as you have to. Understood?'

'Yes, sir. And the other objective?'

'Will be to stand at Choltitz's shoulder and, if it comes to the crunch, make sure that he carries out his orders – or, if necessary, give the orders yourself – for the firing of the explosives.'

'Yes, sir. And . . . ah . . . afterwards?'

The two men gazed at each other. 'My dear Johann,' Himmler said. 'I am giving you the opportunity to die for the Fatherland. What higher honour can there be than that?'

'Up there,' Liane said, 'is my apartment. The fourth floor.'

James looked up at the curtained windows. But then, most of the windows in the building were curtained. 'Is anyone living there now?'

'I have no idea.'

'But we're going there?'

'No, no. We are going to . . . Shit! Act.' Two German soldiers had come round the corner. Liane immediately bowed her back and pulled her shawl over her head, tapping the ground with her stick. With her threadbare clothes and her deliberately filthy hair – she had rubbed it with mud and dirt – she looked at once old and unhealthy.

James, at her shoulder, carrying a small satchel, was equally decrepit, wearing a soiled beret and shabby, dirty clothes, his boots a mass of cracks, and was also walking with a stick. He did not suppose he would recognize himself, just as he could hardly believe that they had made their way through an entire retreating army; but then a great many people had been doing that, either to remove themselves from the vicinity of the next battle or, if they had got too close to their erstwhile conquerors, from the clutches of their vengeful fellow countrymen.

He had never doubted Liane's courage, but always in the past when they had operated together, they had been working to his plans and he had been in control. This was the first occasion on which he had been the junior partner, and he had been astounded not only by her total confidence and self-assurance, but by the way she had submerged herself in the role she felt necessary, refusing to bathe even when water was available, deliberately and extravagantly allowing herself to become more and more dishevelled and odorous through the three weeks of their journey, aided by the hot July going into August sun. And she had required him to do the same.

Now she hobbled unhesitatingly towards the two soldiers, who exchanged comments in German before switching to poor French. 'Hey, old woman,' one of them said. 'You got a pass?'

'Pass?' Liane gave a high-pitched cackle. 'What do I want with a pass?'

'You have to have a pass,' he explained. 'Or we shall have to arrest you.'

'You'll take me in?' Liane give another cackle. 'Give me something to eat. Give him—' she jerked her thumb over her shoulder '—something to drink? That's all he wants, drink.'

The soldiers had come right up to her, now they recoiled. 'Jesus!' the first one said. 'She smells like a dead dog.'

'Get away with you,' said the other. 'Be off.'

'You said you'd arrest me, give me something to eat,' Liane protested.

'Off,' he said again. 'And you.' He aimed a kick at James, which sent him staggering.

Liane shouted curses as she hobbled down the street, James following. 'Whew!' he commented when they were out of earshot. 'That was a close one.'

'The smell works every time,' she said. 'It is not far now.' A few minutes later they came upon the house, large and four-square, set back from the street in its own grounds. It looked decrepit, and terribly in need of a coat of paint, but that could be said of just about every house in Paris. The quite spacious grounds were also unkempt and unweeded, and the iron gate squealed as it was pushed open. 'This is my home,' Liane said. 'When I am in Paris.'

'You mean . . . the house we've been using for evaders? The brothel?'

She smiled. 'They won't charge you.'

She led the way up the drive, which was in surprisingly good repair, but then, James realized, it would be in regular use. Liane went up the steps and rang the bell. It was some minutes before the door was opened. 'We are closed,' the somewhat raw-boned woman announced.

'One day, Marguerite, ' Liane said, 'you are going to be pleased to see me.'

The woman stared at her, then uttered a shriek. 'Mademoiselle Liane! After so long!' She looked past her.

'My man,' Liane explained. 'Aren't you going to let us in?'

'Oh, mademoiselle.' Marguerite stepped back to allow them entry to a large hall, then closed the door, before turning to the staircase that mounted the far wall. 'Madame!' she called. 'Madame!'

James looked around him. Three doors opened off the hall, one at the back, obviously leading to the kitchen, an elaborate double to his right and a single to his left. Then his attention was drawn to the woman descending the stairs. Tall, elegant, with flowing red hair, she wore a dressing-gown and high-heeled mules. Her features could have been attractive but for the hardness of the expression, nor did they lighten at the sight of her visitors. 'Liane?' she asked. 'My God, Liane. Why did you come back? *How* did you come back?'

'I told you I would come back,' Liane said. 'It just took a little longer than I expected.'

'And you expect to stay here? That is not possible. Who is this?'

'Of course it is possible, and necessary,' Liane said. 'This is Major James Barron of the British Secret Intelligent Service. He is my commanding officer, which means that he is also your commanding officer.'

'And you have brought him here? My God, you must be mad. Do you know what Roess did to me when he returned after you attacked him on that train?'

Liane looked her up and down. 'You do not look too badly damaged to me.'

'He was going to flog me,' Constance said. 'Me!'

'But he didn't, apparently. Now, Constance, stop having hysterics. There is no need for it. The War will soon be over. The Allies are getting closer every day. They will be in Paris by the end of this month, at the outside. All we need is the use of your house for that period. Do you have any evaders in residence?'

'No, no. There have been none for over a month.'

'That is because they are not being shot down any more. And it is ideal. We shall use the attic. And the first things we want are a hot bath and a square meal, and then a change of clothing. I know you can arrange this.'

'We will all be hanged,' Constance said.

'Of course we will not be hanged. You have the best house in Paris, and you cater only to German officers. Why should they suspect you of anything? And if they once suspected that you had harboured me, well, now they suppose that I am dead.' She smiled. 'Again. Now, we also want information about some prisoners sent up from the south a few weeks ago. One of them would have been a woman.'

'A woman?' Constance asked, both interested and suspicious.

'What you do not know cannot harm you. We wish to know where these people are being held and if any of them have been shot.'

'How am I to know this?'

'You will get your girls to ask your clients. Tonight.'

'You do not understand.' Constance's voice was almost a wail. 'You think you can come here and take up just where you left off, two years ago? I told you that Roess arrested me, after you assaulted me. You pretended to be my sister.'

'Yes, yes,' Liane said. 'I remember all of that. But he let you go.'

'Because I told him I was certain that you would return to Paris and come here. He made me swear an oath that when you did, I would inform him so that you could be taken.'

'Well, isn't it fortunate that I could not get back. Now Roess is far away, and you do not have to break your oath.'

'You still do not understand,' Constance said. 'Roess is back. He returned two days ago to take over the Gestapo in Paris.'

'Can she be trusted?' James asked.

He soaked in the hot bath with Liane leaning back against him; their legs were over the sides. Absently he soaped her breasts. 'That feels so good,' she said. 'Constance can be trusted because she knows that if I am taken she will be arrested too. And her girls.'

205

'But if she was promised immunity for handing you over . . .'

'She would not dare do that. The woman, or the man, who betrayed Liane de Gruchy would not only be lynched by the mob the moment the Allies get here, but her name would go down in history as an example of infamy. But it is serious that Roess is back. If he should get his claws into Amalie . . .'

'If she is still alive,' he reminded her.

'She is alive,' she said fiercely.

'So, what is your plan? If Roess is back in charge, things will be tightened up.'

'Let us first see what Constance can turn up.'

By two in the morning the last client had gone. It had been a boisterous evening. The German officers had to know the War was all but lost, but they seemed determined to enjoy themselves, drinking Constance's 'champagne', singing songs and of course taking the girls of their choice upstairs to the bedrooms. From their attic Liane and James could hear much of what was said immediately beneath them, the squeals of laughter or pain, the gasps of pretended orgasm from the girls, and once even the snap of a cane and the real shrieks of agony from the recipient.

They had not switched on the light but James could feel the tension in Liane's body.

'Did you really work here?' he asked.

'Does that make you angry?'

'Nothing you could do could make me angry. But . . . were you ever whipped?'

'Once. By Roess. He did not know who I was.'

'He thought you were Constance's sister. But, my God . . .'

'Oh, yes,' she said. 'I have always intended to kill him. Without knowing if I would succeed. But if he is here . . . and if he has harmed Amalie . . .'

He squeezed her hand. 'But you will not commit suicide.'

Before she could reply, the door opened. They both sat up, James with his revolver and Liane with her pistol thrust forward.

'It is me,' Constance said. 'We have found out that some prisoners from the south arrived here three weeks ago. One was a young woman.'

'And they are still alive? There has been no word of any execution?'

'Not that anyone here knows of.'

'Excellent. And where are these prisoners being held?'

'In the cells beneath Gestapo Headquarters.' Constance shivered. 'I have been there. You cannot get them out.'

'We shall have to see. Who is now the head of the Resistance here in Paris?'

'How am I supposed to know that?'

'Because I am sure you do know it.'

'His name is Emile Duvivier.'

Very good. Arrange a meeting between us.'

'Your think he will come to a meeting? He will be afraid of betrayal.'

'He will come to a meeting with Liane de Gruchy,' Liane said. 'Or I will go to a meeting with him.'

'Liane de Gruchy,' said the short, thick-set man, seated in the corner of the bar. 'I have waited all of my life for this moment. But . . . here in Paris? Undisguised?'

'The Germans think I am dead. Will any of these people betray me, Monsieur Duvivier?'

Duvivier looked around the bar, which was fairly full. 'None of these people. They are all mine. And this gentleman?'

'Major Barron of the British Secret Service.'

'Your mission?'

'To lead a rising against the Boche, here in Paris.'

Although James was in her confidence, her effrontery took his breath away.

Duvivier considered her for several moments, while he drank some wine. Then he asked, 'When were you ordered to do this?'

Liane replied without hesitation. 'Two weeks ago. It has taken us that long to reach here.'

'Ah. Well, those orders are out of date. The Americans have decided to by-pass Paris.'

'What? Paris is the soul of France.'

'They do not think so. They think it would absorb too many men, cost too much *matériel*, and lives, to take Paris if it is properly defended, and they are sure that if they can continue this rapid advance and maybe get to Germany itself by the end of this year, Paris will fall of itself.'

'The end of this year? That is four months' away.'

'What is four months in the context of this war?'

'It is for ever. And you and your people accept this?'

'We do not like it. We have protested. And we have been instructed under no circumstances to start any action on our own, which could involved thousands of civilian casualties.'

'Our people. Who would surely die for the freedom of France. How many people do you have?'

'Almost the entire population is behind us. But if you mean how many have arms, it is less than ten thousand.'

'But they would obtain more arms with every German they kill. What is the size of the garrison?'

'Now that is the silly thing,' Duvivier said. 'It is dwindling every day. Even a month ago it was more than a hundred thousand. But so many drafts have been called away, either to try to stop the Allies, or back to Germany, that I do not think there is more than half that number now.'

'Then we start the rising, now.'

He frowned at her. 'Our orders—'

'Were issued by some half-witted staff officer with no sense of the moral value of freeing Paris.'

'You are asking my ten thousand ill-armed people to take on fifty thousand professional soldiers equipped with the latest weapons?'

'For a couple of days, yes.'

'A couple of days? They will take their time. Do you know what they did in Warsaw?'

'A couple of days,' Liane insisted. 'Listen to me, Duvivier. Warsaw was supposed to be relieved by the Russians. But they never came. Because the Russians did not care how many Poles were killed, as long as they killed Germans as well and occupied their attention. We are not Poles and out there are not Russians. There is a Free French corps fighting with the Allies. If we start an uprising now and broadcast it on the radio so that the whole world knows what we are doing, the Allies, much less our own countrymen, must come to our aid or they will be damned throughout history.'

Duvivier looked at James. 'I agree with her,' James said.

Duvivier finished his wine, went to the bar for a refill and sat down again. 'When?'

'How long will it take you to alert all your people?'

'Three days.'

'Three days. That will be Tuesday. All right. Dawn on Tuesday. I will meet you here at four in the morning. And I need a squad of twenty well-armed and determined men.'

'To do what?'

'I will attack Gestapo Headquarters.'

'That will be suicide.'

'Not if we take them by surprise. You will not fail me.'

'Four o'clock, on Tuesday morning, with a picked squad,' Duvivier said and shook her hand, 'And may God help us if you are wrong about Allied support, mademoiselle.'

'I will say amen to that,' James remarked, as they made their way back towards the brothel. He wore an ill-fitting jacket and trousers, and Liane an equally ill-fitting and shabby dress, with her hair concealed beneath a headscarf, but he did not suppose there was much chance of her being recognized in any event, for the various German soldiers that they passed were clearly in a state of some agitation.

'Three days,' she said. 'Three more days for Amalie to endure hell.'

'Well, if she's survived a month in their hands . . .'

'That was before Roess arrived. If he discovers that my sister is in his cells . . . You know he had her there once before?'

'I know. But there is nothing we can do until Duvivier is ready to move. And you do realize that once an uprising starts they are liable to execute all prisoners out of hand.'

'That is why we are assaulting the Gestapo Headquarters the moment that it starts. Now . . .' She paused, staring across the street. 'My God!'

'Eh?' Liane grabbed his arm and dragged him round the corner, then stood against the wall, breathing deeply. 'What in God's name is the matter?'

'Gabrielle Chartrin.'

'Who?'

'Oh, for God's sake, James. You must remember Gabrielle.

209

From the farm. You met her. And I told you about her German boyfriend. Now she is just round the corner.'

'Jesus! How? I mean, in Paris?'

'I don't know what she is doing in Paris. But she recognized me.'

'Are you sure? With your hair tied up—'

'Gabrielle would recognize me anywhere and anyhow. She has known me for years.'

'And you think she will betray you?'

'I would never have supposed so. But . . .'

'Her brother did. Then we must do something about her right away.'

'I did not want this to happen.' Liane sounded quite distressed. 'That family has been so good to me, so loyal . . . Philipe betrayed me because he could not have me. Gabrielle—'

'Had, or perhaps still has, a German boyfriend. It has to be done, Li. Somehow we have to lure her to the brothel. We must go back to her, and you must chat her up.'

Liane drew a deep breath. 'You are right, of course. But you stay here. I will bring her to you.' She went back round the corner, looked left and right along the crowded street and saw Gabrielle again. She went towards her, then realized that she was talking with a German officer. Shit, she thought, and turned back. But Gabrielle had seen her and was pointing. The German officer shouted and people closed on her. Many of them had to be French, but they were instinctively obeying the conqueror's command, as they had done for the past four years.

After four years, Liane thought. One moment of bad luck.

Eleven

The Brightest Day

James could only watch in horror as policemen arrived and Liane was handcuffed, her precious shoulder-bag ripped away, and she was marched up the street in the direction of Gestapo Headquarters. She made no effort to resist the clutching hands. He could not believe that Liane would tamely accept her fate; she would await her opportunity with that deadly patience that was her outstanding characteristic as a guerilla leader. But if the opportunity never came . . .

The temptation to draw his revolver and dash into their midst was overwhelming. But it would be a pointless act of suicide and would certainly not save Liane. So . . . Gabrielle had clearly not recognized him, which was hardly surprising. She had only known him for a couple of days, and he could not now look less like a British officer, therefore the whole business had been dumped in his lap.

It was odd how helpless, how lonely, he felt. Giving orders, whether over the radio or in person, even leading the guerillas into battle, or fighting fierce defensive actions such as the Vercours, had never affected his confidence; because of his confidence in Liane. He had been utterly shattered by the thought that she might have been killed. That she had re-emerged, unharmed and, after that brief moment of despair, as confident as ever, had restored his faith in her immortality.

Now it was he must make the final decision. She was going to be delivered to Roess, a man who had sought her and hated her for four years, whom she had once hit so hard as to put him in hospital for several weeks and, James guessed, affect his mind. He had never met Roess, but he had heard enough

211

about him, from both Liane and Joanna . . . and Rachel, who had briefly been his prisoner. Roess liked to enjoy his victims, especially if they were attractive women. When he was presented with the most attractive woman in the world, with so much already between them, he would wish to enjoy her to the maximum. The question was, how long it would take him to reach that maximum and how much of that 'enjoyment' could Liane stand. But he knew he could not stand a moment of it. He hurried back to the bar.

'You wish to go in now? Without adequate preparation?' Duvivier hunched his shoulders. 'That is madness. Suicide.'

'It is Liane de Gruchy's life. Do you wish to be responsible for ending it?'

'You make it hard, monsieur. You are asking me to sacrifice how many lives, for one, however famous.'

'Do you not suppose lives will be lost if we wait until Tuesday?'

Duvivier pulled his nose. 'By then we will at least know if the Allies are prepared to come to our rescue.'

'But you would be committed whether they agreed to help or not. Now you can tell them that the rising has already begun.'

Duvivier finished his wine; James reckoned that he must have had quite a lot to drink, although like most Frenchmen it did not seem to have affected him greatly. 'I cannot alert sufficient of my people before this evening,' he said. 'Mademoiselle de Gruchy will have to survive until then.'

'This evening,' James agreed. He knew he could not improve on that. 'And then?'

'Then . . . I will tell you what we are going to do.'

'Now, then,' Roess said, studying the map that was spread on the desk in front of him. 'These sites obviously have to be approved by General von Choltitz, but I am having lunch with him this morning, and I am sure he will agree to our proposals.' He looked around the anxious faces of the officers grouped beside him. 'Come, come, gentlemen. I am aware that we are in a dangerous situation, which may well turn out badly. But as we must do out duty to the Reich, for God's sake let us be cheerful about it.' He raised his head in irritation as the door to the office opened without a knock.

'Ah, Marach!' Captain Marach had served with him the last time he had worked in Paris, and he did not appear to have changed in the intervening two years, seeming still a fresh-faced and somewhat excitable youth. 'What is troubling you?'

Marach stood to attention and drew a deep breath. 'We have taken a prisoner, Herr Colonel.'

'My dear Marach, I understand our cells are full of prisoners no one has yet got round to interrogating. Do we really need another one?'

'This one, sir. I have outside Liane de Gruchy.'

Roess gave a snort of derision. 'Liane de Gruchy is dead. She was killed in the Battle of Vercours.'

'I have her outside, sir.'

'If this is some kind of joke, Marach—'

'It is her, Herr Colonel. We have positive identification.'

'Positive identification? Do you know the number of people who have positively identified Liane de Gruchy? And you . . . you have never even seen her.'

'I did see her, sir, two years ago, when she was working in Madame Constance's house. That was just before . . .' He gulped as Roess glared at him. 'I know she was disguised then, sir, but I could never forget her face. Or her voice. And besides, sir, we have a positive identification, from a woman who knew her when she lived in the Massif Central. She is the one who denounced her, not half an hour ago.'

Could it possibly be true? De Gruchy's body had never been found. But as she had not been heard of, either, for more than a month, it had seemed certain that she had to be dead. If she had actually survived again, and was now here . . . He felt almost sick with excitement. But he had to preserve the ice-cold calm that was expected of him. 'Who is this woman?'

Marach took out his notebook. 'Her name is Gabrielle Chartrin.'

Roess frowned. 'Chartrin? I know that name. Her brother was a member of the Resistance. He assisted us in our first assault on the Vercours. By God! Yes, she would know de Gruchy. She is a member of the Resistance herself. Is she under arrest?'

213

'Well, no, Herr Colonel.'

'Why not? Because she denounced another woman as de Gruchy? It is some trick. They are always up to tricks, these people.'

'With respect, Herr Colonel, this woman, Chartrin, well . . .' Marach looked embarrassed. 'She belongs to Captain Dieter Hammerach.'

'Belongs?'

'In a manner of speaking, sir. Captain Hammerach was stationed in Aumont, after your coup in capturing the man Moulin. While there he apparently formed an . . . attachment to this woman and when, following the Allied invasion of the South of France, our troops were pulled out, he was transferred to Paris and he, ah, brought this young woman with him.'

'Good God! What is the German army coming to? This Hammerach did all this, knowing this woman to be a member of the Resistance?'

'Well, sir, I don't think he did know that.'

'I will see this fellow. And his doxy.'

'And Mademoiselle de Gruchy?'

It was Roess' turn to draw a long breath. 'If it is de Gruchy. Has she been searched?'

'Yes, Herr Colonel. She was carrying a pistol in her bag. As far as we have been able to ascertain she has no other weapon.'

'But she is restrained?'

'Oh, yes, sir. She is handcuffed.'

Roess nodded. 'Very good, gentlemen, I will see you later.'

The other officers, looking totally confused by the conversation, filed from the room. Marach followed them but returned a moment later. 'Captain Hammerach, Herr Colonel.' Roess regarded Dieter coldly. 'Mademoiselle Chartrin,' Marach announced. He might have been a majordomo at a grand reception. Roess' eyes were colder yet. 'And Mademoiselle de Gruchy.'

Roess leant back in his chair. He had also only ever seen Liane in disguise, with flamboyant red hair and an abundance of rouge and lipstick and eye shadow. She had not struck him then as being the most beautiful woman in France, as was her reputation, yet she had been attractive enough for him to wish to make her his mistress. And, like almost every man who had ever met her, he had fallen in love with her voice. Now he looked at a truly beautiful woman, for all her shabby clothes. As she wore no make-up, her features were utterly exposed, and the headscarf had been taken away to allow her hair, straight and blonde, to rest below her shoulders. Her eyes were the clearest blue. Her arms were pulled behind her back by the handcuffs.

He gazed at her, and she gazed back. But there remained her voice. 'Speak,' he commanded.

Liane considered for a moment, and he felt his muscles tensing. Then she seemed to accept the situation. Her shoulders gave a slight twitch, as if she might have shrugged. 'Good morning, Johann,' she said. 'How is your head?'

His jaw had dropped. Now he snapped it closed again. 'Better than yours is going to be.' He looked at Gabrielle, who was trembling. 'You denounced this woman? Why?'

'She is a faithful servant of the Reich,' Hammerach said.

'I did not ask you,' Roess pointed out. 'Answer the question, girl.'

Gabrielle licked her lips. 'She was responsible for the death of my brother.'

'Well, only indirectly. But you knew her from Aumont. You must have known she was a Resistance leader, then.'

'I . . . well . . .'

'You, and no doubt your family, are guilty of aiding and abetting an enemy of the Reich. That carries the death penalty.'

'But, Herr Colonel—' Dieter protested.

'Oh, get out!' Roess snapped. 'Be thankful I do not have you cashiered for associating with an enemy of the state.'

Dieter opened his mouth, then closed it again. He gave Gabrielle a despairing glance and left the office.

'Now,' Roess said.

His secretary appeared in the doorway. 'Excuse me, Herr Colonel, but your luncheon appointment with the general . . .'

'Damn,' Roess said. 'Very good, Margrit. Marach, I leave you in charge. Place these two in Cell Twenty-Seven. You understand me?'

'Yes, Herr Colonel. But . . . both in the same cell?'

215

'Yes, in the same cell.'

'You cannot do this,' Gabrielle protested. 'She will kill me.'

'You will chain them each to the wall, facing each other,' Roess said. 'But in addition, either you or Margrit will be with them at all times.'

Marach clicked his heels. 'Yes, Herr Colonel.'

Roess got up and stood in front of Liane. 'I once told you that I liked to hear women scream. Do you remember that, Liane?'

'And did I not scream?'

'But now I know you were acting. When I return, this afternoon, we shall take the business more seriously.' He held her chin between his fingers and moved her head to and fro; she never took her gaze from his face. 'Oh, indeed. We shall have an amusing time. Marach,' he said. 'I wish her fed a good meal and given some wine to drink. I do not wish her senses to be impaired by any extreme discomfort.' He smiled. 'Until I inflict it. Oh, one more thing. Do not under any circumstances release her hands. You will have to feed her yourself.'

'Ah . . . suppose she wishes to go to the toilet?'

'Well, then, you will accompany her and assist her. Will you not enjoy that?' He left the office.

'You will have to assist me, Margrit,' Marach said.

'Me, Herr Captain?' Margrit was a small, rather plump woman with fair hair and somewhat crumpled features.

'I know nothing of women.' Margrit raised her eyebrows, and he hurried on. 'I mean, in their private, er, matters.'

Margrit's lip curled. 'Very well, Herr Captain. And this one?'

'How can you arrest me?' Gabrielle protested. 'Did I not deliver this woman to you?'

'You are an enemy of the Reich,' Margrit said, obviously intending to take control as Marach did not seem able to do so. 'You will not speak unless spoken to. Will you come quietly, or do you wish to be handcuffed?'

Gabrielle licked her lips. 'I will come with you. But I protest most strongly.'

'You protest,' Margrit said scornfully. 'Sergeant!' The sergeant came in. 'Hold her arms.'

The sergeant grasped Gabrielle's arms, pulling them behind her back. Gabrielle gave a little shriek. 'Colonel Roess said that nothing was to be done to these women until he returns,' Marach protested.

'No, no, Herr Captain. He said that nothing was to be done to de Gruchy. He made no reference to this one except to say that she must be placed in the same cell. So . . .' She stood in front of Gabrielle. 'Are you still going to protest, mademoiselle?' Gabrielle opened her mouth and uttered another little shriek as Margrit stepped against her, grasped the collar of her dress and pulled it down with all her strength, ripping the material to the waist. Then she did the same to the petticoat beneath. 'Now, there,' she said. 'You are all exposed, and I am sure you are such a modest, well-brought-up young lady. Now you will have to walk through the entire building with your tits hanging out.' She pulled the torn material left and right further to expose the heaving breasts. Gabrielle burst into tears. 'Now,' Margrit said. 'If you utter another sound I will take off your knickers as well, eh?'

Marach was also breathing heavily, and now at last he glanced at Liane, but she was not to be tempted to speak; she had no intention of providing these people with any more amusement. She had to brace herself for what was coming, for survival in the face of extreme pain and humiliation. But James was still free. And thus there was still hope.

Constance listened to what James had to tell her with terrified consternation. 'Then we are done,' she said.

'We are going to get her out of there.'

'You?'

'And Duvivier's people.'

'That is madness.' She fanned herself, sitting on the bed once shared by James and Liane. 'I feel quite faint.'

'Do you feel nothing for Liane?'

'Well, I am very sorry for her, of course. I loved that woman, you know. We could have done great things together. But now . . .' She stood up. 'I must go and see my mother.'

'I think you should stay here.'

'I may never see my mother again.'

217

'Constance,' James said. 'You do not have a mother.'
Constance stared at him, eyebrows arched. 'Liane has told me
all about you,' James explained.

'I am going out,' Constance said.

'I'm sorry. I cannot allow you to do that.'

'You do not trust me.'

'That is exactly it.'

'You seem to forget that this is my house, filled with my
people.'

'And you have forgotten that you are a whore, who has
come to this bedroom of her own free will. You are attracted
to me, and you are going to spend the next few hours having
sex with me, which will leave you so exhausted you will be
unable to move until this evening.'

She glared at him. 'You flatter yourself. I don't even like
you. I don't like any men, and I especially dislike Englishmen,
but you are the bottom of the list.'

'Well, that is very agreeable, because I don't like you either,
and in any event, I am not in the mood for sex. But that is
what I am going to tell your girls.'

'Don't you think I will tell them the truth?'

'Of course you will. This evening. Now help me tear up
these bedclothes.'

'You are mad. Why do you wish to tear my bedclothes?'

'Because I wish to use the strips to tie you up. And gag
you.'

'You would not *dare*.'

'Constance, we don't know each other very well. But if
Liane were here, she would tell you that I am twice as ruthless as she is.' He opened his haversack and took out his clasp
knife and opened it. 'You have a choice of remaining here,
lying on this bed in comparative comfort save for being bound
and gagged, with every prospect of being able to resume your
life and career after I have gone, until tomorrow morning; or
of lying here, in no comfort at all and, as far as you are
concerned, with nothing to look forward to as your throat will
be cut from ear to ear. The choice is yours.'

When Constance had been attended to, he lay beside her.
He figured he was going to need all his energy in a few
hours' time. But he couldn't sleep. He kept thinking of Liane

at the mercy of Roess, undergoing utter hell … but she would be thinking of him, knowing that he would be coming for her.

At half-past three he got out of bed, grinned at Constance who, after a restless period, had subsided, red in the face, glaring at him. 'Who knows,' he said. 'If you're unlucky, you may see me again.'

He closed and locked the door, pocketed the key and went down the stairs. At the foot he encountered Marguerite. 'Is madame ready for her bath?' she inquired.

'Madame is sleeping. She is quite exhausted. I'm afraid it is a long time since I have had a woman. She asked me to tell you that she will call you when she is ready.'

'We open in two hours' time.'

'I am sure she knows that. Good afternoon to you.'

Duvivier waited in a crowded bar, which was not unusual on a Saturday afternoon. But every man was in a state of some excitement. 'They are ready,' Duvivier said. 'We are ready. My men are in position. Well, most of them. We will seize our objectives at half-past four. You must not begin your assault until we open fire, and then you must allow at least ten minutes for the Boche to react.'

'I understand.' James looked around the somewhat villainous faces. 'Which are my men?'

'These are all your men.'

'I asked for twenty.'

'Well, you have got forty. When they heard it was to rescue Liane de Gruchy, I had difficulty in preventing my entire force from volunteering. Use them well.'

General von Choltitz believed in the good things of life, and French wine was near the head of his list. Thus the luncheon had gone on for some considerable time. Certainly no one seemed to be in any hurry to leave the table. 'This will probably be our last opportunity to enjoy a good meal,' he told his officers. 'So we may as well indulge ourselves.'

'Is there news of the Allied advance, Herr General?' someone asked.

'Oh, indeed. The British are moving up the coast, securing

219

the seaports. One would suppose their objective is Antwerp, which is the most important port north of Le Havre. And the Americans are advancing through the centre.'

'When will they be here?'

'They would be here in about two days, if they were coming here.'

'Sir?'

'They do not appear to be intending to assault Paris,' Choltitz explained. 'Our reconnaissance indicates that they are swinging to the right, meaning to bypass us, cut us off and leave us to be collected later. So we do not even have to destroy the city, for a little while, at least. I will tell you frankly, gentlemen, that that is an order I am most reluctant to give.'

'The charges are all placed, Herr General,' Roess said.

'I am sure that you have done a very good job, Colonel. However . . . we shall see.'

'With respect, sir, do the locals know the Allies are bypassing the city?'

'I should not think so. Do you suppose they might attempt a rising? What is your opinion on that, Roess? You know these people.'

'I doubt they will try anything, Herr General. Especially now.' He paused to look triumphantly around the table.

'Explain,' Choltitz said.

'This morning,' Roess said, 'I arrested Liane de Gruchy.'

There was a rustle. 'It was reported that de Gruchy died in the Vercours incident,' someone said.

'I know. She has been reported dead on more occasions than I care to remember. But she is at this moment in my cells, waiting interrogation. I am commencing that when I leave here.'

'And you are positive it is her?' Choltitz asked. 'Is she not a mistress of disguise?'

'She is. Or was. But I know her personally.'

'Well,' Choltitz said. 'I think I would like to see this fearsome creature. Shall we, gentlemen?'

'Oh, indeed, Herr General.' They spoke as one.

Roess frowned. He had not anticipated this reaction. 'You understand that she is awaiting interrogation.'

'That is why we wish to see her now,' Choltitz explained.

'Before you set about destroying her fabled beauty.' He stood up. 'Show me your prize, Colonel.'

The time was twenty to five.

Liane sat on the floor of the cell. Her wrists were still handcuffed behind her and to an iron upright set into the wall; she had lost a lot of feeling in her arms but apart from that she was in no discomfort, although the floor was hard. She had been fed, spoonful after spoonful, by the very nervous Marach, and given two glasses of wine to drink. 'You understand, Fräulein,' Marach had said, 'I am obeying orders, as I am bound to do.'

'So I forgive you,' Liane said. 'As you must forgive me, when you are dangling from the end of a rope.'

Marach swallowed, and Margrit, who had stood above them through the meal, snorted. 'Don't tell me you are afraid of her, Herr Captain.'

Marach had stood up. 'Remember that she is not to be touched,' he said and left the cell.

Margrit had continued to stare at Liane for some minutes before returning to stand above Gabrielle, also sitting, handcuffed against the opposite wall. 'But you can be harmed, my little dove,' she said.

Gabrielle has spent most of the afternoon weeping. 'Why are you doing this to me?' she had sobbed. 'I gave her to you. I was avenging my brother. I have never harmed the Reich. Oh!'

Margrit had kicked her in the thigh. 'I am going to ask the colonel to give you to me,' she had said. 'I think he will do that. I am going to skin you alive and make a lampshade out of you. You will make a pretty lampshade.'

Gabrielle had again burst into tears. But for the past hour she had been silent, as Margrit had also had little to say. They were waiting. For oblivion? Preceded by pain? Liane refused to believe the first, but she could not preclude the second. And now at last there were feet in the corridor. Liane frowned. There were quite a few feet, and a good deal of loud talk and laughter. Instinctively she squared her shoulders and pushed herself flat against the wall. The cell door swung open, and Marach held it wide to allow eight men into the room. They

221

all wore the uniforms of senior officers and they were all very jolly, except for Roess, who was not looking terribly pleased.

'So where is this demon?' asked the man wearing a general's insignia, which enabled Liane to identify him as Choltitz.

'Get her up,' Roess snapped, and Marach hurried forward, joined by Margrit, who had been standing to attention. Between them they grasped Liane's arms and pulled her to her feet.

'My word,' Choltitz remarked. 'She is quite exceptional. Do we really have to hang her, Roess?'

'She is guilty of every crime you can imagine, Herr General. However, the execution does not have to be immediate. If you would like to attend the interrogation—'

'I think I would prefer a private interview before the interrogation begins. Can that be arranged?'

'You understand, Herr General, that this woman is highly dangerous.'

'Well, can she not remain restrained?'

'Well, sir, if you are prepared to take the risk—'

'Some risks are amply worth taking.' Choltitz frowned and stopped looking at Liane. 'What is that noise?'

'Those are explosions,' one of the other officers said.

'Explosions. What—'

The telephone on the desk was ringing. Marach picked it up. 'Yes?' He listened, his expression slowly registering consternation. Then he replaced the phone. 'A group of terrorists have seized the *hôtel de ville*, Herr General. And there are attacks on our people in several other places.'

'Good God!' Choltitz snapped. 'To your posts, gentlemen. Turn out the troops. This must be ended immediately.' The officers ran from the room. 'Your people too, Roess,' Choltitz said. 'Turn them out.'

'With respect, sir, these cannot be more than isolated incidents. You have fifty thousand men in the city—'

'And there are half a million Frenchmen. I want every man on the streets. You people will recapture the *hôtel de ville*. Now.'

Roess gulped. 'Yes, Herr General. And these people? The woman—'

'She will be here when you get back.'

222

'Yes, sir.'

'And I will see her, later. I will be just in the mood for it then.' He hurried from the cell.

Roess looked at Liane, who looked back, her face expressionless. 'I should shoot you now,' he snarled.

'But that would disappoint the general,' she pointed out.

He glared at her for several seconds, then turned to Margrit. 'You stay with them. Do not leave them for a moment. Understood?'

'Yes, Herr Colonel.'

'Marach, come with me.' The two officers left the cell. 'And lock that door,' Roess commanded.

'But, Herr Colonel—' Margrit protested.

'We'll be back,' Marach assured her.

They disappeared, while the building filled with stamping feet and shouted orders. Margrit and Liane looked at each other. 'I wonder who will get here first,' Liane remarked. 'Your people, or mine?' Margrit raised her hand. 'Uh, uh,' Liane said. 'The general would not like that.' She slid down the pipe to resume her seat.

James and his men crouched in the shelter of the building across the street from the Gestapo Headquarters. All around them were the sounds of battle, some close at hand, others distant; Duvivier had raised the entire city. Now they watched the black-uniformed men running from the doorway, assembling on the pavement, while from the archway leading to the inner courtyard there issued a stream of both cars and motorcycles with sidecars. All were filled with soldiers, and several also mounted machine-guns. The men around him twitched. 'Easy,' he said. 'Easy. Let them go. And remember, no grenades, we want the prisoners alive. Now!'

Duvivier had equipped him with a tommy-gun and a haversack containing five spare drums. He ran across the street and fired a burst at the men who appeared in the doorway. They disappeared in a welter of flying blood and James was up the steps and into the lobby. More men appeared on the main staircase and the surrounding balcony, but ran into a wall of fire from the men behind James and came tumbling down. One or two returned fire, but hastily as they retreated to their various offices and slammed the doors. James heard a chorus of screams and burst into a lower office, where three female secretaries were clustered against the wall. One of them was actually brandishing a pistol. 'Drop it,' James shouted.

For reply, she brought it up and levelled it, and he shot her in the chest. She felt backwards, the pistol thudding to the floor. The other two raised their hands, shouting, 'Nein! Nein!'

'Speak French,' he commanded. 'I know you do.' They gazed at him, and at the men behind him; they knew rape, at the very least, was close. 'Take us to the cells,' he said. 'Quickly.'

'We will be shot.'

'You will be shot if you do not.' He grabbed the arm of the youngest looking, a frothy blonde who was clearly terrified. 'Move!'

He pushed her out of the door into the lobby. The building was still filled with firing, but this was on the upper floors. They went along the lobby and down the steps at the end. Now the prisoners in the cells were shouting, but the one James wanted was at the start of the lower corridor. 'James!' Liane shouted. 'It's locked.'

James slung the tommy-gun and drew his revolver, and Gabrielle screamed. He looked through the bars at Margrit, who had risen and drawn a pistol of her own. 'You shall not have her,' she snarled. James shot her through the head.

'I saved your life,' Gabrielle said. 'You owe me your life.'

'We can deal with her later,' Liane said, rubbing her wrists as James released the handcuffs. 'It is Amalie we want.'

'And Roess?'

'Him too. But Amalie comes first.'

'They are on the run everywhere,' Duvivier said. 'Now they are the ones with only pockets of resistance. And, my friends, the Allies are coming. Or at least, Leclerc's Free French division. They will be here tomorrow.'

'Is it over?' Amalie asked. 'Is it really over?' She had survived her month-long captivity very well, mainly because no one had known who she was and, as there had been several women taken in the fighting in the Vercours, she had been able to lose herself.

Liane hugged her. 'For us, it's getting closer every day.'

James looked out of the window at the flames; the evening was drawing in. There were only a few fires but they dominated the night sky. 'Have any officers been taken?'

'Some,' Duvivier said. 'But we have taken none of the Gestapo or the SS. And if you are thinking of Roess, no one has seen him. He is either still holding out at headquarters or he has fled the city.'

'No,' Liane said. 'He cannot have done that.'

James squeezed her hand. 'We'll get him,' he promised. 'Tomorrow.'

'We must blow the city,' Roess said. 'While we still control enough of it. With a single telephone call, I can destroy Notre Dame, the Arche de Triomphe, the Louvre, the Tuileries . . .' He gave a savage grin. 'The Folies, and all the bridges across the Seine. We will leave them nothing of value.'

'No,' Choltitz snapped.

'Our orders—'

'I am countermanding our orders. This is one of the most beautiful cities in Europe. I will not be a party to its ruin.'

'The bridges, at least, can be considered military objectives, Herr General,' Marach ventured.

'A few fallen bridges will not keep out the enemy.'

'Then what are we to do?' asked a staff officer. 'We cannot surrender to the Resistance. They will hang us all.'

'We will defend ourselves until Leclerc's men take over the city,' Choltitz declared. 'Then we will surrender with dignity.'

'I cannot surrender,' Roess remarked quietly. 'Even to Leclerc. If I am taken, I will be tried as a war criminal.'

'Then I suggest that you fight to the last, and at the last, shoot yourself.'

Roess gazed at him for several seconds. Then he said, 'If you will excuse me, Herr General. Heil Hitler.'

He left the office and was followed a moment later by Marach. 'What are we going to do, Herr Colonel? Our headquarters is held by the enemy. And the Wehrmacht is getting ready to abandon us . . .'

'They are swine,' Roess agreed. 'We need to think very clearly, Marach. We will go first to your apartment.'

225

'Sir?'

'We must get rid of our uniforms, and we cannot go to my place; the guerillas will find out my address quickly enough.'

'Yes, sir. But they will find out that I also am a Gestapo officer and come after me.'

'I know that. But we need to get rid of these uniforms. We are much the same size. Your clothes will fit me.'

Marach followed him into the yard, where machine-gun positions had been set up. 'You mean to try to leave the city in civilian clothes? It will be very dangerous. If we are caught we will be lynched.'

'It is very dangerous now,' Roess agreed. 'But in a week's time things will have settled down. People will be coming and going again freely. We will simply walk away.'

'But . . . we cannot stay in my apartment for a week. We will be discovered before then.'

'We are not going to stay in your apartment.' Roess went to the gate and surveyed the street, watched by the curious machine-gunners. But it was now utterly dark except for the fires, and the shooting had died down. 'We are going to a place no one in the Resistance will ever think of looking for us, and where we will be quite safe for a week.'

'What is happening?' Louise asked. She was the senior of Constance's girls, a buxom young woman in her middle twenties with long black hair. The other five girls crowded behind her as they peered through the half-open door.

'It is a revolution,' Marguerite said. 'There are fires everywhere.'

'It is the Resistance,' Claudine said. 'Rising against the Boche!'

'But the shooting has stopped,' Marie objected. 'They have failed.'

'Do you think there will be any clients tonight?' Natalie asked.

'I wish Madame Constance would come home,' Jeanne said.

'Silly girl,' Marguerite said. 'Madame Constance has not gone out.'

'Then where is she?' Louise asked. 'She must have heard the shooting.'

'Well . . .' Marguerite frowned. 'When the English major went out this afternoon, he said she did not wish to be disturbed. She is in the attic.'

'That was four hours' ago,' Louise said. 'And she never sleeps when we are open.'

The girls looked at each other, then ran for the stairs, half falling over each other in their haste to reach the attic. Marguerite, much older, followed more slowly.

'The door is locked,' Natalie panted.

Louise banged on the panels. 'Madame? Madame? Are you in there? Open the door.'

They listened. 'I hear something,' Claudine said. 'The bed creaked.'

'Madame!'

Natalie, more enterprising, stooped to look through the keyhole. 'There is no key.'

Marguerite had reached them. 'That swine of an Englishman must have taken it.'

'Then we must break the door down,' Louise decided.

'Madame Constance will be very angry if you damage her house,' Marguerite objected.

'She will be grateful if she is lying dead in bed,' Louise pointed out illogically. 'Fetch the axe.'

They were all in a hugely excited state, and a few moments later the door was in a collapsed state. Louise switched on the light – amazingly there was still electricity – and they stared at their employer in consternation. Marguerite released the gag, while the girls untied the strips of sheet. 'My God!' Constance exploded. 'That bastard! Get me a cognac.'

Natalie hurried off.

'He thought I was going to tell the Boche what he was about. Well, I am going to do that. I am going to have him strung up by the balls. Who is downstairs?'

'Nobody,' Louise said. 'Did you not here the shooting? It was everywhere this evening.'

Constance swung her legs off the bed. 'Shooting? My God! And no clients? God, my throat is dry. Where is that fucking girl?'

Natalie appeared, empty-handed. 'Madame,' she gasped, 'Madame! There are two men—'

227

Constance pushed the girls aside as she went to the stairs. 'Clients,' she said. 'Get yourselves ready.' She descended the stairs as regally as she could, halting on the lower landing to gaze at the two rather dishevelled men standing beneath her. 'Get out,' she said. 'This house is reserved for German officers.'

'I am very glad to hear it,' Roess said. 'See that you let no one else in.'

Two days after the rising, Leclerc's division arrived. By then most of the garrison had surrendered or been killed, as had quite a few other people; the Resistance had long memories and quite a few scores to settle. Others had merely been humiliated. Liane handed Gabrielle over to the women fighters, who took her and several other female collaborators to the Place de la Concorde and there shaved their heads before turning them loose. She had more important things to do, such as meeting General de Gaulle, who arrived as soon as the city was secure. James was not included in this interview, as the great man was too busy to receive itinerant British officers.

'You did not miss anything,' Liane told him when she returned. 'He's a pompous bore. But he gave me this.' The cross of the Legion d'Honneur was pinned to her bodice.

'Oh, that's lovely!' Amalie cried. 'Do I get one too?'

'We'll have to work on that. Now, James, I have something to show you.' She took them to her apartment. The concierge remembered her and gave her the key. 'Is it all right?' she asked. 'Up there?'

'It is fine, mademoiselle. I cleaned it up myself. There is no sign of, well . . . anything unpleasant. You will find it exactly as it was, well, before you had to leave.'

'I am quite scared,' she confessed to James and Amalie as they went up the stairs. 'Even if . . .' She unlocked the door, hesitated and then went in.

'It even smells sweet,' Amalie said, prowling through the rooms. 'Where did it happen? Where did you kill Biedermann?'

'In the bedroom.' Liane watched her hurry off. 'She won't find anything.'

James took her in his arms. 'But here is where it all began.'

'Well . . . I suppose it really began on the day I drove you and Pierre and Henri Burstein up to the border.'

'With Joanna.'

'With Joanna. James, you will find out what happened to her?'

'I'll try.' He hesitated, and she smiled.

'But I think it all began the night before, when we slept together for the first time. I don't think, without that, anything else would have happened.'

'You're going to marry me.'

She made a moue. 'I am known as a professional killer. I have been a whore. And I have had a lesbian lover. Do you think you can turn me into a housewife?'

'It'll be fun trying. Now, my darling, I simply have to contact London, let them know I'm alive and get instructions on what I do next.'

'They'll want you back there.'

'Probably. But you'll come with me. I think you should meet the brigadier, and there may even be another gong in it.'

'Um. But there is someone we must see first. Constance.'

'Ah.'

'She has been a faithful friend for four years. She has operated the Paris part of the Route for your evaders.'

'And you trust her.'

'Of course I do.' She frowned. 'Why should I not?'

'Well . . . she didn't seem too happy about my turning out all Paris to rescue you, so when I left the brothel last Saturday afternoon, I tied her to the attic bed.'

'My God! That was three days' ago. She'll be splitting mad.'

'I'm sure the girls will have released her by now.'

'She'll still be angry. Listen, you will come with me, and we'll make it up with her. We'll invite her to our wedding. She'll like that.'

Amalie preferred to stay in the flat and wallow in luxury. Liane and James made their way through the still hysterical crowds, James having his back slapped and his hands wrung time and again and Liane being repeatedly hugged and kissed. They felt quite exhausted by the time they reached the brothel, which stood stark and lonely as always and apparently deserted. 'It is always like this in the middle of the afternoon,' Liane explained. 'It is when they sleep.' She went up the steps and rang the bell, and again.

The bolt rasped and the door swung in. 'We are closed,' Marguerite said. 'Go—' she gazed at Liane and her jaw dropped.

'Didn't you expect us to come back?' Liane asked.

Marguerite had closed her mouth. Now it opened again. 'Go,' she whispered. 'Quickly. Run! Colonel Roess—'

She was wrenched away from the door and sent sprawling across the floor. Then the door was slammed to, but James had stepped past Liane and hurled his shoulder against it, and it struck him and swung back in. Off balance, he fell forward, behind Marguerite, which probably saved his life, as a pistol exploded and the bullet slammed into the wall above his head.

'James!' Liane screamed, unsure whether he had been hit. But James had drawn his revolver and returned fire, blind as his eyes were not accustomed to the gloom. As he did so, he rolled across the floor.

'Keep clear!' he shouted.

But Liane was already inside, slamming the door behind her and throwing herself full length beside Marguerite, who was now screaming herself. The man behind the door had been sent staggering by James' charge, but now he recovered his balance and fired again several times. James felt the impact of a bullet striking him, but there was no immediate pain. Yet when he attempted to fire he could not squeeze the trigger. Only dimly he heard the sound of more shots, and then Liane was cradling him in her arms. 'James,' she said. 'James.'

'Who . . . who was that?' he whispered.

'A man called Marach. A Gestapo officer.'

'Here?'

Liane looked at Marguerite, who was getting to her hands and knees.

'He came with Roess.'

'Where is Roess?'

'Upstairs.'

Liane looked at the stairs, which remained empty. 'Help me,' she said.

Marguerite was a big, strong woman, and between them they half lifted, half dragged James to the office.

'Listen,' he said. 'Marach—'

'Is dead.' Liane closed and locked the door, and they laid James on the floor. Liane tore open his shirt, sucking breath between her teeth.

'How bad?' he asked.

'There is no air. Your lungs are all right, but it is not good. We have to bind this up, Marguerite, until we can get a doctor.'

'But we have nothing.'

'Take off your dress and tear it into strips.' Liane took off her own shirt and set an example.

'Listen,' James said. And then gasped as the pain began.

'I know,' she said. 'Marguerite, Madame Constance keeps a bottle of brandy in her desk. 'You stay here with Major Barron and feed him, a little at a time. You say Roess is upstairs? How many men are with him?'

'There is no one with him, mademoiselle. There was only Captain Marach.'

'And where is Madame Constance? Upstairs with Roess?'

'Madame Constance is dead, mademoiselle. Roess shot her in front of me, in front of the girls. It was to frighten us into obeying him.'

'And he succeeded. Now James—'

'You must get help,' James muttered.

'To deal with Roess? That is a pleasure I have promised myself for too long. I will soon be back. And then we will get help for you.'

'Liane . . .'

She blew him a kiss and closed the door behind herself.

She knew that Roess and everyone in the house had to have heard the shots, and indeed she was aware of a stealthy rustle of sound from above her. But no one was venturing on to the stairs . . . as yet, because only a few moments had passed since the exchange. She checked her magazine; there were three shots left. Hastily she crossed the hall and picked up Marach's gun. He had only fired twice and had nine cartridges left. She tucked the pistol into her waistband and looked up the stairs. Once she started climbing she was totally exposed. But there was also the service staircase, used by the girls to take their clients up to the bedrooms. There too she would be exposed, but even Roess could not watch them both at the same time, and they were some distance apart.

Much would depend on how many of the girls had survived and whose side they would be on. Although she had used the house regularly throughout the War and had even serviced the clients from time to time in her search for information, she did not know any of the girls, other than Constance herself, at all well. She did know that they had resented her presence, both on account of her superior brains and beauty, the way Constance had always treated her as someone different and superior and, above all, as they knew who she was, as someone whose presence meant danger for them all. On the other hand they had to know that Roess was a fugitive, living on borrowed time. They were not stupid.

She opened the door to the reception room, which was empty, returned to the hall and fired a single shot up the stairs. She listened to some crashing and shrieks, and darted through the reception room to the second staircase. This she took in a series of leaps before realizing that there was someone at the top, half hidden in the shadows, panting. It was Claudine. 'Not a sound,' Liane whispered.

'But . . .' She had obviously been placed there as a sentry. 'He will kill me.'

'Go downstairs,' Liane told her and moved along the corridor. At the far end Louise was also on sentry duty. She turned to look at her and uttered a shriek. Instantly the door of Constance's own bedroom opened. Liane fired three times and then her bolt clicked on the empty chamber. The sound was loud enough to reach the bedroom, and the door swung open to reveal Roess, his lips drawn back in a wolfish snarl.

'Well, mademoiselle,' he said. 'No more bullets? That was careless of you. But then, you are only a woman.' Liane dropped her empty gun. 'Now I am going to send you where I sent your sister. I watched her die, you know, drowning in a bath of ice-cold water. Oh, it was a petty sight.' He levelled his gun. 'In the gut, I think. The womb.'

Liane threw herself to one side, at the same time drawing

Marach's pistol and firing three times. There was a chorus of screams from the girls as Roess fell to his knees, half turned away from her by the impact of the shots. He was gasping and bleeding from three wounds, one in his arm and two in his body, but she could see that none of them was fatal. She went forward and stood above him, surrounded now by the girls.

'Bitch,' Roess gasped. 'Bitch from hell.'

'Where you are going,' she said and shot him in the stomach. 'From Madeleine,' she said.

He gave a shriek and drew up his legs.

Liane used her toe to roll him on to his back and shot him in the groin. 'That is for Amalie, four years ago.'

Another shriek, but now he was dying. Liane shot him in the head. 'And that is for France.'

'Oh, sir! Is it really true?' Rachel threw both arms round the brigadier's neck and hugged him.

'I say, sergeant,' he protested. 'Steady on.'

'But you say the wound is not life threatening. He's alive. And he's going to stay alive.'

'It would appear so, yes.'

'And he's coming home?'

'Within the week. You won't believe this, but he's bringing that de Gruchy woman with him. They are both quite heros, you know.'

'They always were, sir.'

'Yes. Well, I actually am looking forward to meeting the famous Liane at last. Even if, well . . .'

Rachel frowned. 'She's not wounded too?'

'No, no. But it seems James has married her. A bedside ceremony, what? Isn't that odd. Now, I must be off.' He bustled through the door.

Rachel sat behind James' desk. She felt curiously winded. But hadn't she always known that James and Liane would marry? If they both survived. And they had done that. So . . .

The door opened. She stared at Joanna.

'I thought I'd better keep out of sight until that old buzzard left,' Joanna said. 'Mrs Hotchkin was giving me a cup of tea.'

'But you're alive. And out of Germany. Everybody's alive.

Have you heard about James? And Liane?' Rachel got up and Joanna sat down.

'Yes,' she said. 'Maybe I'll get to congratulate them some time. I'm going to need those letters of absolution.'

'Of course. I still have them. Well . . .'

They gazed at each other.

'I'm at the Dorchester,' Joanna said. 'Why don't you shut up shop and come over there with me. We could have lunch. And, well, maybe tea as well.'